Privacy and Security in the Digital Age

Privacy and data protection are recognized as fundamental human rights. Recent developments, however, indicate that security issues are used to undermine these fundamental rights. As new technologies effectively facilitate collection, storage, processing and combination of personal data, government agencies take advantage for their own purposes. Increasingly, and for other reasons, the business sector threatens the privacy of citizens as well.

The contributions to this book explore the different aspects of the relationship between technology and privacy. The emergence of new technologies threaten increasingly privacy and/or data protection; however, little is known about the potential of these technologies that call for innovative and prospective analysis, or even new conceptual frameworks.

Technology and privacy are two intertwined notions that must be jointly analyzed and faced. Technology is a social practice that embodies the capacity of societies to transform themselves by creating the possibility to generate and manipulate not only physical objects, but also symbols, cultural forms and social relations. In turn, privacy describes a vital and complex aspect of these social relations. Thus technology influences people's understanding of privacy, and people's understanding of privacy is a key factor in defining the direction of technological development.

This book was originally published as a special issue of *Innovation: The European Journal of Social Science Research*.

Michael Friedewald is a Senior Researcher and Head of the ICT research unit at the Fraunhofer Institute for Systems and Innovation Research in Karlsruhe, Germany. His areas of research are the social and economic impacts of emerging technologies and their implications for policy making. In recent years he has worked extensively on privacy, data protection and surveillance. Michael holds Master Degrees in Electrical Engineering and Economics and a PhD in Science and Technology Studies from RWTH Aachen University, Germany.

Ronald J. Pohoryles is Chairman of the Board of Directors of the ICCR Foundation Vienna, Austria and Paris, France and Assistant Professor of Comparative Political Systems, with experience in social science research for over 35 years. His research expertise covers European integration emphasising public policy analysis, science and technology and integrated technology assessment. Overall, his work relates to a comprehensive understanding of sustainability, bringing together economy, environment, society and democracy. He has co-ordinated more than 100 research projects. His publications include numerous articles and books on the above topics.

Privacy and Security in the Digital Age

Edited by
Michael Friedewald and Ronald J. Pohoryles

LONDON AND NEW YORK

First published 2014
by Routledge
2 Park Square, Milton Park, Abingdon, Oxon, OX14 4RN, UK

and by Routledge
711 Third Avenue, New York, NY 10017, USA

Routledge is an imprint of the Taylor & Francis Group, an informa business

© 2014 ICCR Foundation

All rights reserved. No part of this book may be reprinted or reproduced or utilised in any form or by any electronic, mechanical, or other means, now known or hereafter invented, including photocopying and recording, or in any information storage or retrieval system, without permission in writing from the publishers.

Trademark notice: Product or corporate names may be trademarks or registered trademarks, and are used only for identification and explanation without intent to infringe.

British Library Cataloguing in Publication Data
A catalogue record for this book is available from the British Library

ISBN 13: 978-1-138-78730-8

Typeset in Times New Roman
by Taylor & Francis Books

Publisher's Note
The publisher accepts responsibility for any inconsistencies that may have arisen during the conversion of this book from journal articles to book chapters, namely the possible inclusion of journal terminology.

Disclaimer
Every effort has been made to contact copyright holders for their permission to reprint material in this book. The publishers would be grateful to hear from any copyright holder who is not here acknowledged and will undertake to rectify any errors or omissions in future editions of this book.

Contents

Citation Information	vii
Notes on Contributors	ix

1. Introduction: Technology and privacy
   Michael Friedewald and Ronald J. Pohoryles   1

2. Developing accountability-based solutions for data privacy in the cloud
   Andrew Charlesworth and Siani Pearson   7

3. Legally compatible design of future biometric systems for crime prevention
   Matthias Pocs   36

4. Privacy issues in public discourse: the case of "smart" CCTV in Germany
   Norma Möllers and Jens Hälterlein   57

5. Biocybernetic adaptation and privacy
   Knud Böhle, Christopher Coenen, Michael Decker and Michael Rader   71

6. Generational views of information privacy?
   Priscilla M. Regan, Gerald FitzGerald and Peter Balint   81

7. Public attitudes towards privacy and surveillance in Croatia
   Jelena Budak, Ivan-Damir Anić and Edo Rajh   100

8. Reconciling privacy and security
   Marc van Lieshout, Michael Friedewald, David Wright and Serge Gutwirth   119

9. The proposed Regulation and the construction of a principles-driven system
   for individual data protection
   Paul de Hert, Vagelis Papakonstantinou, David Wright and Serge Gutwirth   133

10. Limits and challenges of the expanding use of covert CCTV in the
    workplace in Spain – beyond jurisprudential analysis
    José R. Agustina and Fanny Coudert   145

11. Evaluating privacy impact assessments
    Kush Wadhwa and Rowena Rodrigues   161

12. Regulating privacy enhancing technologies: seizing the opportunity of
    the future European Data Protection Framework
    Gerrit Hornung   181

Index   197

Citation Information

The chapters in this book were originally published in *Innovation: The European Journal of Social Science Research*, volume 26, issues 1–2 (March–June 2013). When citing this material, please use the original page numbering for each article, as follows:

Chapter 1
Introduction: Technology and privacy
Michael Friedewald and Ronald J. Pohoryles
Innovation: The European Journal of Social Science Research, volume 26, issues 1–2 (March–June 2013) pp. 1–6

Chapter 2
Developing accountability-based solutions for data privacy in the cloud
Andrew Charlesworth and Siani Pearson
Innovation: The European Journal of Social Science Research, volume 26, issues 1–2 (March–June 2013) pp. 7–35

Chapter 3
Legally compatible design of future biometric systems for crime prevention
Matthias Pocs
Innovation: The European Journal of Social Science Research, volume 26, issues 1–2 (March–June 2013) pp. 36–56

Chapter 4
Privacy issues in public discourse: the case of "smart" CCTV in Germany
Norma Möllers and Jens Hälterlein
Innovation: The European Journal of Social Science Research, volume 26, issues 1–2 (March–June 2013) pp. 57–70

Chapter 5
Biocybernetic adaptation and privacy
Knud Böhle, Christopher Coenen, Michael Decker and Michael Rader
Innovation: The European Journal of Social Science Research, volume 26, issues 1–2 (March–June 2013) pp. 71–80

CITATION INFORMATION

Chapter 6
Generational views of information privacy?
Priscilla M. Regan, Gerald FitzGerald and Peter Balint
Innovation: The European Journal of Social Science Research, volume 26, issues 1–2
(March–June 2013) pp. 81–99

Chapter 7
Public attitudes towards privacy and surveillance in Croatia
Jelena Budak, Ivan-Damir Anić and Edo Rajh
Innovation: The European Journal of Social Science Research, volume 26, issues 1–2
(March–June 2013) pp. 100–118

Chapter 8
Reconciling privacy and security
Marc van Lieshout, Michael Friedewald, David Wright and Serge Gutwirth
Innovation: The European Journal of Social Science Research, volume 26, issues 1–2
(March–June 2013) pp. 119–132

Chapter 9
The proposed Regulation and the construction of a principles-driven system for individual data protection
Paul de Hert, Vagelis Papakonstantinou, David Wright and Serge Gutwirth
Innovation: The European Journal of Social Science Research, volume 26, issues 1–2
(March–June 2013) pp. 133–144

Chapter 10
Limits and challenges of the expanding use of covert CCTV in the workplace in Spain – beyond jurisprudential analysis
José R. Agustina and Fanny Coudert
Innovation: The European Journal of Social Science Research, volume 26, issues 1–2
(March–June 2013) pp. 145–160

Chapter 11
Evaluating privacy impact assessments
Kush Wadhwa and Rowena Rodrigues
Innovation: The European Journal of Social Science Research, volume 26, issues 1–2
(March–June 2013) pp. 161–180

Chapter 12
Regulating privacy enhancing technologies: seizing the opportunity of the future European Data Protection Framework
Gerrit Hornung
Innovation: The European Journal of Social Science Research, volume 26, issues 1–2
(March–June 2013) pp. 181–196

Please direct any queries you may have about the citations to
clsuk.permissions@cengage.com

Notes on Contributors

José R. Agustina, Department of Criminal Law and Criminology, Faculty of Law and Political Sciences, Universitat Internacional de Catalunya, Barcelona, Spain

Ivan-Damir Anić, Institute of Economics, Zagreb, Croatia

Peter Balint, Department of Public and International Affairs, George Mason University, Fairfax, Virginia, USA

Knud Böhle, Institute for Technology Assessment and Systems Analysis, Karlsruhe Institute of Technology, Karlsruhe, Germany

Jelena Budak, Institute of Economics, Zagreb, Croatia

Andrew Charlesworth, Centre for IT and Law, University of Bristol, Bristol, UK

Christopher Coenen, Institute for Technology Assessment and Systems Analysis, Karlsruhe Institute of Technology, Karlsruhe, Germany

Fanny Coudert, Interdisciplinary Centre for Law & ICT, Faculty of Law, Katholieke Universiteit Leuven, Leuven, Belgium

Michael Decker, Institute for Technology Assessment and Systems Analysis, Karlsruhe Institute of Technology, Karlsruhe, Germany

Gerald FitzGerald, Department of Public and International Affairs, George Mason University, Fairfax, Virginia, USA

Michael Friedewald, Fraunhofer Institute for Systems and Innovation Research, Karlsruhe, Germany

Serge Gutwirth, Law Science Technology & Society (LSTS), Vrije Universiteit Brussels, Brussels, Belgium

Jens Hälterlein, Faculty of Social Sciences, Department of Sociology of Organization and Administration II, Potsdam University, Potsdam, Germany

Paul de Hert, Law Science Technology & Society (LSTS), Vrije Universiteit Brussels, Brussels, Belgium

Gerrit Hornung, Chair of Public Law, IT Law and Legal Informatics, University of Passau, Passau, Germany

NOTES ON CONTRIBUTORS

Marc van Lieshout, TNO Information and Communication Technologies, Delft, the Netherlands

Norma Möllers, Faculty of Social Sciences, Department of Sociology of Organization and Administration II, Potsdam University, Potsdam, Germany

Vagelis Papakonstantinou, Vrije Universiteit Brussels, Brussels, Belgium

Siani Pearson, HP Labs, Bristol, UK

Matthias Pocs, Stelar Security Technology Law Research, Hamburg, Germany

Ronald J. Pohoryles, ICCR Foundation Vienna, Austria and Paris, France

Michael Rader, Institute for Technology Assessment and Systems Analysis, Karlsruhe Institute of Technology, Karlsruhe, Germany

Edo Rajh, Institute of Economics, Zagreb, Croatia

Priscilla M. Regan, Department of Public and International Affairs, George Mason University, Fairfax, Virginia, USA

Rowena Rodrigues, Trilateral Research & Consulting, London, UK

Kush Wadhwa, Trilateral Research & Consulting, London, UK

David Wright, Trilateral Research & Consulting, London, UK

Introduction

Technology and privacy

Privacy and data protection are recognized as fundamental human rights.[1] They underpin human dignity and other values such as freedom of association and freedom of speech. Indeed they have become two of the most important human rights of the modern age. However, new technologies undermine individual rights because they facilitate the collection, storage, processing and combination of personal data for the use not only of government agencies, but also of businesses.

Technology and privacy are two intertwined notions that must be jointly analyzed and faced. Technology is a social practice that embodies the capacity of societies to transform themselves by creating the possibility to generate and manipulate not only physical objects, but also symbols, cultural forms and social relations. In turn, privacy describes a vital and complex aspect of these social relations. Thus technology influences people's understanding of privacy, and people's understanding of privacy is a key factor in defining the direction of technological development. Either policy-making takes into account this rich and nuanced interplay between technology and privacy or we run the risk of failing to govern the current, concomitant technology and privacy revolutions.

Modern technologies have not "created" challenges to privacy: if we take the example of online social networks, even without them, communication within the framework of "social networks" takes place. Information shared with friends or colleagues in the traditional way might be "leaked" by one of these and give rise to gossip, rumors, etc. However, the sheer quantity involved in online social networks leads to new qualities: while traditional information channels are limited to a normally known group of people and, hence, the "leak" can be traced, the worldwide net is accessible to everybody who has a certain level of technical knowledge. The information, even if restricted to a small group of users, can be used by others, be it for commercial ends, political reasons or personal malicious purposes. The use of modern technology requires personal responsibility, but this can only be based upon ICT literacy.

Hence, innovation in the field of privacy, especially with regard to new technologies, also requires innovative legal and political frameworks that can ensure that the implications of ICT are not only known, but also adequately governed. This task is often threatened by the understanding of privacy as such, perceptible through the many ways in which privacy is addressed and analyzed.

A good example here is the use of mobile communication devices. The recent European Directive on Data Retention has made people aware of the conflict between the comfort of using such devices and the threat to their privacy.[2] However, there is little awareness that the data can be used for other purposes than "just" ensuring security, as this directive alarmingly makes clear. The data can be used for purposes such as the analysis of traffic flows, tourism statistics, regional statistics, etc. If the data, for instance, are gained through the statistics of mobile communication operators, which store the data anyway, the danger for privacy becomes obvious. After all, these data are not anonymized and can be misused for all kinds of private and public purposes. The key concept of privacy has generated four main ideas.

Privacy as a multifaceted concept

Privacy is not only respect for confidentiality, although it implies this. Privacy is not only the right to be left alone, although it includes this. Privacy is not only the right to control one's own life, although it entails this. Nor is privacy only data protection, although it also concerns this. Privacy is all these things together, and more, because privacy is the word we use to describe an important aspect of one of the main, vital and constitutive polarities that shape human beings, that is, the tension between the individual and the community. How do new technologies impact on this complex and rich concept? What are the privacy issues arising from different emerging technologies? Multidisciplinary analysis is needed in order to appreciate the various philosophical, political, legal, ethical and social meanings of the word "privacy" in the contemporary technological world.

Data protection is both wider and more specific than the right to privacy. The relationship between these concepts is certainly something that needs to be addressed in order to arrive at a new concept of privacy. Data protection goes wider because it not only aims to ensure the protection of personal data, but also tends to protect other related rights and interests such as the freedom of expression, and the freedom of thought, conscience and religion. At the same time it also enables the free flow of information in a non-discriminatory way. Yet data protection is also more specific, because it only applies in situations in which personal data are processed. The application of data protection rules does not require an answer to the question of privacy violation: data protection applies when the legal conditions are fulfilled.

Furthermore, data protection rules are not a prohibition by default; they channel and control the way personal data is processed. Such data can only be legitimately processed if certain conditions pertaining to the *transparency* of the processing and the accountability of the data controller are met. Privacy, however, sets *exclusionary* limits that shield the individual against state (and other) powers, thus warranting a certain level of *opacity* of the citizen.

Privacy as a moving target

The concept of privacy has evolved with time. People also define and value it differently depending on context. Moreover, privacy is often balanced against other values, such as society's safety and security. There is little empirical data on citizens' perceptions of various aspects of privacy, especially how it relates to actual behavior. Empirical research on how people value privacy, however they define it, is thus needed in order to understand how real citizens understand the right to privacy and its value within a social model and system of fundamental rights.

Yet with the "technology revolution" the notion of privacy has started a new journey – beyond the legal sphere – which is probably leading privacy back to its original roots, the relation between the citizen and the "polis". We are immersed in new contexts (think, for instance, of ICT (information and communication technologies) implants, with which it becomes possible for a technologically "enhanced" body to communicate with nearby computers and exchange data) and new concepts (for example, the idea of genomic and proteomic information), not to mention issues raised by technologies such as biometrics, smart surveillance systems, body implants and neurotechnology, among others.

These new technologies have specific features that make them quite different from traditional industrial technologies. Compared with the technologies that drove the industrial revolution – which were complex, based on collective action, social infrastructure and technical know-how – emerging technologies are lighter. They are decentralized, dispersed and disseminated, and their control and use are largely in the hands of the individuals, citizen groups and small enterprises. Also the substance and aim of their operation is different – manipulation of information as substance of human interaction as opposed to production of solid objects – therefore the characteristics of cause and effect are based on a different set of principles.

Privacy as a salient topic in technology policy-making

There is a need for a new social debate on privacy rights that includes issues such as the new boundaries of the private domain, new business ethics and the balance between civil rights and governmental spheres of competence. This is probably something governments need to consider. It is necessary to produce a new taxonomy of privacy problems – including all those posed by new technologies – that could help policy-makers and decision-takers to better weigh up privacy against countervailing values, rights, obligations and interests. Consequently this implies a change in the relationship between science and politics.

The post-modern technological system is highly embedded in politics. Researchers are under increasing pressure to demonstrate the policy relevance of their findings and to deliver tangible results. In turn, policy-makers are under pressure to justify their choices of technologies to be developed and socio-economic goals to be achieved.

Because they challenge assumptions at the root of our current morals, emerging technologies are provoking a crisis – or at least a basic uncertainty with regard to moral standards – that is either sanctioned by law or remains at the level of tacit presuppositions. This leads to a growing gap between citizens, technology and politics, most evident when the individual's private sphere conflicts with the notion of common good.

Privacy as an issue of personal responsibility

Privacy is both an issue of political regulation, and one of personal concern, in the sense that it concerns the balance between public/personal security and liberty. The difficulty, when it comes to the introduction of new technologies, is the way in which these are used, perceived and handled, not only by state actors in order to ensure security in the public space, but also by individual users in their own, increasingly virtual space. Major concerns have arisen following the widespread use of "social networks": users tend to underestimate the dangers of publishing private matters and, hence, tend to underestimate the importance of carefully choosing what they want to keep private. Once published in virtual space the data never disappear without a trace. Even if the information is more often than not only accessible to a specified group of recipients, it can be made public by users who might be unaware of the necessity to keep private things private, or who are malicious enough to hack those networks and use the data for their own purposes. The internet is in fact not a private sphere at all.

Another telling example of the Janus-faced characteristics of modern ICT is the example of smart grids: smart grid technologies enable people (1) to understand how their household uses energy, (2) to control expenditure of electricity, (3) to experience fewer and shorter power outages, and (4) to control energy devices in households. In this respect these technologies empower customers by providing them in a timely way with relevant information on their energy use, and with an overarching regulatory framework for reducing costs and their carbon footprint. This might, however, resonate as a "sanctity of the home" issue, as personal details of daily life and individual habits should not be accessible. Additionally, very important concerns are that the privacy implications of smart grids are not yet fully understood and that formal privacy policies, procedures or standards are still insufficient on the side of the entities that are involved in the development of smart grids. Against this background, privacy issues need to be the utmost concern when analyzing the behavior of customers, as well as in attempts to increase their participation in active demand and to empower end users.

The contributions

This thematic issue contains 11 articles that focus on three different aspects of the relationship between technology and privacy. The four articles in the first part deal with aspects of privacy raised by specific new technologies.

One of these is cloud computing, that is, computer systems where information and/or applications are stored online, allowing access by the user over the Internet; recently cloud computing has raised many security and privacy concerns. In their article, Charlesworth and Pearson deal with the challenges presented by cloud computing for data protection. They see a general deficit in the current approach to regulation and advocate the principle of accountability in the governance of new technologies. They examine both procedural and technical solutions to demonstrate that accountability is a solution to juridical privacy and security risks.

In the next article in this part of the journal, Pocs deals with the question of how to ensure that respect for fundamental rights is taken into account in the design of future biometric systems for crime prevention. For this purpose Pocs suggests how technology design could render the violation of a legal norm impossible.

The third contribution is Möllers and Hälterlein's analysis of the public discourse on surveillance technologies and privacy. Drawing on the case of "smart" closed-circuit television in Germany, they show how privacy concerns are socially constructed and change over time, before raising questions for further investigation.

Finally, the research note by Böhle et al. deals with the optimization of human–computer interaction through biocybernetic adaptation. This approach increasingly uses body-related data to detect internal human states (emotion, feelings, possibly even intentions and thoughts) that can be used to control technical systems. It thus raises fundamental data protection and privacy questions. The authors outline possible opportunities, discuss privacy challenges and potential regulatory actions to be taken.

The articles in the second part focus on the important questions surrounding citizens' perceptions of privacy, and challenges to privacy arising from new technologies and their application.

In their contribution Regan et al. investigate whether there are any differences in attitudes towards ICT and information privacy among members of different generations. They find that the empirical basis is rather too small to draw some general conclusions, but discover some interesting patterns.

In the following paper, Budak et al. empirically investigate attitudes towards privacy, data protection, surveillance and security in Croatia. They reach the conclusion that citizens can be divided into three types related to demographic groups in society: "pro-surveillance" oriented citizens; citizens concerned about being surveilled; and citizens concerned about privacy and data protection.

Van Lieshout et al. finally consider the relationship between privacy and security and, in particular, the traditional "trade-off" paradigm that used to be very popular among policy-makers and the surveillance industry. By refusing this simplistic model, they explore whether and how, in a democracy, one can reconcile the trend towards increasing security with the fundamental right to privacy. They present a research agenda for exploring the "real" relationship between privacy and security attitudes in a multidisciplinary and transdisciplinary way.

Finally, the third part covers legal aspects of privacy and data protection – including the consideration of new instruments for their protection. Although we initially stressed that privacy and data protection are two separate concepts that should not be understood as synonymous, data protection remains an important field when it comes to government regulation of emerging sciences and technologies. In that respect the European Commission's initiative for a new data protection regulation is probably the most important development in recent years.

De Hert et al. present an initial analysis of the proposed regulation, highlighting the treatment of basic data protection principles and elements and elucidating their merits and shortcomings.

Agustina and Coudert analyze the expanding use of legitimate covert CCTV in the workplace in Spain. The authors focus on the legal reasons that support court decisions from 2000 to the present and add some criminological and ethical perspectives to better comprehend not only its legal rationale, but also some other collateral effects that employers should take into account in implementing covert surveillance. The results of the study guide the development of a more detailed rationale for improving legal and decision-making analyses in this field.

Wadhwa and Rodrigues's article focuses on privacy impact assessments (PIA). These have been intensively discussed in recent years and have been taken up in Article 33 of the proposed European regulation on data protection, while Article 23 more generally sets out the obligation to follow the principle of data protection by design. Based on good practices, it outlines and evaluates criteria that could be used to turn PIA into an effective instrument taking into account the interests of all stakeholders.

Hornung points out in his article why attempts to introduce privacy by design and privacy enhancing technologies (PETs) have been notoriously unsuccessful in the past few years. He emphasizes that the current reform of data protection law is a unique opportunity to implement at least basic instruments to supplement and foster the development and introduction of privacy by design and PETs.

Acknowledgement

This special thematic issue is a joint initiative of the EU projects PRACTIS[3] and PRESCIENT.[4] PRACTIS analyzes the potential impact of emerging technologies and their convergence on the fundamental individual and structural values in which the European legal right to privacy is rooted, as well as on societal perceptions and conceptions of privacy. PRESCIENT aims to contribute to the development of new instruments for the governance of science and technology, in particular, privacy and ethical impact assessments. PRACTIS as well as PRESCIENT are funded through the Seventh Framework Programme for Research in the area of "Science in Society".

Michael Friedewald
Co-ordinator PRESCIENT; Fraunhofer ISI
Ronald J. Pohoryles
Editor, Innovation; Partner, PRACTIS

Notes

1. Although privacy and data protection are often used synonymously they are listed as separate rights in the European Charter of Human Rights (Articles 7 and 8 ECHR).
2. In fact there are attempts to top up this Directive through a European citizen initiative. The Commission promised to evaluate the Directive and to re-consider it after two years. However, the report was not delivered last autumn when it was due.
3. PRACTIS stands for "Privacy – Appraising Challenges to Technology and Ethics"; see http://www.practis.org
4. PRESCIENT stands for "Privacy and Emerging Sciences and Technologies: Towards a common framework for privacy and ethical assessment"; see http://prescient-project.eu

Developing accountability-based solutions for data privacy in the cloud

Andrew Charlesworth[a] and Siani Pearson[b]

[a]*Centre for IT and Law, University of Bristol, Queens Road, Bristol, BS8 1RJ, UK;* [b]*HP Labs, Long Down Avenue, Stoke Gifford, Bristol, BS34 8QZ, UK*

> Contemporary developments in information and communication technologies make "command and control"-based legislation, for example, EU Directive 95/46/EC, a decreasingly credible means of providing appropriate privacy protection for personally identifiable information (PII) across wide areas of commercial activity. Current legislation provides limited transparency and oversight, fails to encourage privacy innovation, and lacks the flexibility to effectively and efficiently regulate new technologies and globalized business practices. There is a growing consensus that regional, and ultimately global, data privacy regimes will have to adopt new regulatory approaches, and that such approaches should incorporate, as a key element, a greater focus on "accountability". This raises two key questions: what is meant by "accountability", and how might it translate into practical mechanisms for achieving privacy protection? This article considers these questions in the context of "cloud computing", examining how procedural and technical solutions can be co-designed to demonstrate accountability in order to resolve jurisdictional privacy and security risks within the cloud.

Introduction

Data privacy regulation in the EU operates through the rights it provides to data subjects and consequent obligations it places on data controllers. A key premise of this regulatory regime is that data subjects are placed in a position to assess where, when and how their data is being processed by a data controller, or by those processing data on behalf of a data controller (data processors), and are able to identify where and when breaches of their rights have occurred. If this rights and obligations framework is rendered ineffective, whether accidentally or deliberately, it becomes difficult, if not impossible, to realistically apply existing regulatory techniques for protecting data privacy to actual commercial data processing practice.

Yet contemporary personal data processing takes place in an increasingly complex technological environment. Here, even relatively simple transactions, such as purchasing a ringtone via a mobile phone, may involve a web of personal data transactions between several data controllers and data processors in multiple jurisdictions (Charlesworth 2006). As new information processing technologies develop, the disjoint between a regulatory framework based on 1980s understandings of data processing and transfer, implemented via similarly dated and rigid "command and control" regulatory mechanisms based on laws backed by civil and criminal sanctions and applied by (quasi) governmental regulatory agencies, continues to grow. This disjoint has provided not just the impetus for ongoing reform of the EU data privacy regime, but also a welcome opportunity to examine new regulatory techniques, and assess the extent to which they and developing technology-based solutions can be effectively integrated into a coherent regulatory regime. The purpose of this article is to explore aspects of this wider field of examination through an examination of how data privacy in a developing technology environment – cloud computing – might plausibly be provided.

Cloud computing is a means by which highly scalable, technology-enabled services can be easily offered to customers via the internet on an as-needed basis. However, the convenience and efficiency of this approach comes with a range of potential privacy and security risks. These risks have posed two key problems for cloud service providers (CSPs). The first is how to respond effectively to potential commercial customers, and to consumers, over fears that use of cloud services might result in confidential data leakage and loss of privacy. The second stems from the cross-border nature of cloud services, which may leave cloud service customers and CSPs facing difficulties when attempting to demonstrate satisfactory compliance with national implementations of the current EU data protection regime, notably the restrictions placed on cross-border data transfer of personally identifiable information (PII) of individuals.

In the commercial/consumer context, discussion of privacy is premised upon the protection and appropriate use of the PII of customers, as well as the meeting of expectations of customers about its use. For organizations, privacy thus entails the application of laws, policies, standards and processes via which PII is managed. This article is concerned with privacy in the specific sense of data protection, as defined by EU Directive 95/46/EC, and is thus concerned with data that is PII: that is, information that can be linked to an identifiable individual, either directly, for example, a phone number or social security number linked to a name, or indirectly, by triangulation of various types of data held by the data controller, for example, search engine search terms. It focuses on the corporate entity as a customer seeking to contract for services in the cloud, either for its own use, or to offer to its end-users, as such an entity is most likely to have the resources to adopt the proposed path of technical and procedural solutions suggested here. However, the solution discussed here is not EU-specific, and is compatible with the differing privacy principles and practices underlying contemporary American (Levin and Nicholson 2005) and Asia-Pacific (Kennedy, Doyle, and Lui 2009, Alhadeff, Van Alsenoy, and Dumortier 2011) regulation and legislation, as well as a self-regulatory approach (Newman and Bach 2004). It is therefore in keeping with the attempts to develop a more internationally uniform approach to data protection exemplified by the Madrid Resolution on International Standards, adopted at the 2009 International Conference of Data Protection and Privacy Commissioners (2009), discussed below.

The term "accountability" is susceptible to a variety of different meanings within and across disciplines. For example, the term has been used for a number of years in computer science to refer to an imprecise requirement that is met by reporting and auditing mechanisms (see, for example, Cederquist et al. 2005). In this article, the context of its use is corporate data governance (the management of the availability, usability, integrity and security of the data used, stored or processed within an organization), and it refers to the process by which a particular goal – the prevention of disproportionate (in the circumstances) harm to the subjects of PII – can be obtained via a combination of public law (legislation, regulation), private law (contract), self-regulation and the use of privacy technologies (system architectures, access controls, machine-readable policies).

The article proposes the incorporation of complementary regulatory, procedural and technical provisions that demonstrate accountability into a flexible operational framework to address privacy issues in a cloud computing scenario. The structure of the paper is as follows: consideration of open issues that relate to cloud computing and privacy; an explanation of accountability and how this might apply in cloud computing; proposal of legal mechanisms, procedures and technical measures that tie in with this approach; an assessment of this approach; and conclusions.

A brief overview of cloud computing

Although there is no definitive definition for cloud computing, a definition that is commonly accepted is provided by US National Institute of Standards and Technologies:

> Cloud computing is a model for enabling ubiquitous, convenient, on-demand network access to a shared pool of configurable computing resources (e.g., networks, servers, storage, applications, and services) that can be rapidly provisioned and released with minimal management effort or service provider interaction. (Mell and Grance 2011)

This shared pool of resources is unified through virtualization or job scheduling techniques. Virtualization is the creation of a set of logical resources (whether it be a hardware platform, operating system, network resource or other resource) usually implemented by software components that act like physical resources; for example, an actual PC running the Linux OS can host a virtual PC that uses the Windows OS in order to run Windows compatible programs. In particular, software called a hypervisor emulates physical computer hardware and thus allows the operating system software running on the virtual platform (a virtual machine or VM) to be separated from the underlying hardware resources.

Cloud computing has several deployment models, of which the main ones are public (widely accessible), private (a cloud infrastructure operated solely for an organization) and hybrid (a composition of two or more clouds). Cloud computing technology underlies numerous end-user (e.g. Google's Apps) and commercial (e.g. Salesforce's customer relationship management) services. This article is concerned primarily with the commercial model, where business customers are purchasing cloud services from providers via which the PII of third parties will be processed.

Cloud computing enables a self-service-based allocation of technology resources or technology-enabled services. It has three main service models: infrastructure as a service (IaaS), platform as a service (PaaS) and software as a service (SaaS). In IaaS, consumers can deploy and run arbitrary software, which can include operating systems and applications, but without controlling the underlying cloud infrastructure. In PaaS, consumers deploy onto a cloud infrastructure consumer-created or acquired applications that have been created using programming languages and tools supported by the provider. In SaaS, consumers just use providers' applications running on a cloud infrastructure. Using IaaS or PaaS, one or more VMs are created in order for a program to be run within those – when the task is finished, the VMs and the temporary disk space are released. In fact, IaaS providers can provide storage and VM services that are complementary but allow for persistency of data between use of multiple VMs. An allocated VM could be started to carry out a task and stopped once the task is completed; this is logically separate from managing the lifecycle of a VM (as the VM can be deleted when the data are no longer needed). Using a SaaS approach, on the other hand, the customer is one of the users of a multi-tenant application developed by the cloud service provider, and the customers' data is stored in the cloud, to be accessible the next time the customer logs in. The data would only be deleted at the end of the lifecycle of the data, if the customer wishes to change service provider, etc. Hence the risks of data exposure vary according to the service model.

Cloud computing services use "autonomic" or self-regulating technologies, which allow services to react and make decisions on their own, independently of CSP operators and transparently to customers, based on pre-set policies or rules; autonomic processes might, for example, independently scale up service provision in reaction to a customer's use, or transfer data processing within a virtual machine from a physical server location in the US to another in Japan, based on the comparative use of the physical servers.

In most of these cloud computing models, multiple customers share software and infrastructure hosted remotely – a process known as multi-tenancy. Hence, one instance of software, and the physical machine it runs on, serves clients from different companies, although security mechanisms are used to provide a protected VM environment for each user. Therefore, cloud computing can be thought of as an evolution of outsourcing, where an organization's business processes or infrastructures are contracted out to a different provider. A key difference is that with cloud computing it can be difficult, if not impossible, to identify exactly where the organization's data actually is. This is partly because CSPs may have server farms in several countries, and it may not be possible for the CSP to guarantee to a customer that data will be processed in a particular server farm, or even country. For example, Salesforce.com has five data centers, housing about 3000 computer servers. There are four data centers in the United States, one in Singapore and one under construction in Japan (Jones 2011). Amazon Web Services and Google have multiple data centers worldwide, details of the locations of which are often confidential. Offshoring, a term traditionally used where business processes are relocated to a different country, is thus also seen as a common element of cloud service provision.

It is also the case that, just as their customers use cloud services to obtain variable amounts of service provision according to their needs over time (usually referred to as "scalability"), CSPs may themselves lease processing and storage capacity from other service providers to meet their own requirements. Thus when a customer processes data using a CSP, that data may simultaneously reside in a jurisdiction outside that of both the customer and CSP, and on a third party's computer systems.

Cloud computing provides a market opportunity with a huge potential both for efficiency and new business opportunities (especially in service composition), and is almost certain to deeply transform our information technology infrastructures, models and services. Not only are there cost savings owing to economies of scale on the service provider side and pay-as-you-go models, but business risk is decreased because there is less need to borrow money for upfront investment in infrastructure. However, from a legal perspective, several of the key characteristics of cloud computing services including outsourcing, offshoring, virtualization and autonomic technologies may be problematic, for reasons ranging from software licensing, and the content of service level agreements (SLAs), to determining which jurisdiction's laws apply to data hosted "in the cloud", and the ability to comply with data privacy laws (Pearson and Charlesworth 2009; Marchini 2010). This article is concerned with the latter two points.

Privacy issues in cloud computing

Conforming to legal data privacy requirements in the EU, and meeting client data privacy expectations with regard to PII, requires corporations to demonstrate a context-appropriate level of control over, and security of, such data at all stages of its processing, from collection to destruction. In the computing environment which existed when Directive 95/46/EC was drafted, such a requirement would probably not have been unduly onerous, with data being processed in-house or by data bureaux. Data controllers would have been able to set clear conditions on where PII was to be processed and who was to process it, and would, if necessary, have been able to conduct audits and site inspections to verify that any specified data processing requirements were being met (Platten 1996).

In the cloud environment, where a data controller contracts with a CSP to process PII, it may be hard to identify where data is being processed at any given moment, and whether the data is being processed on a physical server owned by the CSP, or on a server owned by a third party who has leased capacity to the CSP. The constantly shifting nature of this arrangement means that traditional oversight mechanisms, such as audit powers and site inspections, become largely ineffective. The advantages of cloud computing – its ability to scale rapidly (through subcontractors), store data remotely (in unknown places) and share services in a dynamic environment – can thus become disadvantages in maintaining a level of privacy assurance sufficient to meet legal requirements, or to sustain confidence in potential customers.

While subcontracting and offshoring have always carried some risk for commercial entities, use of cloud services can clearly magnify those risks. It is not just consumers who are worried about privacy and security concerns in the cloud (Gellman 2009). The European Network and Information Security Agency (ENISA)'s cloud computing risk assessment report states "loss of governance" to be one of the top risks of cloud computing, especially for Infrastructure as a Service (ENISA 2009). "Data loss or leakages" is also one of the top seven threats listed by Cloud Security Alliance in their "Top Threats to Cloud Computing Report" (CSA 2010a).

Key privacy-related issues that arise for those providing and using cloud services are:

- Outsourcing – outsourcing of data processing invariably raises governance and accountability questions. Which party is responsible (statutorily or contractually) for ensuring legal requirements for PII are observed, or appropriate data handling standards are set and followed? (CSA 2009) Can they effectively audit third-party compliance with such laws and standards? To what extent can processing be further subcontracted, and how are the identities, and bona fides, of subcontractors to be confirmed? (Marchini 2010). What rights in the data will be acquired by data processors and their subcontractors, and are these transferable to other third parties upon bankruptcy, takeover, or merger (Gellman 2009)? "On-demand" and "pay-as-you-go" models may be based on weak trust relationships, involve third parties with lax data security practices, expose data widely and make deletion hard to verify.

- Offshoring – offshoring of data processing increases risk factors and legal complexity (Abrams 2008). Issues of jurisdiction (whose courts can/will hear a case), choice of law (whose law applies) and enforcement (whether a legal remedy can be effectively applied) need to be considered (Kohl 2007). A cloud computing service that combines outsourcing and offshoring may thus raise very complex issues (Mowbray 2009).
- Virtualization – there are security risks in sharing machines, for example, loss of control over data location, and who has access to it. The virtualized aspects of cloud computing can bring new threats, such as:
  o "escape" to the hypervisor, where the an attacker uses a guest virtual machine to attack vulnerabilities in the hypervisor software (IBM 2010);
  o cross-VM side channel attacks, where the attacker breaches the isolation between VMs allowing extraction of data via information leakage owing to the sharing of physical resources (Ristenpart et al. 2009).
  Other vulnerabilities may arise from data proliferation, dynamic provisioning, the difficulty in identifying the location of physical servers or the lack of standardization.
- Autonomic technology – if technological processes are granted a degree of autonomy in decision-making, for example, automatically adapting services to meet changing needs of customers and service providers, this challenges enterprises' abilities to maintain consistent security standards, and to provide appropriate business continuity and back-up, not least as it may further obscure where data processing will take place within the cloud (McKinley et al. 2006).

As cloud computing exhibits all of the elements above, proposed privacy solutions need to address a combination of issues. This may require the employment of new perspectives and unique mechanisms, rather than just a combination of known techniques. For example, privacy problems when transferring PII across borders within a group of companies can be addressed via Binding Corporate Rules, and yet this approach would not be available to a corporation seeking to adopt a public cloud computing solution, as the PII it seeks to process will be handled by third-party CSPs (and possibly their subcontractors).

Overall, the speed and flexibility of adjustment to vendor offerings, which benefit business and motivates cloud computing uptake, bring a higher risk to data privacy and security. This is a key user concern, particularly for financial and health data.

Mapping legal and regulatory approaches

Effective corporate governance is vital to compliance with the type of regional block regulatory governance models which underpin Binding Corporate Rules in Europe and Cross Border Privacy Rules in Asia-Pacific Economic Cooperation (APEC) countries. Organizations that process PII must safeguard it (including limiting its use and disclosure) or face legal, financial and reputational penalties. Where there are inadequate information governance capabilities in the cloud, this has the potential to severely restrict the outsourcing of key business processes using cloud-based service marketplaces.

Companies, governmental organizations and regulators are increasingly aware of the need to integrate privacy into the technology design process (Microsoft Corp. 2007; ICO 2008) However, tools and technical controls alone cannot fully address privacy issues in cloud computing, owing to diverse privacy obligations upon, and privacy practices within, organizations (Bamberger and Mulligan 2008). CSPs and marketplace providers need to design their processes to ensure those obligations and practices can be mapped against a combination of technical and procedural measures, which together provide broad assurance that appropriate contextual safeguards apply to PII processing in the cloud. Context is key to requirements. Identical information collected in different contexts by different entities might involve totally divergent data protection criteria (6 2002; Nissenbaum 2004).

Such a mapping exercise requires an understanding of the rationales for, and the objectives of, the protection of PII, and how these translate to the cloud computing environment. If cloud computing is to reach its full potential, where customers are willing to entrust PII to such a service marketplace, these criteria need to be met:

- a determination of risks and requirements involved in a given interaction situation, for example, consideration of the underlying legal, policy and social context;
- a determination of what protective measures (procedural and/or technological) are appropriate, based on this information;
- effective ways of providing assurance and auditing that potential partners protect PII, in accordance with contextually appropriate protective measures;
- a degree of transparency, in the sense of visibility into the data protection obligations and processes of potential suppliers.

Requirements arising from applying privacy legislation to the cloud have been the subject of increasing commentary (Pearson 2009). A key issue is the need to respect cross-border transfer obligations. As this is particularly difficult to ensure within cloud computing, it is suggested that legislation will need to evolve to allow compliance in dynamic, global environments.

Accountability

To date, national and international data privacy protection approaches have been heavily influenced by public law, and often premised upon "command and control" regulatory strategies. However, such legislative and regulatory mechanisms have declined in effectiveness as technological developments render the underlying regulatory techniques obsolete. Effective privacy protection for PII in some business environments is thus heavily compromised, and the ability of organizations to meaningfully quantify, control, and offset, their business risk is significantly impeded.

> It enjoins upon "data controllers" a set of largely procedural requirements for their processing activities, and therefore conveys the impression that formal compliance will be enough to legitimise their activities. It encourages a box-ticking mentality, rather than a more systemic, and systematic, approach to fulfilling its values. (ICO 2006)

The EU data protection regime, in particular, lacks effective regulatory responses for key developing technologies, such as mobile e-commerce and cloud computing (Charlesworth 2006). Equally, self-regulation, in isolation, has failed to gain significant traction as a plausible alternative for effective privacy protection, as existing self-regulatory practices often suffer from weak risk assessment and limited compliance checking (Charlesworth 2003).

What is needed, therefore, is a new approach capable of meeting the four criteria set out above, designed around:

- a goal-oriented legislative framework, which
  - requires adherence to the fair information principles (FIPs) that underpin most existing international data privacy regimes and remain at the heart of regulatory practice;
  - is genuinely technology neutral, and not prescriptive about the procedural and technical mechanisms through which compliance with the FIPs is to be achieved and assessed, but requires those mechanisms adopted to be verifiably appropriate in context and effectively operated in practice;
  - penalizes failure to comply with the FIPs in a manner that encourages parties engaged in the processing of PII to engage in preventative privacy-enhancing behaviors, for example, privacy by design processes, privacy impact assessments, adequate risk assessment and effective contractual allocation of responsibilities and liability, and the adoption of technical measures;
  - provides a meaningful role in policy development and legislative enforcement for subjects of PII and public interest groups, that extends beyond the individual subject access rights and limited rights to seek compensation for breaches that characterizes current EU practices;
- harmonized and pragmatic administrative policies, which recognize and legitimize a broad spectrum of regulatory approaches, practices and tools capable of adaptive/flexible context-sensitive application, both to existing practices, and to developing issues raised by technical and business innovation.

As such, it is suggested that there is a need for a fundamental shift in data privacy regulation, away from the existing top-down "command and control" EU legislative framework, towards a new regulatory paradigm based on the principle of "accountability".

What is Accountability?

The concept of "accountability", much like the concept of privacy, has varying definitions across different contexts. This section examines the development of the principle in the data privacy context and suggests that a contemporary definition must necessarily incorporate a pragmatic and flexible application of elements of public law (legislation, regulation), private law (contract), self-regulation and technology-based (system architectures, access controls, machine-readable policies) processes in order to obtain most effective means of preventing disproportionate (in given circumstances) harm to the subjects of PII.

In the data protection context, the principle of accountability made an early appearance in the Organisation for Economic Co-operation and Development's (OECD's) *Guidelines on the Protection of Privacy and Transborder Flows of Personal Data* (OECD 1980):

> a data controller should be accountable for complying with measures which give effect to the [other] principles [in the OECD Guidelines].

Initially, it appears that this required little more than that a regulated organization should identify a person or persons to take responsibility for its compliance – a fairly narrow interpretation of accountability.

EU Directive 95/46/EC clearly required data controllers to engage in processes that could form the basis of a wider concept of accountability, but it did not explicitly link those processes to an overarching accountability principle. This may explain the weaknesses in the Directive and in national implementing legislation, such as the UK Data Protection Act 1998 (DPA 1998), which despite providing for transparency elements such as pre-processing regulatory notification, information provision requirements and data subject access, failed to provide effective external (or encourage effective internal) means of harnessing these elements for the prevention or remediation of data privacy failures. A large part of the regulatory failure (in the UK context at least), the resulting lack of faith in the regulatory framework amongst the general public and the lack of motivation amongst data controllers to comply with the DPA 1998 at all, or to innovate to maintain and develop the level of privacy protection in new ICTs, can be traced to this "accountability gap" (Charlesworth 2006, 50).

Crompton, Cowper, and Jefferis (2009) have noted that, in contrast to the EU's "adequacy" regime, "accountability" is increasingly popular in jurisdictions such as Australia, the United States (e.g. Title V, Gramm–Leach–Bliley Act of 1999) and Canada (e.g. Sch. 1, Principle 1, Personal Information Protection and Electronic Documents Act (PIPEDA), 2000).

Principle 1 – Accountability

> [...]
> An organization is responsible for personal information in its possession or custody, including information that has been transferred to a third party for processing. The organization shall use contractual or other means to provide a comparable level of protection while the information is being processed by a third party. (Sch. 1, Personal Information Protection and Electronic Documents Act (PIPEDA) 2000, Canada)

As discussed below, accountability in this context means placing a legal responsibility upon an organization that uses PII to ensure that contracted partners to whom it supplies the PII are compliant, wherever in the world they may be. Our accountability model reflects the basic premise of this approach, but extends it by suggesting ways in which organizations might take the "accountability" approach further in order to develop a reflexive, continually evolving, privacy process. This is complementary to the approach suggested by the APEC Privacy framework and explored in terms of practical implementation through the APEC Privacy Pathfinder projects (Alhadeff, Van Alsenoy, and Dumortier 2011).

Weitzner et al. (2006) argued for a form of accountability based on a policy shift from hiding information to ensuring that only appropriate uses occur. This requires information use to be transparent so it is possible to determine whether a use is appropriate under a given set of rules. A history of data manipulations and inferences can be maintained (providing transparency) and can then be checked against a set of policies that are supposed to govern them (providing accountability). This provides retrospective accountability, in the sense that, if actor A performs action B, then we can review B against a predetermined policy to decide if A has done something wrong, and so hold A accountable.

The weakness with this approach is that it is inflexible when dealing with context-sensitive or changing privacy environments – it can deal effectively only with circumstances that fall within a prescribed set of rules, and then only after the fact. Reducing the risk of disproportionate harm to data subjects, and thereby reducing negative consequences for the data controller(s) requires the inclusion of prospective processes and reinforcement of good practices such that liability does not arise in the first place (Pearson and Charlesworth 2009). This is a reflexive privacy process, which is not static and where there is an on-going assessment of harm and process of privacy review throughout the contractual/service provision chain. Our use of the term "accountability" thus differs from Weitzner's to the extent that adherence to policy becomes less critical than achieving a proportionate and responsive process for reacting to context-dependent privacy risks.

More recently, the significance and utility of the principle of accountability in introducing innovations to the current legal framework in response to globalization and new technologies has been highlighted in two reports by the EU Article 29 Working Party, *The Future of Privacy* (2009) and *Opinion 3/2010 on the Principle of Accountability* (2010), and the global data protection standards of the Madrid Resolution adopted by the International Conference of Data Protection and Privacy Commissioners (2009):

> 11. Accountability principle.
> The responsible person shall:
> a. Take all the necessary measures to observe the principles and obligations set out in this Document and in the applicable national legislation, and
>
> b. have the necessary internal mechanisms in place for demonstrating such observance both to data subjects and to the supervisory authorities in the exercise of their powers [. . .].

The "Galway Project" of privacy regulators and privacy professionals provided an initial definition of accountability, in the context of this latest regulatory sense:

> Accountability is the obligation to act as a responsible steward of the personal information of others, to take responsibility for the protection and appropriate use of that information beyond mere legal requirements, and to be accountable for any misuse of that information. (CIPL 2009)

A rather more complex formulation emerged from the second meeting of the same group during the "Paris Project", where accountability was defined as:

> a demonstrable acknowledgement and assumption of responsibility for having in place appropriate policies and procedures, and promotion of good practices that include correction and remediation for failures and misconduct. It is a concept that has

governance and ethical dimensions. It envisages an infrastructure that fosters responsible decision-making, engenders answerability, enhances transparency and considers liability. It encompasses expectations that organisations will report, explain and be answerable for the consequences of decisions about the protection of data. Accountability promotes implementation of practical mechanisms whereby legal requirements and guidance are translated into effective protection for data. (CIPL 2010, 2)

Both the EU Article 29 Working Party deliberations and the work of the Centre for Information Policy Leadership are reflected in the recent Commission proposal for a new Data Protection Regulation (EU Commission 2012a, 2012b). The Commission consulted widely while preparing the draft Regulation (EU Commission 2012b, 2–5) and, while the Regulation itself does not specifically make reference to the principle of accountability, the Commission makes it clear that the shift in the draft Regulation away from protection of personal data by means of the bureaucratic process of notification (widely perceived to be cumbersome and inappropriate) will be compensated for by ensuring that data controllers can ensure and demonstrate that they are in compliance with all the obligations in the draft Regulation. It is important to note that this accountability approach will also have implications for data processors established in the EU, in that there will be accountability obligations requiring them to maintain documentation of their processing operations, to carry out data protection impact assessments of risky processing activities and ensure an adequate level of protection for data they transfer outside the EU (Buttarelli 2012, 3).

The Commission notes in its Memorandum to the draft Regulation that:

Article 22 takes account of the debate on a "principle of accountability" and describes in detail the obligation of responsibility of the controller to comply with this Regulation and to demonstrate this compliance, including by way of adoption of internal policies and mechanisms for ensuring such compliance. (EU Commission 2012b, 10)

While space does not allow for detailed examination of the implications of the draft Regulation in this article, it is clear that, if implemented in anything like its current form (and there is already significant commercial opposition to the Proposal), it will have significant implications for the future practices of CSPs, subcontractors and end users (Buttarelli 2012, 6).

Broadly speaking, an accountability approach in accordance with current regulatory thinking requires organizations to:

- commit to accountability and establish policies consistent with recognized external criteria;
- provide transparency and mechanisms for individual participation, for example including sharing these policies with stakeholders and soliciting feedback;
- use mechanisms to implement these policies – including clear documentation and communication (encompassing the organization's ethical code), gaining support from all levels within the organizational structure, tools, training, education, on-going analysis and updating;
- allow validation – provide means for external enforcement, monitoring, and audit;

- provide mechanisms for remediation – these should include event management (e.g. dealing with data breaches) and complaint handling (Bruening 2010).

It seems plausible that the third item above can be extended to encompass both pre-emptive approaches (to assess risk and avoid privacy harm) and reactive approaches that provide transparency and audit throughout the entire life cycle of PII.

Potential hazards of accountability

It is clear that the concept of accountability has recently been the subject of significant interest in regulatory and business circles, to the point where it almost appears to be viewed as the "magic bullet" for the current problems that face privacy regulators, commercial and governmental PII users, and data subjects. There has been some skepticism expressed as to what a principle of "accountability" can actually add to existing privacy protections (ALRC 2008, 1134), but at present there appears to be relatively little critical assessment of the notion of accountability as a data privacy panacea. It is worth noting that a move towards "accountability" may, depending upon how accountability is defined and implemented, raise issues for both the subjects of PII and for commercial entities.

Adequacy of accountability implementations

When one examines how accountability might be implemented in practice, then existing descriptions of accountability in practice may appear to resemble, quite strongly, existing forms of self-regulation. Consider:

1. The organisation takes appropriate measures to establish processes and procedures that implement its privacy policies. It carries out risk analysis and mitigation based on their understanding of its obligations under an accountability approach. The organisation may enlist the consultation of the supervisory authority or recognized accountability agent in this process and complete the appropriate documentation.
2. The organisation self-certifies that it meets the requirements of accountability.
3. The supervisory authority or recognized accountability agent reviews such filings and provides some form of acceptance of the certification.
4. The organisation submits to enforcement by the supervisory authority or recognized accountability agent. The supervisory authority or accountability agent will hear and resolve complaints from individuals. It will also conduct appropriate organisation spot checks to ensure that they continue to meet the criteria to which they have self-certified.
5. Supervisory authorities, recognized accountability agents, trade associations, and government agencies engage in raising the awareness of organisations about the obligations that an accountable organisation must meet, and the benefits that flow from being accountable. ("Measuring Accountability" in CIPL 2010, 6)

Two issues stand out from that description. First, both the largely self-regulatory US Safe Harbor Agreement, and wholly self-regulatory private sector arrangements, such as those provided by Truste, would appear to meet those criteria – despite ongoing questions about the extent to which either actually provide adequate privacy protection (DiLascio 2004; Leathers 2009). Second, individuals (and/or public interest groups) appear to have no obvious role in the process, except to the extent that they may make complaints.

The first issue raises the question of whether the focus on "accountability" might be simply a means of introducing light-touch self-regulation by the back door, and could thus legitimately be seen as a way of watering down existing privacy protections, notably those granted to EU citizens. The second issue may raise questions about what the future role of the public (or representatives of the public) in data privacy regulation might be. While there is an argument that a data privacy regime based on accountability might reduce the burden on data subjects of policing the marketplace for enterprises using data irresponsibly (CIPL 2009, 10), there is no significant discussion of what role, if any, they might have, as stakeholders, elsewhere in the accountability process.

At present, the key theoretical discussions and practical proposals have largely emerged from fora dominated by regulators and corporations, and largely closed to input from elsewhere. While a comprehensive analysis and critique of the concept is beyond the scope of this article, it is clear that, for accountability to play a meaningful role in the protection of data privacy, and in the construction of trust in the use of new technologies, such as cloud computing, both legislators and regulators will need to consider carefully how legislation and regulatory practices can ensure that a data privacy framework focused on accountability actively encourages the meaningful engagement of all stakeholders, and provides plausible compliance and enforcement mechanisms. The discussion below is thus to some extent dependent upon the development of an accountability framework, nationally and internationally, which does more than simplify the ways in which corporations and governments can meet legislated responsibilities, but which is ultimately seen by the public as a more credible and legitimate response to their data privacy concerns than that which went before.

Regulatory pressures

That having been said, a focus on accountability may also raise some red flags for corporate users of PII. Accountability-based regimes may result in greater liability than data privacy legislation alone, on the basis of measures that organizations can be seen to have explicitly or implicitly promised to deliver to third parties, such as consumers.

> 64. The proposed system can only work if data protection authorities are endowed with meaningful powers of sanction. In particular, when and if data controllers fail to fulfil the accountability principle, there is a need for meaningful sanctions. For example, it should be punishable if a data controller does not honour the representations it made in binding internal policies. Obviously, this is in addition to the actual infringement of substantive data protection principles. (EU Article 29 Working Party 2010, 17).

If accountability is defined broadly, then measures that individual organizations take, perhaps with the intention solely of developing internal privacy-enhancing corporate governance processes, may come to be regarded as *de facto* sectoral obligations under an accountability approach, failure to comply with which may then result in sanction by regulators. This effect of this type of development is demonstrated in the example of the US Federal Trade Commission (FTC) and the privacy role it developed on the internet, via the use of deceptive trade practices jurisdiction over the use of online privacy policies. Neither the expansion of the FTC's regulatory role, nor the regulatory pressures and obligations placed on internet companies, were necessarily obvious or desired outcomes of the decision by some internet firms to adopt more transparent data privacy processes (Hetcher 2000a, 2000b). Thus, the likely development of regulatory practices based on notions of accountability may not be easy to assess given:

- the range of, and relations between, potential regulators (i.e. not just privacy regulators);
- the dynamics between regulators and regulatees, both generally and in specific sectors; and
- the prevailing political climate and public sentiment.

Exploration of possible regulatory strategies arising from adoption of an accountability principle is thus important. It will be necessary to ensure that the strategies adopted can provide adequate privacy protection, but also that they avoid unnecessary overlap between national regulatory remits (e.g. in the UK between the Information Commissioner's Office and the Financial Services Authority) or unnecessary divergences between different national and regional jurisdictions (e.g. between the US and EU data privacy regulatory regimes), and can thus provide consistent, predictable and efficient regulatory practices and outcomes. The possibilities of international "regulatory interoperability" are being actively explored by the US and EU, with the aim of building upon previous interoperable mechanisms such as the EU/US Safe Harbor Agreement and the use of Binding Corporate Rules. In the words of Daniel Weitzner, deputy Chief Technology Officer for internet policy at the White House

Given the global reach [of data] there is a greater sense of the need for global interoperability – based on common principles but with different implementations and enforcement mechanisms. (Cited in Franklin 2011)

Accountability as a way forward for privacy protection in cloud computing

Solutions to privacy risks in the cloud involve reintroducing an element of control. For the corporate user, privacy risk in cloud computing can be reduced if organizations involved in cloud provision use a combination of privacy policies and contractual terms to create accountability in the form of transparent, enforceable commitments to responsible data handling (Pearson 2009, ICO 2006). Specifically, accountable organizations will ensure that obligations to protect data (corresponding to user, legal and company policy requirements) are observed by all processors of the data, irrespective of where that processing occurs.

Through contractual agreements, all organizations involved in the cloud provision would be accountable. While the corporate customer, as the first corporate entity in the cloud provision, would be held legally accountable, the corporate customer would then hold the initial cloud service provider (CSP1) accountable through contractual agreements, requiring in turn that the CSP1 hold its service providers accountable contractually as well. This is analogous to some existing cases in outsourcing environments, where the transferor is held accountable by regulators even when it is the transferee that does not act in accordance with individuals' wishes (Crompton, Cowper, and Jefferis 2009).

The following elements are key to provision of accountability within the cloud:

- Transparency – individuals should be adequately informed about how their data is handled within the cloud and the responsibilities of people and organizations in relation to the processing of PII should be clearly identified. As with other disaggregated data environments, transparency in cloud computing is important not only for legal and regulatory reasons, but also to avoid violation of social norms (Dolnicar and Jordaan 2006). In the context of this paper, transparency means a level of openness about an entity's handling of PII that permits meaningful accountability.
- Assurance – the corporate user provides assurance and transparency to the customer/client through its privacy policy, while requiring similar assurances from the SP through contractual measures and audits.
- User trust – accountability helps foster user trust. When it is not clear to individuals why their personal information is requested, or how and by whom it will be processed, this lack of control will lead to suspicion and ultimately distrust (Lacohée, Crane, and Phippen 2006). There are also security-related concerns about whether data in the cloud will be adequately protected (CSA 2009).
- Responsibility – most data protection regimes require a clear allocation of responsibility for the processing of PII, as existing regulatory mechanisms rely heavily upon user and regulator intervention with responsible parties. Disaggregated data environments, such as mobile e-commerce and cloud computing, can hinder determination of that responsibility. Predetermining responsibility, via contract, as information is shared and processed within the cloud, pre-empts perceptions of regulatory failure, which may erode user trust. It also permits companies to assess their trading risks in terms of potential financial losses and data privacy breaches. This knowledge can be used to establish organizational and group privacy and security standards, and to implement due diligence/compliance measures which conform to regulatory parameters, but which are otherwise negotiable between contracting organizations, based on relevant operational criteria (Charlesworth 2006).
- Policy compliance – accountability helps ensure that the cloud service complies with laws, and the mechanisms outlined in this article also help compliance with cloud provider organizational policies and user preferences, and with auditing.

With a legal and regulatory approach, location is paramount to enforcement. With accountability, location either becomes less relevant to the customer/client, because of assurances that data will be treated as described regardless of jurisdiction, or becomes transparent through contracts specifying where data processing will take place. In the accountability model, the corporate user works with legal and regulatory bodies to move data between jurisdictions through mechanisms such as Binding Corporate Rules and intra-company agreements. For the corporate user, the flexibility to move customer/client data between jurisdictions has a big impact on cost.

With accountability, regulators enforce the law on the "first in the chain" in regard to the misdeeds of anybody in the chain, including those further along. However, whether any regulatory framework will be effective depends upon a number of characteristics including the background of the regulator (country, resources available to prosecute, etc.). This approach is more effective if action can be taken against an organization that has a presence in the regulator's home jurisdiction.

Accountability is included in various privacy frameworks, including Canada and the United States and the APEC privacy framework. In the EU it applies in the restricted sense that data controllers (DCs) are directly responsible for the actions of their data processors (DPs) (and thus for clouds of DPs and sub-DPs). The difference in approaches becomes more obvious where there are multiple DCs; if these are responsible separately (DCs in common, but not joint DCs) it is hard to police via the EU model, as the data subject (DS) may be unable to identify and enforce rights against a specific DC in a cloud computing environment with a mix of DCs and DPs.

The key issue in responsibility (and accountability) terms under EU law is who is making the decision about the particular processing purpose, and not who is carrying out the processing. A central problem in the mobile e-commerce and cloud computing environments is that it is unclear to the DS if, and if so, where, a breach is taking place, so that they can enforce rights against the relevant DC. The contractual approach provides a mechanism for avoiding that accountability-negating uncertainty, in a manner that permits the DC to demonstrate compliance with the substantive law (and boost user trust), without undue reliance upon the flawed mechanism in the legislation. The accountability process is expanded outwards by the initial DC to DPs and other DCs by contract, then information that the initial DC derives from the accountability processes can be passed upwards to the regulator and downwards to the DS, so that both can perform the functions envisaged by the legislation.

As such, accountability can play a role in ensuring that laws that apply to cloud computing are enforced. There is a role for regulators in the form of criminal penalties for misuse. Also, there is a role for technology, as considered below.

Co-designing procedural and technical solutions for accountability

Accountability promotes implementation of practical mechanisms whereby legal requirements and guidance are translated into effective protection for data. Legislation and policies tend to apply at the data level, but the mechanisms can be at various levels, including the system level and data level. A toolbox of measures could be provided for data controllers, to allow construction of custom-built solutions, whereby the controllers might tailor measures to their context (taking into account consideration of the systems involved, type of data, data flows, etc.).

It is possible to co-design legal mechanisms, procedures and technical measures to support this approach. Design elements may be integrated to support:

- prospective (and proactive) accountability, using preventive controls;
- retrospective (and reactive) accountability, using detective controls.

Preventive controls can be used to mitigate the occurrence of an action continuing or taking place at all (e.g. an access list that governs who may read or modify a file or database, or network and host firewalls that block all but allowable activity). Preventive controls for cloud include risk analysis and decision support tools (e.g. privacy by design and privacy impact assessment), policy enforcement (e.g.

machine-readable policies, privacy-enhanced access control), trust assessments, obfuscation techniques and identity management.

Detective controls are used to identify the occurrence of a privacy or security risk that goes against the privacy or security policies and procedures (e.g. intrusion detection systems, policy-aware transaction logs, language frameworks and reasoning tools). Detective controls for the cloud include audit, tracking, reporting and monitoring. In addition, there are corrective controls (e.g. an incident management plan, dispute resolution), which are used to fix an undesired result that has already occurred. These controls complement each other: a combination of these would ideally be required in order to provide accountability.

Provision of accountability would not just be via procedural means, especially for cloud, which is a highly automated and dynamic environment: technology can play an important role in enhancing the solution – by enforcing policies, providing decision support, assurance, security, etc. We now consider procedural measures, technical measures and how these may be co-designed.

Procedural measures

Procedural is used here in the sense of governance, business practices (e.g. strong privacy policies) and contractual agreements. Privacy policies can be defined at a number of levels and be reflected within internal and external corporate policy statements, contracts, SLAs, security policies, etc. Policies are passed on when sharing information with third parties and organizational policies are used to help ensure legal compliance. In general, they should be based upon established privacy principles, such as the OECD privacy principles (OECD 1980) and regulatory requirements specific to the region(s) in which the company is operating.

For our approach, cloud computing providers should move away from terms and conditions of service towards contracts between the client and the initial service provider (SP), and between that SP and other cloud providers. This approach is consistent with industry self-regulation (for example, Truste certification; Truste 2009). At issue in cloud computing is that most policies have a clause that frees the company to change its policy at any time, often, but not always, with some form of notice. These clauses may need to be re-examined in the cloud environment, where data is perhaps not as easily destroyed or returned to its original owner.

The corporate user has options that the consumer does not in using contracts as a governance measure for control within the cloud environment. Contractual obligations are those imposed on an entity by incorporation in a contract of similar legally binding agreement between that entity and other party. The corporate user has experience in using contracts to control offshoring and outsourcing relationships. These experiences can be leveraged in the cloud.

SLAs for the cloud are still being developed and there are still a number of open issues (SLA@SOI 2009). SLAs can be informal or formal with the former being more in the nature of a promise than a contract and the latter being ancillary to a contract between parties, with breach of an SLA term not being in general as severe as a breach of contract. Moreover, third parties (i.e end-users) would not easily be able to rely on the terms of an SLA between a cloud computing company and a corporation selling such services onwards (i.e. the customer), as there are processes for varying the terms, without the need to renegotiate the whole SLA with customers.

Nevertheless, specific contractual agreements can be used between the cloud provider and the corporate user, just as contracts are used today with traditional SPs. SPs can pass on obligations to subcontractors via contracts – they would require written permission to subcontract with agreements that must be no less restrictive than the agreement the corporate user has with the SP, and reserve the right to enter at will into additional confidentiality agreements directly with the subcontractors. Such contracts have to be plausibly capable of supporting meaningful enforcement processes, and capable of at least some degree of meaningful oversight/audit. The contracts can be used to:

- address the issue of location – by requiring prior written consent for transfers to any third country;
- restrict use of data, especially additional uses by the CSP;
- prevent copying or reproducing of data without express written permission, except as technically necessary to fulfil the agreement (e.g. backup protection);
- restrict employee access to the associated data (e.g. on a need to know basis), require that the SP provide employee privacy training, and require employees to sign confidentiality agreements;
- specify security levels – at least the same level of care applied to the SP's own similar data, but not less than a reasonable level of care, implementation of any security measures required by applicable laws;
- require immediate notification by specified means (e.g. via telephone with written follow-up), for any suspected data breach, and cooperation in resolving;
- reserve the right to audit;
- require upon request or at termination, that PII be delivered back to the data controller or data subject, and all copies be destroyed.

In summary, procedural measures for accountability include determining the capabilities of CSPs before selection, negotiating contracts and SLAs, restricting the transfer of confidential data to CSPs and buying insurance. Organizations should also appoint a data protection officer, regularly perform privacy impact assessments on new products and services, and put mechanisms in place to allow rapid response to data subject access and deletion requests.

Technical measures

A key technical measure developing for accountability is the use of sticky policies, where machine-readable policies (defining allowed use and associated obligations) are attached to data within the cloud and travel with it. In this approach, customers allow cloud (service) providers to have access to specific data based on agreed policies and by forcing interactions with interchangeable independent third parties called Trust Authorities (Pearson and Casassa Mont 2011). The access to data can be as fine-grained as necessary, based on policy definitions, underlying encryption mechanisms (supporting the stickiness of policies to the data) and a related key management approach that allows (sets of) data attribute(s) to be encrypted specifically based on the policy. Access to data is mediated by a Trust Authority that checks for compliance with policies in order to release decryption keys. By these means users can be provided with fine-grained control over access and use of their data within the cloud, even in public cloud models.

In such an approach, the machine-readable policies would include preferences or conditions about how PII should be treated (for example, that it is only to be used for particular purposes, by certain people or that the user must be contacted before it is used). When PII is processed, this is done in such a way as to adhere to these constraints. Existing policy specification, modeling and verification tools that can be used as a basis for this representation include EPAL (IBM 2004), OASIS XACML (OASIS n.d.), W3C P3P (Cranor 2002) and Ponder (Damianou et al. 2001). Policies can be associated with data with various degrees of binding and enforcement. Trusted computing and cryptography can be used to stick policies to data and ensure that that receivers act according to associated policies and constraints, by interacting with trusted third parties (Casassa Mont, Pearson, and Bramhall 2003; Pearson 2005).

Although it is not usual to hide data within the cloud, there is still the possibility of obscuring it in some contexts; for example, sensitive data can in some cases be obfuscated in the cloud (Mowbray, Pearson, and Shen 2010) and multi-party security (zero knowledge) techniques can be used (Yao 1986).

It is necessary to utilize security techniques within the cloud to protect PII from unauthorized access or modification, and to protect backup, protect and manage multiple data copies and delete PII. To limit who has access to personal information within an organization, privacy-aware access control (Casassa Mont and Thyne 2006) deployed within that organization can make decisions and enforce access control policies, intercepting queries to data repositories and returning sanitized views (if any) on requested data.

If trusted infrastructure (Pearson 2005; TCG 2009) can be made available within the cloud, it could help to ensure that the infrastructural building blocks of the cloud are secure, trustworthy and compliant with security best practice; determine and provide assurance regarding location (Pearson and Casassa Mont 2006); and provide a basis for enhanced auditing of platforms (Pearson 2005; TCG 2009). Furthermore, trusted virtual machines (Dalton et al. 2009) can support strong enforcement of integrity and security policy controls over a virtual entity; for different groups of cloud services, there could be different personae and virtualized environments on each end-user device.

An array of technical work is presently emerging in this area. The Cloud Security Alliance (CSA) – a non-profit organization formed to promote the use of best practices for providing security assurance within cloud computing – has a Governance, Risk Management and Compliance stack (CSA 2010b) that includes three very relevant activities: a CloudTrust protocol that can be used to promote the transparency of CSPs (CSC 2010), CloudAudit (CSA 2010c), which aims to provide a technical foundation to enable transparency and trust in private and public cloud systems, and the Trusted Cloud Initiative (CSA 2010d), which is working towards certification of "trusted clouds". Haeberlen (2010) has provided a primitive audit for cloud, and has proposed an approach for accountable virtual machines (Haeberlen et al. 2010). HyTrust Appliance (HyTrust 2010) is a hypervisor consolidated log report and policy enforcement tool that logs from a system perspective. Chen and Wang of CSIRO have produced a prototype in which CSPs are made accountable for faulty services and a technique that allows identification of the cause of faults in binding Web services and have presented this as "accountability as a service" (Chen and Wang 2010; Yao et al. 2010). There has also been research into the development of provenance systems for the cloud (Davidson et al. 2011). Technical measures for accountability can include encryption for data security mitigation, privacy infomediaries and agents to help increase trust.

Co-design of procedural and technical measures

An effective approach will require a combination of procedural and technical measures to be used and co-designed. In essence, this would use measures to link organizational obligations to machine-readable policies, and mechanisms to ensure that these policies are adhered to by the parties that use, store or share that data, irrespective of the jurisdiction in which the information is processed (ideally, with a technical basis for enforcement backing up contractual assurances that incorporate privacy). In such a model, natural language policies in the contract are associated with lower-level policies that are machine-readable and that can be acted upon automatically within the cloud without the need for human intervention. These policies define the use constraints of the associated PII. In this approach, as with that of Weitzner et al. (2006), the data is accessible, but its use is constrained.

The primary problem in the cloud is how this can be policed and enforced. One option may be to adopt an approach based on the Creative Commons copyright license model. This uses a combination of natural language policies (e.g. legal rules), machine-readable policies (reflecting those rules) and plain English policies (indicating the scope of the rules to non-lawyers) to make licensees aware of their obligations and provide a basis against which their behavior can then be audited (Creative Commons 2009). The strongest binding between technical and procedural approaches would be if the wording in the contracts can be translated into machine-readable policies that are bound to data, and then enforced within the cloud. However, this binding cannot be an exact one from laws to human-readable policies to machine-readable policies, owing to interpretation of the law, and furthermore only a restricted part of this translation process can be easily automated. Translation of legislation/regulation to machine-readable policies has proven very difficult, although there are several examples of how translations of principles into machine-readable/actionable policies can be done, for example;

- Privacy Incorporated Software Agent (PISA) project – deriving and modelling privacy principles from Truste (Kenny and Borking 2002);
- SPARCLE project – transforming natural based policies into XML code that can be utilized by enforcement engines (IBM 2008);
- REALM project – translating high level policy and compliance constraints into machine-readable formats) (IBM 2006);
- The work of Breaux and Antón – extracting privacy rules and regulations from natural language text (Travis, Breaux, and Antón 2008); and
- OASIS LegalXML – creating and managing contract documents and terms (OASIS 2007).

An approach that could be used is to add a technical descriptor at the bottom of a contract that describes what a cloud SP should do. For example, there could be a policy text in words that forms part of the contract, then a legal XML expression corresponding to this also within the contract. In addition, there could be a mapping from legal XML expression to a policy associated with data covered by the contract, and this policy might be expressed in a language like XACML. However, there are currently gaps between these layers, so further work is needed to allow, and provide, an automatic translation. In addition, the mapping needs to be agreed, perhaps involving a third party to pre-define clauses and their meanings. A similar approach could be taken to that proposed for assurance control policies (Elahi and Pearson 2007), to avoid having to use a fine-grained ontological approach. In general, there is a tension between flexibility of expression and ease of understanding of such policies. There is a role for standardization as these technical policies need to be understood by multiple parties so that they can be dealt with and enforced by policy decision points and policy enforcement points within the cloud infrastructure. Current technical policies of this type are access control policies and obligations and security policies. The EnCoRe (2008) project has sought to define the necessary policies at different levels and address the problem of policy refinement (Casassa Mont et al. 2011).

As an extension of this approach, there can be a role for infomediaries, for example, as a Trust Authority (Casassa Mont, Pearson, and Bramhall 2003), to check that policies apply before allowing the decryption of data, and to play a role in auditing at this point. They could help check the situation before authorizing access to personal information, for example, via identity-based encryption, or via secret sharing techniques where the decryption key is broken down and shared between multiple parties, a certain number of whom need to agree in order to be able to build up the decryption key. Potentially, privacy infomediaries (Gritzalis, Moulinos, and Kostis 2001) could be used in other ways that help provide accountability, for example, by acting as insurance brokers and paying claims in case of privacy breaches. Who plays the role of privacy infomediary could vary according to the context; it could be a trusted identity provider for a federated set of services, a web proxy at an enterprise boundary, or a consumer organization.

Mechanisms for checking compliance will be a mixture of procedural and technical, involving both auditing and regulatory aspects. There is also a role for risk and trust assessment (including reputation management; Pearson, Sander, and Sharma 2009) before issuing contracts, to help satisfy regulators that best practice is being carried out, and in measuring metrics specified within SLAs. Decision support tools might be useful for lawyers representing the cloud providers, and to determine appropriate actions that should be allowed and to assess risk before PII is passed on – this could be part of a Privacy Impact Assessment (Warren et al. 2008). In addition, automated access control decision-making could incorporate privacy policy checking.

Utilizing procedural and technical co-design for accountability in the cloud

In essence, it is suggested that it is necessary to build upon the accountability proposals so far elucidated by extending the notion of retrospective accountability to include prospective effects. This is because the policies by which we will be judging our actors in the cloud will be continually changing, the context and technological environment will be evolving, and the potential privacy harms will not be constant or equal. Liability must still be determined in the event of a breach, but the negative impact of breaches in the cloud environment makes it imperative to build in processes and reinforce good practices such that liability does not arise in the first place. As such, businesses organizations contracting to supply or to utilize cloud services should be prepared to take the accountability practices a step further and incorporate reflexive privacy requirements into their agreements. This entails moving away from reliance upon static compliance mechanisms (in the sense of contracting parties being compliant with privacy law, and so reducing the risk of sanctions) and utilizing developmental, contractual and technical processes that encourage contracting parties to review and improve their privacy standards on an ongoing basis. Thereby, an ongoing process of privacy review is provided throughout the contractual chain.

Accountability in our sense is to be achieved via a combination of *private* and *public* accountability. Public accountability is derived from an active interaction between subjects of PII; regulatory bodies, such as Information Commissioners; and data controllers. It is premised upon highly transparent processes. Private accountability, in contrast, is derived from the interaction between data controllers and data processors, and is premised on contract law, technological processes, and practical internal compliance requirements. The objective of such accountability is not to meet "a set of largely procedural requirements for...processing activities", but rather to reduce the risk of disproportionate (in context) harm to the subjects of PII, and thus reduce or permit the amelioration of negative consequences for the data controller. It reflects an acceptance that absolute reduction of harm to the subjects of PII is an impossible goal in a disaggregated environment, such as a cloud service, and that the ability to respond flexibly and efficiently (or systemically and systematically) to harms arising will provide a more efficient form of privacy protection than enforcing blunt and/or static "tick-box" compliance criteria.

Hence accountability is in two halves. As shown in the top part of Figure 1, public accountability is provided by two means:

- transparency and stakeholder (data subject and regulator) consultation via an "evergreen" PIA process and data processor privacy audit; and,
- accountability via the ability of stakeholder's to assess performance against publicized policies and practices.

An "evergreening" PIA process is a cyclic continuous improvement process. In other words, unlike a privacy audit document, which is a snapshot of privacy compliance at the time of the audit, the PIA is designed so that processes can be checked against its recommendations, and those recommendations can be continually developed in the light of environmental changes. The data controller can point to the PIA process as involving and informing both data subjects and regulators (as stakeholders). The PIA process in turn feeds into risk reduction and risk amelioration strategies, such as privacy-enhancing contractual terms, and insurance policies against data private breaches and liabilities to data subjects. These too can be exposed to public scrutiny as a means of demonstrating data controller awareness of privacy risks, and the accountability processes through which such risks are to be managed, thus promoting stakeholder trust.

As shown in the bottom part of Figure 1, private accountability is provided by means of contractual provisions and technological tools that enforce reactive, and reward proactive, accountability practices amongst providers and subcontractors. Private accountability builds upon the risk information obtained from the PIA in the light of evolving cloud accountability or trust standards, i.e the PIA provides the

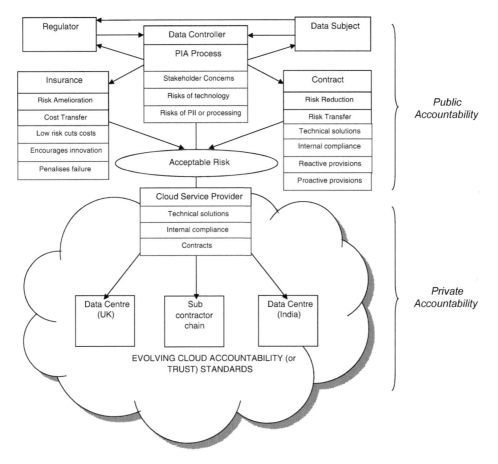

Figure 1. Accountability model.

context against which changing environmental conditions can be evaluated, permitting the effective/efficient deployment of appropriate technical, administrative or contractual privacy solutions across data centers and through subcontractor chains. Such accountability mechanisms need not be open to a high degree of public scrutiny (and may be commercially sensitive), but can be shown to be derived from a process that is visible to stakeholders.

Accountability and good privacy design go together, in that privacy-protecting controls should be built into different aspects of the business process. This should be a reflexive process in that it is underpinned by a non-static compliance mechanism that is an ongoing process of privacy review throughout the contractual chain. There will be developmental, contractual and technical processes in play that encourage an organization's cloud contractors to review and improve their privacy standards on an ongoing basis – this discourages "cheating" by contractors, rewards effective privacy protections, and prioritizes the prevention of disproportionate (in context) privacy harms over inconsequential (in context) privacy harms. This contrasts with the application of privacy protection in a "box-ticking fashion", where checking "our contractor is 'adequate' according to this set of static criteria" is likely to either waste resources on low-risk privacy harms or fail to identify developing high-risk privacy harms. Audit information can be produced, for example, by logging, use of third parties and tracking (Golle, McSherry, and Mironov 2006). In particular, sticky policy techniques can be used to ensure an audit trail of notification and disclosure of data to third parties (Casassa Mont, Pearson, and Bramhall 2003). Third-party certifiers or auditors can periodically verify data protection controls, and also underpin a range of new accountability-related services that offer a cloud computing infrastructure assurances as to the degree of privacy offered (e.g. analogous to privacy seal provision for web services (Cavoukian and Crompton 2000) and mechanisms for privacy assurance on the service provider side (Elahi and Pearson 2007)).

While this approach can provide a practical way forward, it has limitations. First, while contracts provide a solution for an initial data controller to enforce its policies along the chain, risks that cannot be addressed contractually will remain. For example, data generally has to be unencrypted at the point of processing, creating a security risk and vulnerability owing to the cloud's attractiveness to cybercriminals. Secondly, only large corporate users are likely to have the legal resources to replace generic SLAs with customized contracts – although it is possible that the cloud model will benefit SMEs without the requisite experience in-house by permitting them to buy services for security accountability from larger corporate users, thus increasing the degrees of assurance that they are able to provide. Finally, adding requirements to the vendor chain will increase the cost of the service. Use of contracts will be most effective for more sensitive or more highly regulated data that merits additional and more costly protection. However, we believe that this approach should be scalable. It is an upcoming challenge to strengthen this approach and make it more workable by developing intelligent ways in which accountability and information stewardship can be provided. This goes beyond traditional approaches to protect data (such as the "confidentiality, integrity, availability" model), in that it includes complying with and upholding values, obligations, and enhancing trust.

Conclusions

It is posited that, at present, the EU data privacy regulatory structure places too much emphasis on recovering if things go wrong, and not enough on trying to get organizations to "do the right thing" for privacy in the first place. Recent proposals for reform of data privacy regulation, both within the EU, and in the wider international arena, include encouraging the development of new regulatory processes that place a clearer emphasis on pro-active "accountability". Such discussions are still at a relatively early stage, and appear to have been largely confined to fora that are less than representative of the full range of data privacy stakeholders. It is suggested that there is considerable scope for critical evaluation of the theoretical underpinnings, and the possible practical implications, of an accountability-based regulatory approach from a socio-legal/regulatory theory perspective. Whether such an approach might import weak self-regulation to the EU via the back door, heighten the risk of regulatory capture or risk regulator overreach, are just some of the questions that might be usefully addressed in future research.

With the caveat that questions remain over the interpretation of "accountability", it is suggested that, in the scenario envisaged by this article, development of a hybrid accountability mechanism via a combination of legal, regulatory and technical means, leveraging both public and private forms of accountability, could be a practical way of addressing some current problems inherent in the EU data privacy regulatory structure. It appears to be a particularly appropriate mechanism for dealing with privacy issues that arise and are combined within cloud computing. There is much to be said for a co-regulation strategy based on a corporate responsibility model and underpinned primarily by contract. This places the onus upon the data controller to take a more proactive approach to ensuring compliance, but at the same time works to encourage cloud service vendors and their subcontractors to compete in the service provision arena, at least in part, on the basis of at least maintaining good, and ideally evolving better, privacy enhancing mechanisms and processes.

References

6, P. 2002. "Who Wants Privacy Protection, and What Do They Want?" *Journal of Consumer Behaviour* 2 (1): 80–100.

Abrams, M. 2008. *A Perspective: Data Flow Governance in Asia Pacific and APEC Framework.* Accessed April 15, 2012. http://www.docstoc.com/docs/42620170/A-Perspective-Data-Flow-Governance-in-Asia-Pacific-APEC

Alhadeff, J., B. Van Alsenoy, and J. Dumortier. 2011. "The Accountability Principle in Data Protection Regulation: Origin, Development and Future Directions." Accessed April 15, 2012. http://ssrn.com/abstract=1933731

ALRC. 2008. *For Your Information: Australian Privacy Law and Practice.* Sydney: Australian Law Reform Commission.

Bamberger, K., and D. Mulligan. 2008. "Privacy Decision-making in Administrative Agencies." *University of Chicago Law Review* 75 (1): 75–108.

Bruening, P. J. 2010. "Accountability: Part of the International Public Dialogue about Privacy Governance." *World Data Protection Report* 10 (10): 1–4.

Buttarelli, G. 2012. "Security and Privacy Regulatory Challenges in the Cloud." European cloud computing 2012, making the transition from cloud-friendly to cloud-active, Brussels, European Data Protection Supervisor's Office, March 21. Accessed April 15, 2012. http://www.edps.europa.eu/EDPSWEB/webdav/site/mySite/shared/Documents/EDPS/Publications/Speeches/2012/12-03-21_Cloud_computing_EN.pdf

Casassa Mont, M., S. Pearson, and P. Bramhall. 2003. "Towards Accountable Management of Identity and Privacy: Sticky Policies and Enforceable Tracing Services." In *Proceedings of the 14th International Workshop on Database and Expert Systems Applications 2003*, 377–382. New York: IEEE.

Casassa Mont, M., and R. Thyne. 2006. "A Systemic Approach to Automate Privacy Policy Enforcement in Enterprises." In *Proceedings of PET 2006*, edited by G. Danezis and P. Golle. Lecture Notes in Computer Science 4258, 118–134. Berlin: Springer.

Casassa Mont, M., S. Pearson, S. Creese, M. Goldsmith, and N. Papanikolaou. 2011. "A Conceptual Model for Privacy Policies with Consent and Revocation Requirements." In *Privacy and Identity 2010*, Vol. 352, *IFIP Advances in Information and Communication Technology*, edited by S. Fischer-Hübner, P. Duquenoy, G. Hansen, M. Leenes, and R. Zhang, 258–270. Berlin: Springer.

Cavoukian, A., and M. Crompton. 2000. "Web Seals: A Review of Online Privacy Programs." In *22nd International Conference on Privacy and Data Protection*. Toronto, Canada: Information and Privacy Commissioner of Ontario/Sydney, Australia: Office of the Federal Privacy Commissioner. Accessed April 15, 2012. http://www.privacy.gov.au/publications/seals.pdf

Cederquist, J. G., R. Corin, M. A. C. Dekker, S. Etalle, and J. I. den Hartog. 2005. "An Audit Logic for Accountability." In *IEEE International Workshop on Policies for Distributed Systems and Networks, 2005*, 34–43. New York: IEEE.

Charlesworth, A. 2003. "Information Privacy Law in the European Union: E Pluribus Unum or Ex Uno Plures." *Hastings Law Review* 54 (4): 931–969.

Charlesworth, A. 2006. "The Future of UK Data Protection Regulation." *Information Security Technical Report* 11 (1): 46–54.

Chen, S., and C. Wang. 2010. "Accountability as a Service for the Cloud: From Concept to Implementation with BPEL." In *Proceedings of the 6th IEEE World Congress on Services, 2010*, 91–98. New York: IEEE.

CIPL. 2009. *Data Protection Accountability: The Essential Elements*. Washington, D.C.: Centre for Information Policy Leadership. Accessed April 15, 2012. http://www.huntonfiles.com/files/webupload/CIPL_Galway_Accountability_Paper.pdf

CIPL. 2010. *Demonstrating and Measuring Accountability: A Discussion Document*. Washington, D.C. Centre for Information Policy Leadership. Accessed April 15, 2012. http://www.huntonfiles.com/files/webupload/CIPL_Accountability_Phase_II_Paris_Project.PDF

Council Directive 95/46/EC. 1995. On the protection of individuals with regard to the processing of personal data and on the free movement of such data. OJ L281, 31–50.

Cranor, L. 2002. *Web Privacy with P3P*. Sebastopol, CA: O'Reilly and Associates.

Creative Commons. 2009. Accessed April 15 2012. http://creativecommons.org

Crompton, M., C. Cowper, and C. Jefferis. 2009. "The Australian Dodo Case: An Insight for Data Protection Regulation." *BNA World Data Protection Report* 9 (1): 5–8.

CSA. 2009. *Security Guidance for Critical Areas of Focus in Cloud Computing*. Vol. 2.1. Cloud Security Alliance. Accessed April 15, 2012. https://www.cloudsecurityalliance.org/guidance/csaguide.pdf

CSA. 2010a. *Top Threats to Cloud Computing*. Vol. 1.0. Cloud Security Alliance. Accessed April 15 2012. https://cloudsecurityalliance.org/topthreats/csathreats.v1.0.pdf

CSA. 2010b. *Cloud Security Alliance Governance, Risk Management and Compliance (GRC) Stack*. Cloud Security Alliance. Accessed April 15 2012. http://www.cloudsecurityalliance.org/grcstack.html

CSA. 2010c. *CloudAudit (A6 – The Automated Audit, Assertion, Assessment, and Assurance API)*. Cloud Security Alliance. Accessed April 15 2012. http://cloudaudit.org/

CSA. 2010d. *Trusted Cloud Initiative*. Cloud Security Alliance. Accessed April 15 2012. http://www.cloudsecurityalliance.org/trustedcloud.html

CSC. 2010. *Digital Trust in the Cloud*. Falls Church, VA: Computer Sciences Corporation. Accessed April 15 2012. http://assets1.csc.com/cloud/downloads/wp_cloudtrustprotocolprecis_073010.pdf

Dalton, C., D. Plaquin, W. Weidner, D. Kuhlmann, B. Balacheff, and R. Brown. 2009. "Trusted Virtual Platforms: A Key Enabler for Converged Client Devices." *Operating Systems Review* 43 (1): 36–43.

Damianou, N., N. Dulay, E. Lupu, and M. Sloman. 2001. *The Ponder Policy Specification Language*. In *Policies for Distributed Systems and Networks*, edited by M. Sloman, J. Lobo, and E. C. Lupu. Proceedings of POLICY 2001, Bristol, UK Lecture Notes in Computer Science, Volume 1995/2001, 18–38. Berlin: Springer.

Data Protection Act 1998. (1998) London: Stationery Office.

Davidson, S. B., S. Khanna, S. Roy, J. Stoyanovich, V. Tannen, and Y. Chen. 2011. "On Provenance and Privacy." In *Proceedings of the 14th International Conference on Database Theory*, 3–10. New York: ACM.

DiLascio, T. 2004. "How Safe Is the Safe Harbor – U.S. and E.U. Data Privacy Law and the Enforcement of the FTC's Safe Harbor Program." *Boston University International Law Journal* 22 (2): 399–424.

Dolnicar, S., and Y. Jordaan. 2006. "Protecting Consumer Privacy in the Company's Best Interest." *Australasian Marketing Journal* 14 (1): 39–61.

Elahi, T., and S. Pearson. 2007. "Privacy Assurance: Bridging the Gap between Preference and Practice." In *Proceedings of the TrustBus 2007*, edited by C. Lambrinoudakis, G. Pernul, and A. M, Tjoa. Lecture Notes in Computer Science 4657, 65–74. Berlin: Springer.

EnCoRe. 2008. *Ensuring Consent and Revocation Project Website*. Accessed April 15 2012. http://www.encore-project.info

ENISA. 2009. *Cloud Computing: Benefits, Risks and Recommendations for Information Security*. Heraklion: European Network and Information Security Agency (ENISA). Accessed April 15, 2012. http://www.enisa.europa.eu/act/rm/files/deliverables/cloud-computing-risk-assessment/at_download/fullReport

EU Article 29 Working Party. 2009. *The Future of Privacy: Joint Contribution to the Consultation of the European Commission on the Legal Framework for the Fundamental Right* to *Protection of Personal Data* (WP168). Brussels: European Commission. Accessed April 15, 2012. http://ec.europa.eu/justice/policies/privacy/docs/wpdocs/2009/wp168_en.pdf

EU Article 29 Working Party. 2010. *Opinion 3/2010 on the Principle of Accountability* (WP 173). Brussels: European Commission. Accessed April 15, 2012. http://ec.europa.eu/justice/policies/privacy/docs/wpdocs/2010/wp173_en.pdf

EU Commission. 2012a. *Commission Proposes a Comprehensive Reform of the Data Protection Rules* (press release). Brussels, January 25. Accessed April 15, 2012. http://ec.europa.eu/justice/newsroom/data-protection/news/120125_en.htm

EU Commission. 2012b. *Proposal for a Regulation of the European Parliament and of the Council on the Protection of Individuals with Regard to the Processing of Personal Data and on the Free Movement of such Data (General Data Protection Regulation)*, COM(2012) 11 final, Brussels, January 25. Accessed April 15, 2012. http://ec.europa.eu/justice/data-protection/document/review2012/com_2012_11_en.pdf

Franklin, M. 2011. "White House Insists EU–US Data Protection Rules should be Interoperable." *MLex: Market Intelligence*, September 20. London: MLex.

Gellman, R. 2009. *Privacy in the Clouds: Risks to Privacy and Confidentiality from Cloud Computing*. World Privacy Forum. San Diego, CA: World Privacy Forum. Accessed April 15, 2012. http://www.worldprivacyforum.org/pdf/WPF_Cloud_Privacy_Report.pdf

Golle, P., F. McSherry, and I. Mironov. 2006. "Data Collection with Self-enforcing Privacy." In *Proceedings of the 13th ACM conference on computer and communications security*, 69–78. New York: ACM.

Gritzalis, D., K. Moulinos, and K. Kostis. 2001. "A Privacy-Enhancing e-Business Model Based on Infomediaries." In *Proceedings of the MMM-ACNS 2001*, edited by V. I. Gorodetski, V. A. Skormin, and L. J. Popyack. Lecture Notes in Computer Science 2052, 72–83. Berlin: Springer.

Haeberlen, A. 2010. "A Case for the Accountable Cloud." *ACM SIGOPS Operating Systems Review* 44 (2): 52–57.

Haeberlen, A., P. Aditya, R. Rodrigues, and P. Druschel. 2010. "Accountable Virtual Machines." *Proceedings of the 9th USENIX Conference on Operating Systems Design and Implementation Vancouver, Canada, 2010*, 1–16.

Hetcher, S. A. 2000a. "The *de facto* Federal Privacy Commission." *John Marshall Journal of Computer and Information Law* 19 (1): 109–131.

Hetcher, S. A. 2000b. "The FTC as Internet Privacy Norm Entrepreneur." *Vanderbilt Law Review* 53 (6): 2041–2062.

HyTrust. 2010. *HyTrust Appliance*. Accessed April 15, 2012. http://www.hytrust.com/product/overview/

IBM. 2004. *The Enterprise Privacy Authorization Language (EPAL). EPAL Specification*, Vol. 1.2. Accessed April 15, 2012. http://www.w3.org/Submission/2003/SUBM-EPAL-20031110/

IBM. 2006. *REALM Project Website*. Armonk, NY: IBM Corporation. Accessed April 15, 2012. http://www.zurich.ibm.com/security/publications/2006/REALM-at-IRIS2006-20060217.pdf

IBM. 2008. *SPARCLE Project Website*. Armonk, NY: IBM Corporation. Accessed April 15, 2012. http://domino.research.ibm.com/comm/research.nsf/pages/r.security.innovation2.html

IBM. 2010. *X-Force® 2010 Mid-Year Trend and Risk Report*. Armonk, NY: IBM Corporation. Accessed April 15, 2012. ftp://public.dhe.ibm.com/common/ssi/ecm/en/wgl03003usen/WGL03003USEN.PDF

ICO. 2006. *A Report on the Surveillance Society*. Wilmslow: Information Commissioner's Office. Accessed April 15, 2012. http://www.ico.gov.uk/upload/documents/library/data_protection/practical_application/surveillance_society_full_report_2006.pdf

ICO. 2008. *Privacy by Design*. Wilmslow: Information Commissioner's Office. Accessed April 15, 2012. http://www.ico.gov.uk/upload/documents/pdb_report_html/privacy_by_design_report_v2.pdf

International Conference of Data Protection and Privacy Commissioners. 2009. *International Standards on the Protection of Personal Data and Privacy – The Madrid Resolution*, November 5, Madrid. Accessed April 15, 2012. http://www.privacyconference2009.org/dpas_space/space_reserved/documentos_adoptados/common/2009_Madrid/estandares_resolucion_madrid_en.pdf

Jones, S. D. 2011. "Cloud Software Upgrades Aid Salesforce.com Growth." *Wall Street Journal Online*. Accessed April 15, 2012. http://online.wsj.com/article/BT-CO-20110405-708445.html

Kennedy, G., S. Doyle, and B. Lui. 2009. "Data Protection in the Asia-Pacific Region." *Computer Law and Security Report* 25 (1): 59–68.

Kenny, S., and J. Borking. 2002. "The Value of Privacy Engineering." *JILT* 1. Accessed April 15, 2012. http://www2.warwick.ac.uk/fac/soc/law/elj/jilt/2002_1/kenny

Kohl, U. 2007. *Jurisdiction and the Internet*. Cambridge: Cambridge University Press.

Lacohée, H., S. Crane, and A. Phippen. 2006. *Trustguide Final Report*. DTI Sciencewise programme. Accessed April 15, 2012. http://www.trustguide.org

Leathers, D. R. 2009. "Giving Bite to the EU–U.S. Data Privacy Safe Harbor: Model Solutions for Effective Enforcement." *Case Western Reserve Journal of International Law* 41 (1): 193–242.

Levin, A., and M. J. Nicholson. 2005. "Privacy Law in the United States, the EU and Canada: The Allure of the Middle Ground." *University of Ottawa Law and Technology Journal* 2 (2): 357–396.

Marchini, R. 2010. *Cloud Computing: A Practical Introduction to the Legal Issues*. London: BSI.

McKinley, P. K., F. A. Samimi, J. K. Shapiro, and C. Tang. 2006. "Service Clouds: A Distributed Infrastructure for Constructing Autonomic Communication Services." In *Proceedings of the 2nd international symposium dependable, Autonomic and Secure Computing*, 341–348. New York: IEEE.

Mell, P., and T. Grance. 2011. *A NIST Definition of Cloud Computing*. NIST SP 800-145 2009. Gaithersberg, MD: National Institute of Standards and Technology. Accessed April 15, 2012. http://www.nist.gov/itl/cloud/upload/cloud-def-v15.pdf

Microsoft Corp. 2007. *Privacy Guidelines for Developing Software Products and Services*. Vol. 2.1a. Redmond, WA: Microsoft Corporation. Accessed April 15, 2012. http://www.microsoft.com/Downloads/details.aspx?FamilyID=c48cf80f-6e87-48f5-83ec-a18d1ad2fc1f&displaylang=en

Mowbray, M. 2009. "The Fog over the Grimpen Mire: Cloud Computing and the Law." *Script-ed: Journal of Law Technology and Society* 6 (1): 132–146.

Mowbray, M., S. Pearson, and Y. Shen. 2010. "Enhancing Privacy in Cloud Computing via Policy-based Obfuscation." *The Journal of Supercomputing* 61 (2): 1–25.

Newman, A. L., and D. Bach. 2004. "Self-regulatory Trajectories in the Shadow of Public Power: Resolving Digital Dilemmas in Europe and the United States." *Governance* 17 (3): 387–413.

Nissenbaum, H. 2004. "Privacy as Contextual Integrity." *Washington Law Review* 79 (1): 119–158.

OASIS. n.d. *XACML*. Accessed April 15, 2012. http://www.oasis-open.org/committees/tc_home.php?wg_abbrev=xacml

OASIS. 2007. *eContracts Specification v1.0*. Accessed April 15, 2012. http://www.oasis-open.org/apps/org/workgroup/legalxml-econtracts

OECD. 1980. *Guidelines Governing the Protection of Privacy and Transborder Flow of Personal Data*. Geneva: Organisation for Economic Co-operation and Development.

Pearson, S. 2005. "Trusted Computing: Strengths, Weaknesses and Further Opportunities for Enhancing Privacy." In *Trust Management, Proceedings of the iTrust 2005*, edited by P. Herrmann, V. Issarny, and S. C. K. Shiu. Lecture Notes in Computer Science 3477, 91–117. Berlin: Springer.

Pearson, S. 2009. "Taking Account of Privacy when Designing Cloud Computing Services." In *Proceedings of the Software Engineering Challenges of Cloud Computing: ICSE-Cloud'09*, Vancouver, 44–52. New York: IEEE.

Pearson, S., and M. Casassa Mont. 2006. "A System for Privacy-aware Resource Allocation and Data Processing in Dynamic Environments." In *Proceedings of the I-NetSec06 201*, edited by S. Fischer-Hübner, K. Rannenberg, L. Yngström, and S. Lindskog, 471–482. Berlin: Springer.

Pearson, S., and M. Casassa Mont. 2011. "Sticky Policies: An Approach for Privacy Management across Multiple Parties." *IEEE Computer* 44 (9): 60–68.

Pearson, S., and A. Charlesworth. 2009. "Accountability as a Way Forward for Privacy Protection in the Cloud." In *Proceedings of the CloudCom 2009*, edited by M. G. Jaatun, G. Zhao, and C. Rong. Lecture Notes in Computer Science 5931, 131–144. Berlin: Springer.

Pearson, S., T. Sander, and R. Sharma. 2009. "Privacy Management for Global Organizations." In *Proceedings of the DPM 2009*, edited by J. Garcia-Alfaro, G. Navarro-Arribas, N. Cuppens-Boulahia, and Y. Roudier. Lecture Notes in Computer Science 5939, 9–17. Berlin: Springer.

Platten, N. 1996. "Background to and History of the Directive." In *The EC Data Protection Directive*, edited by D. Bainbridge, 13–32. London: Butterworths Law.

Ristenpart, T., E. Tromer, H. Shacham, and S. Savage. 2009. "Hey, You, Get Off of My Cloud: Exploring Information Leakage in Third-Party Compute Clouds." In *Proceedings of the 16th ACM conference on computer and communications security, 2009*, 199–212. Chicago, IL: ACM.

SLA@SOI. 2009. Accessed April 15, 2012. http://sla-at-soi.eu/

Travis, D., T. D. Breaux, and A. I. Antón. 2008. "Analyzing Regulatory Rules for Privacy and Security Requirements." *IEEE Transactions on Software Engineering* 34 (1): 5–20.

Truste. 2009. Accessed April 15 2012. http://www.truste.org/

TCG. 2009. Trusted Computing Group. Accessed April 15 2012. https://www.trustedcomputinggroup.org

Warren, A. P., R. Bayley, C. Bennett, A. Charlesworth, R. Clarke, and C. Oppenheim. 2008. "Privacy Impact Assessments: international experience as a basis for UK guidance." *Computer Law and Security Report* 24 (3): 233–242.

Weitzner, D., et al. 2006. "Transparent Accountable Data Mining: New Strategies for Privacy Protection." In *Proceedings of the AAAI Spring Symposium on The Semantic Web meets eGovernment, 2006*. Palo Alto, CA: AAAI Press.

Yao, A. C. 1986. "How to Generate and Exchange Secrets." In *Proceedings of the 27th Annual Symposium on the Foundations of Computer Science, 1986*, 162–167. New York: IEEE.

Yao, J., C. Shiping, W. Chen, D. Levy, and J. Zic. 2010. "Accountability as a Service for the Cloud." In *Proceedings of the 2010 IEEE International Conference on Services Computing*, 81–88. New York: IEEE.

Legally compatible design of future biometric systems for crime prevention

Matthias Pocs

Stelar Security Technology Law Research, Hamburg, Germany

> Innovations in emerging technologies have an impact on privacy and fundamental rights. For example, emerging technologies include future biometric systems for crime prevention. In contrast to large-scale biometric systems for migration control, these systems promise to track down terrorists and organized criminals but also entail novel risks for society. One can govern science and technology by means of privacy impact assessments (which are currently being researched). Alternatively there is the approach – used in this paper – that primarily builds on the assumption that technology design can render the violation of a legal norm impossible. Using German and European constitutional law as an example, this paper will present proposals for technology design derived from the law.

Introduction

At the airport the police scan fingerprint traces left on luggage before boarding. Should a terrorist cause the aircraft to crash, the data captured before the flight are searched against already known data from a database of criminals. This is one example of possible future crime detection scenarios where biometric data play a significant role. Police authorities have already tested and used biometric technology (Bundeskriminalamt 2007; Gates 2010; Thomas 1998; Daugman et al. 2004) and research is being funded (Hildebrandt et al. 2011; Bouchrika et al. 2011).

Owing to this development, it is possible that legislators will allow the police to use biometric systems in public places for preventing terrorism and organized and crossborder crime. In this scenario one captures data before knowing that the person checked is a criminal or before a crime is committed. Such precautionary data capture challenges the law (Desoi, Pocs, and Stach 2011; Pocs 2011a; Hildebrandt et al. 2011; Hornung, Desoi and Pocs 2010), particularly because one captures biometric characteristics without the individual having given cause for suspicion, as well as the large number of persons subject to the practice.

One can avoid risks to individual freedoms and democracy by means of technology design. This paper will present proposals for technology design derived from the law. It uses German and European constitutional and data protection law as an example. For the technology it uses future biometric systems for crime prevention as an example. The paper aims to engage in the discussion around the impact of innovations in emerging technologies on privacy. It also aims to contribute to the development of new instruments for the governance of science and technology.

Future biometrics and its opportunities and risks

In future biometric systems for crime prevention, nonsuspects are exposed to specific risks. In order to derive proposals for technology design from the law, one needs to know the special features of that technology as well as its risks to privacy.

Biometric scenarios for crime prevention

The deployment of future biometric systems for crime prevention challenges the law because it differs from the deployment of conventional systems for biometric access and identity card checks. This is particularly because these systems capture biometric characteristics by automatic means in uncontrolled environments where the individuals do not have to cooperate and hence cannot control the data capture.

This paper presupposes two scenarios at the airport. One is biometric data retention for use if an incident occurs during the flight; the other is biometric data capture for instant comparison with wanted lists. In the first scenario, before the take-off of an aircraft all fingerprint traces that are left on luggage are captured and stored as a precaution for crime detection (see Hildebrandt et al. 2011, 5.2). However, owing to the design, one can only use the data concerning a flight if a trusted third party such as a data protection authority cooperates (Pocs 2012a; Pocs, Schott, and Hildebrandt 2012). If then a predefined incident occurs (airplane crash, hijacking, members of criminal networks travelling or similar), the police can use the data to identify known criminals involved.

In the second scenario, facial data (with fingerprint traces this is not yet possible) are captured from CCTV cameras and instantly compared with wanted lists. Both scenarios aim to afford the police clues for detecting criminal networks and, in addition, the second scenario aims to detect and stop criminals on the spot.

Opportunities and risks of the technology

For society, the deployment of future biometric systems affords opportunities and entails risks. On the one hand the deployment could prevent crime. On the other, it entails specific risks (Desoi, Pocs, and Stach 2011; Pocs 2011a; Hildebrandt et al. 2011; Hornung, Desoi, and Pocs 2010):

- the revealing of sensitive information from biometric raw and template data (Working Party 2003, 3.7);
- the ability to connect several databases to create a personality profile owing to the uniqueness, universality (everyone has biometric characteristics) and life-long validity of biometric characteristics;
- the gaining of information about whereabouts, time and destination;
- "false hits";
- secretive data capture (fingerprints and faces leave traces; Working Party 2003, 3.2);
- unauthorized data access ("identity theft");

- function creep of data access (e.g. punishment of minor offences or creation of profiles about witnesses, contact persons, etc.; see in detail Pocs 2011a); and
- follow-up measures by the police at the location of system deployment.

In the future, legislators could allow the police to use systems that automatically capture biometric characteristics and compare them with wanted lists. Then one has to fear that the deployment cannot be checked because the technology affords unlimited possibilities of social control. This paper analyzes the impact of technology on privacy and how to govern science and technology by means of technology design.

Legality of future biometrics

Future biometric systems have to meet requirements from national constitutions like the German *Grundgesetz*, the European Convention on Human Rights and the EU Treaties and Fundamental Rights Charter. First, one has to consider the fundemental rights to informational self-determination (Germany), privacy and data protection (EU). In addition human dignity could be concerned if state authorities use biometric characteristics as single identifiers for the treatment of data subjects as mere "objects". Moreover, the special protection of sensitive data (Article 8 DPD) such as health and ethnic information could be applicable at least to some forms of biometric data. In addition, the right to travel and the freedom of movement could be at risk where the police track and continuously monitor individuals in different places.

Finally several other fundamental rights could be violated: property and free movement/freedom to travel (in case of confiscation); assumption of innocence and equality (if the system or its design suffer from errors); judicial review (in non-transparent systems); and prohibition of arbitration (in case of unspecified purpose of use; Hornung, Desoi, and Pocs 2010).

Governing science and technology by legal technology design

One can govern science and technology by privacy impact assessments. These are currently being researched in general (Friedewald et al. 2010) and particularly with a view to smart surveillance technologies (SAPIENT 2011). Another similar method is to "regulate" the technology design.

However one should bear in mind that technology design does not replace the law, but it can render the violation of a legal norm impossible. The relevant legal norm necessarily precedes the technological design. Therefore one does not make the prohibition of unlawful data processing redundant but instead enforces it by technology design. There are a number of implications to such technological enforcement, which have been discussed extensively (see e.g. Brownsword 2006; Citron 2007). It is questioned whether technology design can still be referred to as "law" (Brownsword 2006). It is also pointed out that automated implementation of legal rules should contain specific safeguards to guarantee, amongst other things, transparency (Citron 2007). In consequence, one cannot necessarily assume that design replaces a legal prohibition, but it is clear that it can enforce preceding constitutional legal norms that legitimize the design.

In order to regulate technology design, one can derive specific requirements for information and communication technology systems from legal rules. One example of such legal technology design has been described (Hammer, Pordesch, and Roßnagel 1993). Legal technology design also promotes the principle of "Privacy by Design" (Pocs 2012b), which in the future will be part of EU law. The following section will identify legal requirements for the design of future biometric systems for crime prevention.

Constitutional requirements in Germany

Laws permitting police to use biometric surveillance systems have to meet German constitutional requirements. In its case law the Bundesverfassungsgericht (Federal Constitutional Court of Germany) specified these requirements.

Anonymization

The legal provision that allows the police to use the system has an impact on the fundamental right to information self-determination according to Article 2(1) together with Article 1(1) *Grundgesetz*. This is because the future biometric system processes biometric data and criminal records. These are personal data within the meaning of Section 3 of the German Federal Data Protection Act (*Bundesdatenschutzgesetz*) and Article 2(a) together with Recital 26 of the EU Data Protection Directive 95/46/EC (DPD). From this, one can also derive the first legal criterion, that is, designing the system in a way that avoids identifiability by anonymizing or pseudonymizing biometric data (Desoi, Pocs, and Stach 2011).

Precision of the legal basis

The legal basis permitting the biometric system must specify, precisely and clearly, the "cause" ("*Anlass*"), purpose and limits of system deployment (Bundesverfassungsgericht 2008, 424). For police measures, legislators need to define a specific suspicion or danger as a requirement (Bundesverfassungsgericht 2004, 55). They can do this by limiting (1) the wanted lists, (2) data capture and (3) subsequent use of information. One has to regard the interplay of these three components in order to assess proportionality (Bundesverfassungsgericht 2008, 432).

First, legislators have to specify conditions for inclusion in databases for comparison, that is, the wanted lists. One needs to distinguish suspects and nonsuspects (witnesses, contact persons, etc.), facts and mere assumptions. From this, one can derive another legal criterion of technology design. One should design the system in a way that enables the police to distinguish between data subjects according to these conditions for inclusion in the wanted list (Pocs 2011a).

Second, legislators need to define conditions for data capture, including the place of system deployment (airport, football stadium, shopping mall, school or similar). Third, legislators need to limit the subsequent information use (courts must not use "hits" as evidence of a crime; Pocs 2012a).

Further, legislators must specify the technology design in a qualified, at least basic, precise and binding manner (Bundesverfassungsgericht 2010, 225). Hence legislators can define certain goals that the technology design must achieve.

Suitability and necessity

The technology deployment needs to be suitable and necessary for achieving its goal. At least, the system deployment must not prove to be unsuitable. For this the data capture needs to be successful in individual cases (Bundesverfassungsgericht 2009). This is very controversial and requires serious scrutiny. Therefore one should not understand technology design as legitimizing biometric systems that do not achieve the stated purpose.

In this case, the biometric system aims at aiding the police in detecting criminal networks. This means that the wanted list must only contain known persons who are suspects based on facts according to conventional constitutional police laws. Persons who match certain profiles based on statistical inferences (e.g. Harcourt 2007; NRC 2008) must not be included. The distinction by the police between suspects and nonsuspects as well as the facts and mere assumptions is crucial.

Further, it is not only false positives or "false hits" that stigmatize individuals. Rather, the mere fact of a match is problematic. This is because the match solely confirms that one belongs to a certain category that might – based on other evidence – be involved in criminal action. Therefore, a match or a "hit" must not imply guilt. Police and courts must not treat innocent people as criminals. This is even true if the hit is not a false hit because the inclusion of a person in a wanted list could be erroneous too. If respective safeguards are not in place, the system deployment will be ineffective and thus unsuitable for achieving the stated purpose.

Legislators have to show that, using the biometric system, police can in fact detect organized crime and terrorism. It is not enough to present facts that sound plausible. Rather one needs to conduct an empirical study. This study has to stand the test of the latest state of the art of criminology and application of its methods.

Apart from suitability, the system deployment is only necessary if no less intrusive and equally effective means is available. One has to take into account all biometric modalities (iris, fingerprint, face, gait, etc.). "Nontraceable" modalities (gait/iris) are less intrusive than modalities with which one leaves traces in many circumstances of daily life (CNIL 2007). The capture of fingerprints and faces also harms the effectiveness of existing biometric systems used for forensics, secret services and witness protection (Pfitzmann 2006).

Proportionality (in the strict sense)

Finally one must balance the impact on individuals and the goals pursued with the system deployment. One assesses the proportionality (in the strict sense) of automated capture of personal data using several criteria.

Detecting criminals. The goals of the system deployment specified in the legal basis are to detect criminal networks and individual criminals. In the case of future biometrics the purpose will have to be limited. The group of wanted persons should be small, that is, only those wanted for very serious crimes. Then the goals pursued by the system deployment are serious.

Public nature. The biometric system captures data in a public place. Accordingly everybody can see or otherwise perceive the biometric characteristics. The public nature reduces the impact on individuals according to the *Bundesverfassungsgericht* (Bundesverfassungsgericht 2008, 404).

However, one can argue against this legal criterion. "Privacy in public" is an important value precisely because the anonymity of the crowd provides an individual with privacy (Nissenbaum 1997). Biometric systems could identify individuals and thus violate this expectation of privacy or render superfluous the legal criterion of the public nature. Moreover the biometric machine/software "perceives" biometric characteristics in an entirely different manner than human beings. Therefore, it is not relevant that police use the system in public. This is because the software can store the data and render it searchable (inferring information not available to the naked human eye).

Data collection as mere aid. Police will only deploy the biometric system in order to look for people who are already known and have given cause for suspicion. The system processes data about a large number of innocent people but only temporarily and deletes them automatically. Hence, the technology use is merely an aid to identify persons and immediately take police measures (Bundesverfassungsgericht 2008, 404). This reduces the impact on individuals. However the following criteria will assert that the impact on individuals is higher.

Lack of cause. The system deployment lacks cause if neither a danger for certain objects of legal protection nor a suspicion of having committed a crime justifies the system deployment (Bundesverfassungsgericht 2008, 402). For such an indiscriminate data capture, the individual has not given cause.

"High scatter". Further, the system deployment involves a high "scatter" of data processing (or a "serious collateral intrusion into privacy"). This is because a large number of persons that have not given cause for the data collection are subject to it (Bundesverfassungsgericht 2008, 402). From this, one can also derive the legal criterion to design the system in a way that avoids a high scatter of captures and comparisons of biometric data.

Feeling like we are being watched. The system deployment could provoke the feeling of being watched. Such a feeling can be a consequence of the high scatter of the data processing (Bundesverfassungsgericht 2008, 403). As an argument from the contrary, this means that avoiding a high scatter also promotes the criterion of avoiding the feeling of being watched.

Adapting behavior. Further, the system deployment could lead to individuals adapting their behavior, which functionally corresponds to impacts on other fundamental rights of the data subjects (Bundesverfassungsgericht 2008, 406).

Transparency. The system deployment might violate the principle of transparency. "Transparency" refers to two concepts. On the one hand, legal protection is hampered if individuals do not know enough about the technology use (Bundesverfassungsgericht 2008, 403). In contrast to video surveillance, it is not only relevant to know about the camera, but also about matches or "hits" (Bundesverfassungsgericht 2008, 406).

On the other hand, transparency can be systemic. Legislators can achieve such a system transparency by involving data protection authorities. Hence the legislator of the European Community did this in Articles 18, 20, 22 and 28(3) of the DPD. It is typical for police measures for searching for wanted persons that transparency for the individuals and access rights have to be limited; therefore the constitution requires checking by completely independent state authorities (Bundesverfassungs-gericht 2001, 361). System transparency is particularly relevant owing to the secretive nature of police measures and the "high scatter" of the future biometric system for crime prevention. From this, one can also derive the legal criterion to design the system in a way that avoids identifiability and processing if the data protection authority does not cooperate.

Data minimization. In Germany the principle of "data avoidance and data frugality" according to Section 3a BDSG is recognized on the constitutional level (Bundesverfassungsgericht 2010, 270). It requires the technology to be designed with the goal of processing as little personal data as possible. If the biometric system does not use anonymization technologies (e.g. "Biometric Template Protection"), the principles are violated and the impact on individuals is more serious.

Use limitation. The principle of use limitation prohibits the use of personal data for other purposes than originally specified (Bundesverfassungsgericht 1983, 65). In the case of future biometrics, one cannot rule out the possibility that legislators later enact a law that permits data access for other purposes. Thus the impact on individuals is more serious. One can also derive design criteria such as designing the biometric system in a decentralized way that avoids concentration of informational power.

Data security. For the system deployment legislators need to safeguard a standard of data security that takes the specific impact on individuals into account (Bundesverfassungsgericht 2010, 224). Depending on the technology design, the police might violate this principle.

Stigmatization. The impact on individuals is more serious if the data subject is put under pressure to offer an explanation (Bundesverfassungsgericht 2010, 212) or is stigmatized (Bundesverfassungsgericht 2005, 351). Biometric (one-to-many) identi-fication systems are subject to specific error rates (TeleTrust-Arbeitsgruppe Biometrie 2006, 15). Individuals could therefore be subject to "false hits" which stigmatize them. Hence the impact on individuals is more serious.

Uniform personal identifiers. Another requirement follows from human dignity according to Article 1(1) *Grundgesetz*: one must not use uniform personal identifiers for comprehensive registration of the data subject (personality profile; Bundesverfassungsgericht 1983, 53). Certainly the police would not deploy the biometric system for comprehensive registration. However owing to their uniqueness, universality and life-long validity, biometric characteristics could be used accordingly and thus render the impact on individuals more serious.

Constitutional requirements in Europe

Laws permitting police measures using biometric surveillance systems have to meet European constitutional requirements. In Europe, Article 8 European Convention on Human Rights protects privacy and Articles 7 and 8 EU Fundamental Rights Charter protect privacy and data protection. The legal basis for data protection law is enshrined in Article 16 of the Functioning of the EU Treaty. This means that the EU will pass secondary law for data protection in the area of police and criminal justice (Commission 2012a).

This paper regards German and EU law as two parallel legal systems and uses both for deriving technology design proposals. This approach is due to a certain rationale. According to the European Court of Justice (ECJ), EU law also takes precedence over the constitutional law of Germany (*Internationale Handelsgesellschaft* C-11/70 (1970) ECR 1125; *Costa v. ENEL* 6/64 (1964) ECR 585). In contrast, the Bundesverfassungsgericht first did not accept this view. This was because the EU had no legal protection that would satisfy the German standard of fundamental rights (Bundesverfassungsgericht 1974, 285). Later this changed since the court held that it would normally not review the compatibility of secondary EU law with fundamental rights (Bundesverfassungsgericht 1986, 387). However the court regards the German fundamental rights as being also applicable to EU law and thus reserves the right to have the last word in exceptional cases (Bundesverfassungsgericht 1993, 175).

ECtHR case law

Before the coming into force of the Treaty of Lisbon in 2009, provisions for privacy and data protection in police and criminal justice were missing in EU primary law. Instead, the Council of Europe was in charge of fundamental rights according to the European Convention on Human Rights (ECHR). The ECHR provides for privacy protection in its Article 8, which is also the basis for the Data Protection Directive 95/46/EC in line with Rec. 46 DPD.

The ECHR is interpreted by the European Court of Human Rights (ECtHR). Its case law gives guidance for the privacy protection in police measures. Further, the Council of Europe adopted a recommendation for the police sector (Recommendation (87)15) which, however, was not often considered (Bygrave 1998, 265).

Introduction. In general, privacy/"private life" has a broad ambit that extends beyond the domestic sphere (*Peck v. UK* 2003). Similar to German constitutional law, the court examines the impact on privacy according to Article 8(1) using several criteria, such as storage of personal data (*Amman v. Switzerland* 2000), consent and awareness, nature of the information, and re-purposing of the information.

According to Article 8(2), the legal authority needs to promote a legitimate aim referred to in that provision, be necessary for achieving that aim, and specify the purpose. The legal authority is necessary if it answers a "pressing social need" and is "proportionate to the legitimate aim pursued". The purpose specification must be sufficiently precise and clear for individuals to foresee the technology deployment (*Kruslin v. France* 1990, para. 33; *Malone v. UK* 1984, para. 68).

Foreseeability. Regarding foreseeability, the ECtHR reaffirmed that the requirement of specifying the scope and manner of technology deployment also applies to police measures (such as phone interception; *Liberty v. UK* 2008; see also nos 2(1) and 5(1) Recommendation R(87)15).

However, it also acknowledges that the requirement of foreseeability cannot be "the same in the special context of interception of communications for the purposes of police investigations". This was because "the object of the relevant law is to place restrictions on the conduct of individuals". In particular, an individual should not "foresee when the authorities are likely to intercept his communications so that he can adapt his conduct accordingly" (*Malone v. UK* 1984, para. 67). Nonetheless, the law needs to provide for the category of individuals exposed to the surveillance, its circumstances, and the conditions for destroying recordings (*Kopp v Switzerland* 1998, paras 73–75; *Kruslin v. France* 1990 A 176-A, para. 35; *Huvig v. France* 1990 A 176-B, para. 34).

Necessity. Regarding the necessity of police powers, the ECtHR only accepts powers of secret surveillance of citizens "only insofar as strictly necessary for safeguarding the democratic institutions" (*Klass v. Germany* 1978, para. 42). Unlike in Germany, "necessary" also means "proportionate". In particular, it is disproportionate to store (DNA) data about non-convicted individuals. Even if the police collected the data for a good reason, they need to delete it as soon as the individual turns out to be innocent. It is unlawful to retain data for the sake of preventing future committal of crimes where most individuals will not commit a crime (*S and Marper v. UK* 2008). This resembles the Bundesverfassungsgericht's criterion of indiscriminate data processing and high "scatter" of data processing mentioned above.

In contrast to the German constitution, the term "necessity" is however broader in the ECHR. In Germany, the suitability and necessity only refer to the introduction of a police measure as a whole. The technology design and its impact on fundamental rights is evaluated no sooner than during the assessment of proportionality in the strict sense. However, the ECtHR understands that "necessity in a democratic society" includes both a "pressing social need" (this is similar the German notion of necessity) and proportionality. Therefore, it seems that these legal principles are not as strictly distinguished as in Germany.

Accordingly, the necessity requires serious scrutiny, especially since the use of biometric systems for the fight against crime is very controversial. As mentioned above, one should not understand technology design as legitimizing biometric systems that do not achieve the stated purpose. Rather, the use of the biometric system must be effective and meet the requirements mentioned in that regard. Otherwise, the system deployment is ineffective and thus prohibited by the ECHR.

Transparency. Since it is typical for police measures that transparency for the individuals is limited, the ECtHR also acknowledges checking by completely independent state authorities (*Kruslin v. France*, para. 30).

Positive obligations. Privacy protection also entails "positive obligations" on the state, for example, to provide IT security measures (*I v. Finland* 2008), access rights (*Von Hannover v. Germany* 2004; *McGinley & Egan v. UK* 1998; *Guerra v. Italy* 1998; *McMichael v. UK* 1995; *Gaskin v. UK* 1989) and rectification rights (*B v. France* 1992; *Cossey v. UK* 1990; *Rees v. UK* 1986).

Sensitive information. The ECtHR also recognizes the need to specially protect sensitive information. It holds that these are data which "call for the most careful scrutiny on the part of the Court, as do the safeguards designed to secure an effective protection" (*Z v. Finland* 1997, para. 96; see also Article 6 Convention 1981 ETS no. 108). Since from biometric data one can also obtain data about health and ethnic origin, this special protection is relevant.

Reasonable expectation. An additional criterion is the reasonable expectations of individuals (*Copland v. UK* 2007; *Halford v. UK* 1995), which reminds of the US approach. However unlike the US courts, the ECtHR does not rule out an impact on privacy solely based on this criterion; it only influences the impact on individuals.

Comparison with the Bundesverfassungsgericht and EU Directive. Legal protection by the ECtHR can be weaker in some instances than that of the *Bundesverfassungsgericht*. First, the legal authority does not have to be a legislative authority. It can also be a merely ministerial order. Further, the doctrine of "margin of appreciation" leaves European states room for manoeuvre with respect to the proportionality assessment, extent of the state's positive obligations, and establishment of facts. However several aspects narrow the margin of appreciation: the importance of the right concerned, the impact on individuals, the purpose of system deployment, and extent of common European standards (*S and Marper v. UK* 2008).

Moreover, it is weaker than the EU Directive is in relation to transparency. Transparency could follow from the requirement of effective remedy for the individual pursuant to Article 13 ECHR. However the Court holds that it is incompatible with the efficacy and purpose of surveillance if the police would have to notify individuals, even if only after the surveillance (*Leander* 1987 A 116, para. 66; *Klass* 1978 A 28, para. 58). The ECtHR offers less legal certainty in two regards. It is unclear what information use is covered by the right to privacy and how it influences the impact on individuals ("somewhat confusing"; Bygrave 1998, 263). It also offers a lower standard of protection ("hurdles not difficult to jump"; Bygrave 1998, 268f.).

Overlap with the ECJ. Sometimes the ECJ also decides on matters that fall within police and criminal justice. In particular, this competence is due to the discrimination between EU nationals. In particular, in EU countries it prohibits national centralized databases for the fight against crime if they do not store data about nationals but only about people from other EU countries. The fight against crime necessarily involves the prosecution of crimes and offences committed irrespective of nationality. Therefore the situation of a Member State's nationals cannot be different in relation to this objective from that of non-national EU citizen (*Huber v. Germany* C-524/06, 16.12.2008, paras. 78f.).

European Union law

In the future, it is the EU that will govern data protection for police and criminal justice. The ECtHR's case law will remain to delineate the minimum level of protection. This is due to the recognition of the so-called "general principles" including the ECHR according to Article 6(3) TEU (codifying *Carpenter* C-60/00 (2002) ECR I-6279; *Nold* C-4/73 (1974) ECR 491, para. 13).

Moreover, since 2010 the EU has the power to accede to the ECHR according to Protocol no. 14 ECHR (amending ETS no. 194). As soon as the EU has acceded, the ECtHR could have the last word. This is the case if Article 8 ECHR and Article 8 Fundamental Rights Charter (FRC) are equivalent (Streinz 2011, 604). According to Article 52(3) FRC, provisions of the ECHR and EU FRC have the same meaning and scope insofar as they are equivalent. However, insofar as EU law offers a higher level of protection, the ECtHR will not restrict privacy and data protection. This is because Article 52(3) FRC only harmonizes the ECHR and FRC as a minimum level of protection.

Since the EU will govern data protection for police and criminal justice, the European Court of Justice is competent. Judicial review by the ECJ could prove beneficial to privacy and data protection in the police sector because, in contrast to the ECtHR, the ECJ applies additional legal mechanisms. These mechanisms include the primacy of EU law (since *Costa v. ENEL* 6/64 (1964) ECR 585), direct effect (for the Treaty since *Van Gend en Loos* 26/62 (1963) ECR 1; and for directives since *Van Duyn* 41/74 (1974) ECR 1337), state liability (since *Francovich and Bonifaci* C-6/90 and C-9/90 (1991) ECR I-5357), equivalence and practical possibility (*Comet BV v. Produktschap* C-45/76 (1976) ECR 2043) and effectiveness (since *Factortame I* C-213/89 (1990) ECR I-2433).

Secondary law of the European Union

The EU will govern police data protection by means of specific secondary law. The future Police and Criminal Justice Data Protection Directive (Commission 2012a) will provide for specific rules in the police sector. The current data protection law of the EU will inspire it. However it will also provide for new rules. It will introduce new principles (Articles 4–11), create and restrict notification of data subjects (Articles 13, 15, 16 and 18), and introduce data breach notification (Articles 28 and 29). Moreover it will give to the data protection authorities stronger powers and stricter duties (Articles 18 and 46), and create remedies and compensation for individuals and bodies (Articles 50–52).

System transparency. The biometric system must be transparent. Legislators can achieve such a system transparency by involving data protection authorities. Hence data protection authorities are involved in a way that is stricter than the requirements of German law because the data protection authority needs to be "completely independent" (C-518/07, 9.3.2010). This is particularly relevant for surveillance measures, in order for the data protection authority to be independent not only of the police authority but also of the ministry of the interior, which influences police work.

Sensitive data. Sensitive data are data about ethnicity, health, etc. (Article 8 (1) DPD), and data about criminal records or similar (Article 8 (5) DPD). Thus the biometric system could process sensitive data because from biometric data one can extract ethnic and health data (Working Party 2003, no. 3.7) and any crime prevention system processes criminal data. This also entails a technology design criterion to separate sensitive data from the captured biometric data and delete them.

Data accuracy. Owing to the abovementioned error rates, the system deployment could violate the principle of data accuracy according to Article 6(1)(d) DPD.

Automated decisions. Further, owing to the above-mentioned error rates, the system deployment could violate the prohibition of automated individual decisions according to Article 15. In relation to the principles of data accuracy and the prohibition of automated individual decision, one can also derive another legal criterion of technology design. One should design the system in a way that ensures compliance with an upper limit of false "hits".

In particular: privacy by design and similar provisions

Privacy by Design. The principle of "Privacy by Design" requires appropriate technical and organizational measures to be taken at the planning stage so as to comply with the data protection provisions (Working Party 2009; see also Article 19 of the future Directive (Commission 2012a)). The principle requires governing science and technology by means of technological design which constitutes the theme of this paper. All design criteria mentioned in this paper promote the principle of privacy by design.

According to Article 23(4) of the future general regulation (Commission 2012b) the Commission could even implement the principle of Privacy by Design by means of specific technical standardization. Similarly there have been first attempts of the EU Commission to implement the principle of Privacy by Design. One example is the RFID PIA Framework (Working Party 2011a). The goal of this Framework was to develop "guidance for the design of RFID applications in a lawful as well as socially and politically acceptable way" (Commission 2009).

Another example of a tool for Privacy by Design is the EU Commission's pursuit of best practices for two associations in the field of online behavioral advertisement. They aim at specifying the opt-out rule in Article 5(3) of the ePrivacy Directive 2002/58/EC (as amended by Directive 2009/136/EC). In particular, the best practices provide for the design of cookies (Working Party 2011b).

The PIA Framework and best practices are only first attempts to implement Privacy by Design and are in need of improvement. To this end this author proposes to adopt two additional rules: (1) a certain report demonstrating how a certain technology design promotes fundamental rights; and (2) a five-step procedure for the interdisciplinary cooperation between lawyers and technologists (Pocs 2012a; Pocs, Schott, and Hildebrandt 2012).

Accountability. The principle of accountability requires technology users to be able to demonstrate that they have chosen and adjusted a legally compatible technology (Working Party 2010, para. 34; see also Article 18 of the future Directive; Commission 2012a). The demonstration adds to Article 5(2) of the current DPD, which only requires "ensuring" compliance.

Accountability enforces Privacy by Design in three steps. Compliance rests with the Privacy by Design requirement. Consistently one has to audit, if appropriate, the fact that one has taken the required design measures. Then one has to be able to demonstrate this. This is why one needs to retain the audit report for the supervisory authority. If one does not comply with one of these steps, according to the Commission, the supervisory authority will be able to impose a dissuasive fine on controllers.

Since Accountability enables the police and others to demonstrate technology design, some also regard Privacy by Design as a part of Accountability (European Data Protection Supervisor 2010, 105). Owing to Accountability, it is possible to demonstrate that one chose and adjusted the technology in a legally compliant way.

Privacy Impact Assessments. Privacy Impact Assessments will be mandatory for use of technology that entails specific risks for privacy and data protection. One can enforce Privacy by Design with PIA in two steps. It obliges technology users to assess in advance specific risks for "rights and freedoms" of data subjects that are entailed by a planned data processing process. Then they have to take measures to mitigate those risks (Clarke 2009). In particular, biometrics is set as a technology that requires the carrying out of PIA (Article 33 of the future General Regulation; Commission 2012b).

PIA adds to the prior checking according to Article 20 of the current DPD because it provides for a legal compatibility test. It takes not only data protection into account, but moreover the "rights and freedoms" of individuals as a yardstick for the assessment. That is, instead of a legal compliance test, there is a legal compatibility test within the norms of the EU Fundamental Rights Charter. Taking fundamental rights as a starting point is sensible because in relation to novel technology applications EU secondary law is full of gaps in the description of technology design.

Summary

To sum up it is apparent that future biometric systems for crime prevention have a large impact on the fundamental rights to privacy and data protection. If the police render crime prevention effective by means of automated capture of biometric data, they need to do this for the protection of fundamental rights too. They should use automatic means to protect those who are subject to the data capture or (false) "hits" and possible follow-up measures by the police. That is, just as with the goal of crime prevention, police need to use automatic means to reduce the risks for individuals and society.

Further, if the police process personal data prior to criminal activity, they should also ensure transparency and supervision prior to violations of privacy and data protection. This too suggests the development of technological measures for Privacy by Design, Accountability and Privacy Impact Assessments as well as legally compatible technology design. The law needs to define these technical measures to satisfy the necessary precision of the legal provision.

Examples of design proposals for future biometric systems

Supporting the above-mentioned legal requirements and design criteria, one can only realize legally compatible technology design together with developers, operators and users. Since the research on the biometric system for crime prevention is work in progress, the following part will present a selection of such design goals they have identified so far.

There are simple measures to reduce the impact on individuals. For example, the system could reduce the number of data captures to random data captures (Bundesverfassungsgericht 2008, 430). However there are also more sophisticated elements of legal technology design. The following section will present them.

Coarse scans (based on Dittmann et al. 2012)

The mere fact that a fingerprint trace is at a certain position on luggage scanned can indicate suspicion or danger if it was not located there before checking in the luggage. For example, the police use such an indication in the following scenario: during luggage handling at the airport, the scanner captures all fingerprint traces on bags, once before luggage handling and once afterwards. Then, the system only compares the numbers of fingerprint traces. If there are more traces afterwards there is reason to believe that someone has manipulated the luggage in the security zone of the airport. Hence technology design should avoid capturing a detailed fingerprint trace whenever sensible.

To this end, the scanner captures traces by means of so-called coarse scans (Dittmann et al. 2012). Coarse scanning limits the pixel resolution of the captured image. Accordingly, one can only roughly see whether there is a fingerprint trace at a certain position of the luggage scanned ("region-of-interest"). However, the image's resolution is so low that one cannot distinguish one fingerprint trace from another; the image is blurred.

This approach of a coarse scan is not only important to speed up the scanning process and render it feasible to scan bags routinely, but also promotes the criteria of:

- avoiding personal data because data are anonymized, people cannot be singled out, treated differently, subject to specific error rates or comparison with incompatible databases, and additional knowledge from databases (wanted lists or Automated Fingerprint Identification Systems (AFIS)) or audio/video material (CCTV recordings or work schedules) cannot be used;
- avoiding a high scatter because detailed scanning is not applied to the entirety of captured data relating to all flights but only to a single bag that is scanned in detail after it has been qualified as manipulated;
- the principle of transparency on a systemic level because one can inform a third party after coarse scans and before detailed scans, that is, it avoids identifiability and processing if the third party does not cooperate; and
- the principle of data minimization because the technology is designed in a way that is not oriented towards processing personal data but only anonymized data; individuals do not have to fear data collection due to which they can be exposed to police follow-up measures.

Comparison within capture device (based on Pocs 2011b)

The future crime prevention system compares the data captured in the location of system deployment (about a large number of nonsuspects) with the wanted list. If it is a central database system, the system combines the movements of all data subjects in an information system of a single police department. Hence technology design should avoid unnecessary concentration of informational power about the movements of nonsuspects.

To this end, one can propose not carrying out the biometric comparison in a central database system but within the capture device. For the comparison within the capture device, the police copy biometric data for the wanted list as index data from the central system into the capture devices. In order to be technically feasible, one needs to reduce the amount of data in a biometric dataset. For this, one can develop a data format using cryptoalgorithms of Biometric Template Protection.

This approach of decentralized comparison promotes the criteria of:

- avoiding a high scatter because, instead of the high number of persons that would be subject to the entirety of capture devices installed in the country, data capture is limited to the number of persons that are subject to a single capture device;

- the principle of data minimization because the capture device does not necessarily copy the data into the central system;
- the principle of use limitation because it satisfies the requirement of (vertical) separation of informational powers;
- the principle of data security because it avoids the need for investment of time, money and expertise that would be needed to protect the captured data from all capture devices;
- avoiding the use of uniform personal identifiers for comprehensive registration because not the location data from all capture devices but only the information about a certain place can be associated with the data subjects.

Distinction between data subjects (based on Pocs 2011a)

In recent years the police obtained powers to collect data without justifying it by relying on a specific danger or suspicion. This broadens the group of persons subject to data collection (witnesses, contact persons, informants, victims, etc.). Further the police have the power to use another Member State's police information system ("Prüm") or the EU's police information system (SIS II). Hence varying traditions in terminology could lead to inadvertent broadening of groups of persons. For these reasons technology design should ensure distinctions between the various groups of persons. The biometric system should only notify hits on the conditions for the inclusion into the wanted list specified by the legal provision.

To this end, one can propose designing the system in such a way that one can distinguish between the data subjects. The data fields used in the police databases enable the police to define the reasons of the registration of a wanted person. However, for the time being, the reasons the police use are not specific enough. They contain nonspecific terms such as "international criminal". They include residual terms such as "other causes". There are also reasons such as "police observation" that do not distinguish between criminals, witnesses and contact persons. Therefore one has to define data fields so that one can distinguish between data subjects in line with the legal provision (suspect/nonsuspect, objects of legal protection with a high priority, etc.).

Further, for EU data exchange, one has to link causes and purposes used in police work with the equivalent terms of the own Member State's database. One can do this by using equivalent data fields and keys in a "table of equivalence". Finally, one has to consider that the police choose wanted lists after having begun to deploy the biometric system. Hence one should be able to evaluate the data processing afterwards and ascertain the actual size of the wanted list. To this end one should create an automatic counter of data subjects that counts the number of individuals that are subject to the wanted list. Otherwise the data needed may not be available anymore for evaluating the system deployment afterwards.

This approach of distinction between data subjects promotes the criteria of:

- precision of legal provision because hits are only notified in the cases permitted by the law justifying the deployment of the biometric system;
- avoiding a lack of cause or suspicion because the data subject has given cause for notification of hits; and
- avoiding a high scatter because the group of persons subject to hits is limited.

Defining and testing of error rates

Biometric (one-to-many) identification systems are subject to specific error rates. Individuals could therefore be subject to false "hits". Technology design should hence limit the number of false hits and safeguard that the police comply with this limit during the system deployment.

To this end, one can propose several measures. As to the limit of false hits, one can choose between comparison algorithms. There are algorithms that are better at reducing the number of false nonmatches and those that are better at reducing the number of false matches. In principle, the latter algorithms should be preferred. Further, one has to establish the total working time of police officers to limit the number of false hits in such a way that every hit is actually re-examined manually. The factors influencing the error rates must not be alterable (physical position of capture device, comparison algorithms and thresholds of (dis-)similarity of faces, fingerprints, etc.).

Moreover one should consider several design requirements. The user interface should render the outcome of the comparison decision transparent. For example the system could display the relevant biometric features and the degree of similarity by means of "traffic lights". The captured data should be deleted without the need for human interaction. The police should train the operators of the biometric system regularly.

Moreover one has to safeguard compliance with the upper limit of false hits during the system deployment. To this end one should define the system during its testing and compare them with the subsequent deployment in real life. These aspects include: the physical position of capture device, comparison algorithms, thresholds of similarity, "population size" (number of data subjects), and the entire variability of data quality in the wanted lists. In addition one has to be able to evaluate the data processing afterwards and ascertain the actual number of false hits. To this end one should create an automatic counter of data subjects which counts the number of individuals that are subject to false hits.

This approach of defining and testing error rates promotes the criteria of:

- avoiding coming under pressure to offer an explanation;
- avoiding stigmatization;
- the principle of data accuracy;
- avoiding automated individual decisions;
- the assumption of innocence;
- equality; as well as
- the right to free movement and freedom to travel.

"Three-step model" (based on Desoi, Pocs, and Stach 2011)

Biometric systems for crime prevention capture personal data without having established whether the captured data will be relevant for the police. This is only done during the data processing, for example, if the security officer observes deviant behavior. Even then, identification is not necessary in every case. Thus technology design should reduce identifiability of data subjects according to the level of danger and suspicion.

To this end, some propose a "three-step model" for biometric surveillance systems (Roßnagel, Desoi, and Hornung 2011; Desoi, Pocs, and Stach 2011). For fingerprint trace collection this means a variation of the scenarios mentioned above: during luggage handling at the airport, the police scan all fingerprint traces on bags. First, they scan the traces by means of coarse scans (Dittmann et al. 2012). Owing to their limited pixel resolution, one cannot use these data for identification.

Second, if there are more traces on the bags after the luggage handling process, one can suspect manipulation of the bags in the security zone of the airport. Then the scanner captures these new fingerprint traces by means of detailed scans. However, these data are not accessible yet. Third, if there is reason to believe that there is a specific danger or suspicion, the officer is authorized to access the data by receiving a decryption key or similar. However, even at this stage, one does not carry out identification yet, only if further investigation requires it.

This approach of reducing identifiability promotes:

- reducing risks for the individuals according to the stages of danger and suspicion;
- avoiding the high scatter of the data processing;
- the principles of transparency and control;
- the principle of data minimization; as well as
- the principle of use limitation.

Exclusive storage of auxiliary data by data protection authority (based on Pocs 2012a)

If the police desire to retain biometric data that enable them to identify suspects in case of an incident, one needs to store data about a large number of innocent citizens. Varying the scenarios mentioned above, the police could scan all faces from CCTV cameras at the airport and store them for the duration of the flight. The police will not need most of the data, but individuals have to be afraid of being exposed to police follow-up measures. Hence, technology design should remove identifiability and only re-personalize the data in the case of an incident.

To this end, one can apply basic technologies of Biometric Template Protection on an institutional level. That is, the captured data are separated into so-called "pseudo identities" and "auxiliary data" and only a trusted third party such as the data protection authority stores the auxiliary data. In order to ensure that no one circumvents this, one also has to take several measures. For example one should separate system rights so that the police department cannot unilaterally change the system programs. Further, one should secure the exchange of keys and signatures between the police and the data protection authority.

Biometric Template Protection technologies, which are needed for the design approach of this subsection, do not work in all scenarios (just as the scenarios mentioned above). This is because they only work after the system extracts features from biometric data, which is necessary for automatic comparison. In that case one can take a similar but less strong approach of double encryption (Pocs, Schott, and Hildebrandt 2012).

Table 1. Overview of proposals for technology design derived from the law using the example of future biometric systems for crime prevention

	"Coarse scans"	Comparison of capture device	Distinction between data subjects	Defining and testing errors	"Three-step model"	Exclusive auxiliary data
Precision of legal provision			×			
Danger and suspicion					×	
Lack of cause			×			
High scatter	×	×	×		×	×
Transparency	×				×	×
Data minimization	×	×			×	×
Use limitation		×			×	×
Data security		×				×
Pressure/stigmatization				×		
Uniform identifiers		×				×
Sensitive data						×
Data accuracy				×		
Automated individual decisions				×		
Assumption of innocence				×		
Equality				×		
Free movement				×		

This approach of institutional pseudonymization promotes the criteria of:

- avoiding a high scatter;
- the principle of transparency by data separation on an institutional level;
- the principle of data minimization;
- the principle of use limitation by institutional separation of informational powers;
- the principle of data security because not all datasets but only one dataset can be attacked at a time;
- avoiding using uniform personal identifiers for comprehensive registration because from the captured facial data random pseudoidentifiers are created and hence diversified so that the biometric data cannot be used as "access keys" to connect several databases; and
- avoiding the obtaining of sensitive data because the system diversifies the captured biometric data and hence one cannot regenerate the original raw or template data from which one could obtain sensitive data about ethnic origin, health, etc.

Conclusion

This paper derives technology design proposals from German and European legal requirements. Its aim is to avoid that individuals need to fear being exposed to unnecessary police measures and "identity theft". Thereby it contributes to the governance of science and technology using the example of future biometric systems for crime prevention (Table 1).

Society can only handle innovations in emerging technologies if governments are paying attention to both the benefits of using technology, in this case, the protection from crime and dangers, on the one hand, as well as protection from consequences of abuse of informational power and carelessness when using that technology, on the other. If we take the opportunities privacy-enhancing design offers, it is possible to achieve both benefits for society.

Acknowledgements

The work in this paper was funded in part by the German Federal Ministry of Education and Science (Bundesministerium für Bildung und Forschung, BMBF) through the Research Programme under contract no. 13N10820 – "Digitale Fingerspuren" (Digi-Dak).

References

Bundeskriminalamt. 2007. *Final Report of the "Fotofahndung" study at Mainz Railway Station.* Wiesbaden, Bundeskriminalamt. Accessed September 21 2012. http://www.bka.de/kriminalwissenschaften/fotofahndung/pdf/fotofahndung_final_report.pdf

Bouchrika, A., M. Goffredo, J. Carter, and M. Nixon. 2011. "On Using Gait in Forensic Biometrics." *Journal of Forensic Sciences* 56 (4): 882–889.

Brownsword, R. 2006. "Neither East Nor West, Is Mid-West Best? *SCRIPT-ed* 3 (1): 15–33.

Bundesverfassungsgericht [1974] 37 BVerfGE 271.

Bundesverfassungsgericht [1983] 65 BVerfGE 1.

Bundesverfassungsgericht [1986] 73 BVerfGE 339.

Bundesverfassungsgericht [1993] 89 BVerfGE 155.

Bundesverfassungsgericht [2001] 100 BVerfGE 313.
Bundesverfassungsgericht [2004] 110 BVerfGE 33.
Bundesverfassungsgericht [2005] 115 BVerfGE 320.
Bundesverfassungsgericht [2008] 120 BVerfGE 378.
Bundesverfassungsgericht [2009] 120 BVerfGE 274.
Bundesverfassungsgericht [2010] 125 BVerfGE 260.
Bygrave, L. 1998. "Data Protection Pursuant to the Right to Privacy in Human Rights Treaties." *International Journal of Law and Information Technology* 6 (3): 247–284.
Citron, D. 2007. "Technological Due Process." *Washington University Law Review* 85 (1): 1249–1313.
Clarke, R. 2009. "Privacy Impact Assessment." *Computer Law and Security Review* 25 (2): 123–135.
CNIL. 2007. Commission nationale de l'informatique et des libertés (CNIL), 2007. *Biometrics*. Paris, CNIL. Accessed September 21 2012. http://www.cnil.fr/english/topics/regulating-biometrics/
Commission. 2009. Recommendation of the European Commission on PIA framework for RFID applications, C(2009) 3200, final.
Commission. 2012a. "Proposal for a Directive of the European Parliament and of the Council on data protection in the police sector." COM(2012)10, final.
Commission. 2012b. "Proposal for a General Data Protection Regulation of the European Parliament and of the Council." COM (2012)11 final.
Daugman, M., and C. Malhas. 2004. "Iris Recognition Border-crossing System in the UAE." *International Airport Review* 2: 49–53.
Desoi, M., M. Pocs, and B. Stach. 2011. "Biometric Systems in Future Crime Prevention Scenarios – How to Reduce Identifiability of Personal Data." In *International Conference of the Biometrics Special Interest Group (BIOSIG 2011)*, 8–11 September 2011, Darmstadt, edited by A. Brömme and C. Busch, 259–266. Bonn: Springer.
Dittmann, J., M. Pocs, C. Vielhauer, and M. Ulrich. 2012. "Fingerspuren in der Tatortforensik." *Zeitschrift für Datenrecht und Informationssicherheit (digma)* 12 (2): 80–83.
European Data Protection Supervisor. 2010. OJ no. C280, 16 October, 1.
Friedewald, M., D. Wright, S. Gutwirth, and E. Mordini. 2010. "Privacy, Data Protection and Emerging Sciences and Technologies: Towards a Common Framework." *Innovation: The European Journal of Social Science Research* 23 (1): 61–67.
Gates, K. 2010. "The Tampa 'Smart CCTV' Experiment." *Culture Unbound: Journal of Current Cultural Research* 2 (1): 67–89.
Hammer, V., U. Pordesch, and A. Roßnagel. 1993. *Betriebliche Telefon- und ISDN-Anlagen rechtsgemäß gestaltet*. Heidelberg: Springer.
Harcourt, B. 2007. *Against Prediction – Profiling, Policing, and Punishing in an Actuarial Age*. Chicago, IL: University of Chicago Press.
Hildebrandt, M., M. Pocs, J. Dittmann, M. Ulrich, R. Merkel, and T. Fries. 2011. "Privacy Preserving Challenges: New Design Aspects for Latent Fingerprint Detection Systems with Contact-less Sensors for Future Preventive Applications in Airport Luggage Handling." In *BioID 2011*, 4–6 March 2011, Brandenburg adH, edited by P. Drzygalo et al. Lecture Notes on Computer Sciences, Vol. 6583, 286–301. Berlin: Springer.
Hornung, G., M. Desoi, and M. Pocs. 2010. "Biometric Systems in future preventive Scenarios – Legal Issues and Challenges." In *Conference of the Special Interest Group on Biometrics and Electronic Signatures (BIOSIG 2010)*, 4–7 September 2010, Darmstadt, edited by A. Brömme and C. Busch, 83–95. Bonn: Springer.
Nissenbaum, H. 1997. "Towards an Approach to Privacy in Public – The Challenges of Information Technology." *Ethics and Behavior* 7 (3): 207–219.
National Research Council. 2008. *Protecting Individual Privacy in the Struggle Against Terrorists – A Framework for Program Assessment*. Washington, DC: National Academies Press.
Pfitzmann, A. 2006. "Biometrie – wie einsetzen und wie keinesfalls? *Informatik-Spektrum* 29 (5): 353–356.
Pocs, M. 2011a. "Gestaltung von Fahndungsdateien – Verfassungsverträglichkeit biome-trischer Fahndungssysteme." *Datenschutz und Datensicherheit* 35 (3): 163–168.

Pocs, M. 2011b. "Abgleich im Erfassungsgerät." In *D-A-CH Security 2011*, 12–16 September 2011, Oldenburg, edited by P. Schartner and J. Taeger, 346–360. Oldenburg: syssec.

Pocs, M. 2012a. "Vier Augen, zwei Behörden und eine Technik für künftige Biometrie-basierte Kriminalitätsbekämpfung." In *Staat und Verwaltung auf dem Weg zu einer offenen, smarten und vernetzten Verwaltungskultur – Gemeinsame Fachtagung Verwaltungsinformatik (FTVI) und Fachtagung Rechtsinformatik (FTRI) 2012*, 15–16 March 2012, Friedrichshafen, edited by J. von Lucke et al. Lecture Notes in Informatics, 97–112. Bonn: Springer.

Pocs, M. 2012b. "Will the EU Commission be Able to Standardise Legal Technology Design with a Legal Method?" *Computer Law and Security Review* 28(6): 641–650.

Pocs, M., M. Schott, and M. Hildebrandt. 2012. "Legally Compatible Design of Digital Dactyloscopy in Future Surveillance Scenarios." In *Optics, Photonics, and Digital Technologies for Multimedia Applications II (SPIE Photonics 2012)*, 2–6 July 2012, Brussels, edited by P. Schelkens et al., Vol. 8436, article number 84360Z. Brussels: SPIE.

Roßnagel, A., M. Desoi, and G. Hornung. 2011. "Ein Drei-Stufen-Modell als Vorschlag zur grundrechtsschonenden Gestaltung." *Datenschutz und Datensicherheit* 35 (7): 694–701.

SAPIENT. 2011. "FP7 research project SAPIENT, 2012". *Surveillance, Privacy and Ethics.* Karlsruhe: Fraunhofer-Institut für System- und Innovationsforschung. Accessed September 21 2012. http://www.sapientproject.eu

Streinz, M. 2011. "Die Rechtsprechung des EuGH zum Datenschutz." *Datenschutz und Datensicherheit* 35 (9): 602–604.

TeleTrust-Arbeitsgruppe Biometrie. 2006. *Kriterienkatalog zur Vergleichbarkeit biometrischer Verfahren (V3.0).* Berlin: TeleTrust. Accessed October 1 2012. http://www.teletrust.de/uploads/media/KritKat-3_final_01.pdf

Thomas, R. 1998. "As UK Crime Outstrips the US, a Hidden Eye is Watching: Police Switch on a Camera that Recognizes Your Face." *The Observer*, October 11, 5.

Working Party. 2003. Opinion of the European Union's Article 29 Working Party on Data Protection of 1.8.2003 on Biometrics, WP80, 12168/02/EN.

Working Party. 2009. "Opinion of the European Union's Article 29 Working Party on Data Protection of 1.12.2009 on the Consultation of the European Commission on the Legal Framework for the Fundamental Right to Protection of Personal Data", WP168, 02356/09/EN.

Working Party. 2010. "Opinion of the European Union's Article 29 Working Party on Data Protection of 13.7.2010 on Accountability", WP173, 00062/10/EN.

Working Party. 2011a. "Opinion of the European Union's Article 29 Working Party on Data Protection of 11.2.2011 on the revised Industry Proposal for a Privacy and Data Protection Impact Assessment Framework for RFID Applications", WP180, 00327/11/EN.

Working Party. 2011b. "Opinion of the European Union's Article 29 Working Party on Data Protection of 8.12.2011 on EASA/IAB Best Practice Recommendation on Online Behavioural Advertising", WP188, 02005/11/EN.

Privacy issues in public discourse: the case of "smart" CCTV in Germany

Norma Möllers and Jens Hälterlein

Faculty of Social Sciences, Department of Sociology of Organization and Administration II, Potsdam University, August-Bebel-Str. 89, D-14482 Potsdam, Germany

In dealing with surveillance, scholars have widely agreed to refute privacy as an analytical concept and defining theme. Nonetheless, in public debates, surveillance technologies are still confronted with issues of privacy, and privacy therefore endures as an empirical subject of research on surveillance. Drawing from our analysis of public discourse of so-called "smart" closed-circuit television (CCTV) in Germany, we propose to use a sociology of knowledge perspective to analyze privacy in order to understand how it is socially constructed and negotiated. Our data comprise 117 documents, covering all publicly available documents between 2006 and 2010 that we were able to obtain. We found privacy to be the only form of critique in the struggle for the legitimate definition of smart CCTV. In this paper, we discuss the implications our preliminary findings have for the relationship between privacy issues and surveillance technology and conclude with suggestions of how this relationship might be further investigated as paradoxical, yet constitutive.

The persistence of privacy

Privacy is a controversial issue in surveillance scholarship because it meets political, thematic and conceptual difficulties. Regarding privacy as a policy instrument, Stalder (2002, 123), for instance, has expressed doubts as to whether privacy can effectively keep surveillance in check, because sanctions of information misuse are not strong enough. On the other hand, Bennett (2011, 493–494) claims that privacy regulations remain flawed but necessary, simply because they are the only actual mechanism to control excessive surveillance. To varying degrees, these positions exemplify a broadly shared conviction that privacy is a fairly weak means for political activism. On a related matter, Lyon (2003a, 1), van der Ploeg (2003, 66–67), and others insist that focusing too much on privacy as a scholarly theme means ignoring more pressing issues that may result from surveillance practices, such as discrimination, social inequality or even shifting conceptions of bodily integrity. The rejection of privacy as a defining theme is widely shared in surveillance research because it is regarded as too narrow to grasp the entirety of the social consequences resulting from surveillance practices. Finally, several scholars have pointed out serious difficulties when privacy is applied as a theoretical concept to analyze whether we have less privacy now than in the past. In response to these conceptions of privacy, Lyon and Zureik (1996, 13) pointed out that understandings of what is private and what is public differ across cultures, and Haggerty and Ericson (2006, 11–12) added that they are also relative to institutional and organizational contexts. They then conclude that such a static definition of privacy is largely inappropriate to the factual complexities of surveillance in present societies.

While we sympathize with the claim that researching surveillance technology exclusively through the lens of privacy is inadequate, we nevertheless face the problem that it cannot be ignored because of its regular occurrence in empirical data. If privacy endures as a substantive empirical subject in surveillance research, we must find an adequate perspective to work with it. The critiques of privacy as a theoretical concept can help guide this perspective: if understandings of privacy are culturally relative, then they are also historically relative, and we can trace their development across time and analyze how they relate to other topics in surveillance research. This means that we can treat privacy as an empirical phenomenon that is constructed and negotiated in social processes, and thus open it up for sociological analysis. This approach somewhat resembles Steeves's understanding of privacy as "a dynamic process of negotiating personal boundaries" (Steeves 2009, 193). However, we would prefer to treat the ends of this negotiation as an open-ended question because personal boundaries are not necessarily the only parameters that are construed under the title of privacy. This shift in perspective decenters privacy and focuses on other issues such as the development and employment of surveillance technology, the organization of labor, or shifts in social control. This perspective might bring privacy back into surveillance research in a useful way, for example, by scrutinizing how the public debate on privacy might affect the development of surveillance technology, or how privacy regulations and their interpretations in practice might affect the organization of surveillance work.

Thus taking a social constructionist stance, this paper analyzes a small portion of the relationship between privacy and surveillance technology. Technology studies have demonstrated that the technical properties of a technological system cannot determine its legitimate use, but that technology is better understood in a mutually constitutive relationship with the social worlds in which it is embedded (MacKenzie and Wajcman 1999, 23). This means that meanings attached to a technology are achieved to an important extent by the social processes relevant to its development and employment. Whereas early technology studies focused on the social shaping in design and appropriation of technologies (Pinch and Bijker 1984; Bijker 1995; Kline and Pinch 1996), subsequent contributions pointed out the importance of the cultural conditions under which a technology is developed (e.g. Klein and Kleinman 2002, 40–46; Jasanoff 2005, 247–249). Applied to surveillance technology, this means that discourses of privacy also shape the circumstances for which it is regarded an appropriate means. Although these negotiations constitute only one facet of social processes, their analysis might nonetheless help understand why surveillance technologies enjoy their immense popularity, even though there is no strong evidence for their effectiveness or a general increase in crime.

This paper suggests that the privacy discourse might have helped the emergence of new surveillance technologies. We outline this seemingly contradictory relationship between privacy critiques and surveillance technology by discussing preliminary results of our analysis of the public discourse of so-called "smart" closed-circuit television (CCTV) in Germany between 2006 and 2010. First, we state our working definition of smart CCTV. Second, we briefly sketch the institutional context in which actors struggle over the legitimate definition of smart CCTV. Third, we delineate our research design by laying out the theoretical and methodological assumptions on which our results are based. Fourth, we briefly summarize the overall structure of the public discourse of smart CCTV, pointing out the various core issues that emerged between 2006 and 2010. Finally, we focus on how privacy issues have been discussed in public discourse, and elaborate on some of our findings. We conclude with some suggestions of how the relationship between privacy and surveillance technology might be further investigated as paradoxical, yet constitutive.

"Smart" CCTV

Scholars still grapple with finding an appropriate term for the new CCTV systems that are currently being developed in the Euro-American world because they come with a variety of functionalities and applications. Functionalities may range from classification, storage and retrieval of video footage, through object tracking, to data mining and the prediction of events based on the captured data (Introna and Wood 2004, 181; for a more detailed overview in terms of technical features see Gouallier and Fleurant 2009). The new CCTV systems are also not limited to one single purpose. Desired applications range from automatic detection of criminal behavior, identification of search-listed criminal or unwanted individuals, through the prosecution of traffic offenders, to prediction of traffic jams and mass panic, as well as the statistical analysis of consumer behavior (e.g. in supermarkets). Although these projected functionalities and applications may seem disparate, the common idea that runs through them is that operators are not required to watch the video screens at all times, but are notified by the system in case of an event of interest. In other words, the shared feature of the new CCTV systems is that all of them are built around the computer, not the camera.

The shift from camera to computer is nicely captured by the term *algorithmic surveillance*, originally coined by Norris and Armstrong (1999) and adapted by Introna and Wood (2004) for facial recognition systems. Some of the more commonly used alternatives are *semantic video surveillance* (Musik 2011), *second generation CCTV* (Surette 2005), and *smart CCTV* (Gates 2010; Ferenbok and Clement 2011). However, none of these terms are entirely satisfying: *algorithmic surveillance* does not discriminate visual from non-visual surveillance and thus might be better used as an umbrella term for all kinds of computer-based surveillance technologies; *second generation CCTV* collapses the complex entanglement of social and technical processes to a linear and evolutionary logic of technological development; and *smart CCTV* might be understood containing a strong normative connotation of technological progress.

For the sake of brevity and owing to the lack of a better term, throughout this paper we apply the term *smart CCTV*, while acknowledging its flaws. Our working definition of smart CCTV refers to *visual surveillance systems* that analyze and interpret video footage by using *pattern recognition technologies*. Because we take a social constructionist stance, the systems' actual properties were less important; instead, we collected documents if they defined the emerging technology as new, smart, autonomous or in similarly descriptive terms. Also, our definition ultimately guided our selection of articles in which we restricted the data collection to articles that (1) discussed visual surveillance, and (2) referred to these surveillance systems as somehow "doing things autonomously".

Situating the controversy

The development of surveillance technology is accompanied by struggles over their legitimate definition. Governmental institutions might strongly demand and extensively fund research and development because global risks, such as terrorism and organized crime, seemingly necessitate more efficient countermeasures. Nevertheless, privacy advocates criticize surveillance technologies because they are seen to pose threats to individual liberties. To varying degrees, these contrasting positions are stabilized in Germany's institutional landscape.

Governmental institutions are often a crucial driving force for the development and implementation of new surveillance technologies because provision and protection of public safety fall under their area of responsibility. In 2007, Germany's Ministry of Education and Research set up extensive funds to stimulate research of smart surveillance technologies. Similarly, the various police offices that are affiliated with the German Ministries of Internal Affairs each have their own in-house research facilities for these technologies. Alongside considerations of security, the flourishing market for security technology strongly motivates governmental institutions to push research and development; of course, this interest is widely shared by private corporations within the industry for surveillance technology. However, smart CCTV systems, similar to analog systems, encounter serious socio-technical problems, as exemplified by the facial recognition project of the Federal Police Office (Bundeskriminalamt) in 2006, in which false alarm rates proved to be problematic for police in terms of effectiveness. More importantly, failures frequently have elicited harsh criticism, weighing the systems' low effectiveness against considerable infringements of privacy rights. Thus, in spite of massive efforts to push research and development, government institutions are probably pressured to justify the appropriateness of smart CCTV against opponents' objections.

In 1970, protection of privacy was formally institutionalized in German law following a decision in the federal state of Hessen. Mayer-Schönberger (1997, 221) claims that a major reason for this was the introduction of electronic data processing into governmental bureaucracies. Since then, the juridical literature on privacy and data protection has expanded significantly and numerous legal regulations have been passed in Germany to protect guidelines and sanction their violations, which is an effect presumably due to the expansion of computer-based work in public and private sectors. Privacy advocates may be organized in non-governmental organizations (NGOs), and privacy is on the agenda of political parties, but with varying degrees of importance. Although privacy is addressed in a range of institutions, control of privacy guidelines is mainly provided by data protection commissioners at communal, federal and national levels. The commissioners' mandate is to assess organizations' surveillance practices and pressure them to meet legal requirements. Yet the legal regulation of CCTV in public spaces remains extremely complicated because it varies not only along Germany's national laws, but also along those of the 16 federal states. In semi-public spaces such as public transportation, the problem is even more intricate because the employment of CCTV not only falls under police regulations, but is also subject to civil law. Similarly, legal regulations are also required to consider the great variety of surveillance technologies and keep track of the critical differences between old and new technologies. Thus, despite considerable efforts to control the use of surveillance technologies, requirements specific to the sovereign rights of the federal states and rapid technological advances of emerging surveillance technologies challenge legal frameworks, courts and data protection commissioners.

Theoretical framework

Our project uses the "sociology of knowledge approach to discourse" (SKAD) which was mainly developed by Keller (2011a, 2011b, 2011c) over the course of the past decade. As its name implies, the most distinctive feature of SKAD, compared with linguistic or ethnomethodological traditions of discourse analysis, is that it draws heavily from the sociology of knowledge traditions.[1] Another distinctive feature of SKAD is that it is compatible with inductive strategies of qualitative research, most importantly grounded theory in the tradition of Strauss (Strauss 1987; Strauss and Corbin 1998). Although SKAD's conceptualization of the relationship between the material and the social could be better elaborated, we contend that it is a framework particularly well suited to exploring the cultural conditions of the development of surveillance technology.

Keller developed the theoretical framework by integrating Berger and Luckmann's (1966) approach to the sociology of knowledge and Foucault's (1972) concept of discourse. It attempts to overcome the shortcoming of both approaches, which is the analytical gap between structure and agency. On one hand, it uses Berger and Luckmann's approach to conceptualize how knowledge shapes and is shaped by social practices, which is a pitfall in Foucault's early structuralist writings. On the other hand, SKAD deems Foucault's concept of discourse to be beneficial because it focuses on the extent to which large-scale knowledge regimes, entrenched in powerful institutions, structure social practices. Keller points out that this is a conceptualization of large-scale social aggregation that was not sufficiently elaborated in Berger and Luckmann's theory. According to Foucault (1972, 49), these large-scale sign structures, which he calls discourses, do not represent the objects to which they refer, but systematically produce them. Translating Foucault's well-known concept into sociological terms, SKAD understands discourses as knowledge that forms patterns of interpretation and action. This knowledge is understood as institutionalized in social and material structures within specific socio-historic contexts. SKAD thus tries to adapt Foucault's (1979) later material-semiotic understanding of the social and material worlds as inextricably linked to each other because there is no practice independent of discourse; simultaneously, discourses exist only by means of practices and artifacts.

Referring to Berger and Luckmann (1966), SKAD agrees that society is an "objective reality" that is institutionalized in social stocks of knowledge. Actors in turn internalize knowledge in socialization processes, and then reproduce and transform knowledge in their everyday practices. For example, when we read in the daily press about plans for a new CCTV system in our neighborhood, it certainly shapes our attitudes towards these technologies: some people may feel safer in monitored spaces, while others might try to avoid them or even engage in organized public protest. It is of crucial importance that these practices do not occur in an arbitrary way, but are bound to the finite number of alternatives provided by shared ways of knowing. Thus, if knowledge structures the ways in which individuals act, think and speak, it is useful to scrutinize which knowledge is acknowledged and accepted as true. A second reason for analyzing discourses in terms of SKAD is that it allows for particular attention to claims that are marginalized or excluded from dominant discourses. If discourses determine what is known to be true, truth-claims that contradict dominant discourses but cannot draw on powerful resources (e.g. degree of organization, public visibility) generally have great difficulty in being acknowledged. Disadvantaged social groups are often excluded from dominant discourses, and the analysis of their exclusion informs us about the distribution of power. Finally, even within the arena of dominant discourses, phenomena often remain contested over longer periods of time; the discourses of surveillance technology are prominent examples of such struggles. Consequently, dominant discourses might compete for the legitimate definition of a phenomenon by seeking to include or exclude issues, or controlling a controversy (Keller 2011b, 47; also see Foucault 1982). Applied to our research, the configuration of negotiations in relation to what they exclude then constitutes the cultural conditions that afford the development of smart CCTV.

Methods

Data collection

In order to link theory and methods, we chose to analyze public documents in which the production and reproduction of social stocks of knowledge could be found. In public arenas like the mass media, discourses not only struggle over the legitimate definition of smart CCTV; they also reach a significant audience whose relation toward smart CCTV they are likely to shape. We thus considered only publicly available documents that explicitly discussed smart CCTV. Among our data set first were daily and weekly newspaper articles on regional and national levels. On the national level we selected widely circulated newspapers, whereas on regional levels we pre-selected newspapers of areas in which smart CCTV was either piloted or officially planned. To cover the widest possible range of discourse, we also collected articles from blogs and online magazines because we assumed that they might present smart CCTV in different ways. Finally, to cover explicitly political discourse, we collected transcripts of parliamentary debates and other parliamentary documents at regional and national levels.

We accessed our source material via online archives of the aforementioned formats. We began with a set of three keywords – "intelligent video surveillance", "smart CCTV" and "automated video surveillance" – which unfortunately returned only about 20 articles. Having subsequently learned that the technical community has a much wider vocabulary for smart CCTV, we expanded the keywords to terms such as "machine learning" and "video analytics", among others. Our expanded list then had 34 combinations of different keywords for smart CCTV, and returned about 400 articles. After two readings of the entire data set, we discarded articles that were clearly not related to smart CCTV as stated in our working definition, or which only mentioned smart CCTV in passing. Our final data set (Table 1) then comprised 117 documents, covering the years between 2006 and 2010.[2] We can see that the public discussion is relatively small, which is probably because smart CCTV in Germany is still in the development phase. Also note that there are only eight parliamentary documents, which indicates that the issue has not yet been widely discussed in the legislative branches of government. We want to emphasize that our focus on these formats was not to disregard other sources, such as documents of NGOs, lobbies and unions, or radio and TV productions, but rather because qualitative analyses, including discourse analysis, are time-intensive.

Table 1. Final data set covering 2006–2010

	Daily and weekly newspapers	Parliamentary documents	Blogs and online formats
2006	8	4	10
2007	20	0	15
2008	7	0	20
2009	3	0	5
2010	6	4	15
Total	**44**	**8**	**65**

Data analysis

We analyzed the material using qualitative methods, drawing heavily on strategies developed in grounded theory (Strauss 1987; Strauss and Corbin 1998). The aim was not to deductively assume that there are discourses in opposition to or in favor of smart CCTV, but to inductively analyze how smart CCTV was problematized. Since we wanted to understand the different meanings of smart CCTV in public discourse, the roles it would play could not be set in advance, but had to be treated as open-ended questions. This blending of theoretical assumptions and inductive methods leads to a common problem in qualitative research: because the analysis iterates between empirical concepts and relevant theoretical sources, a complete rendition of the process would involve a somewhat lengthy and unintelligible chronological presentation of data and concept building. For the sake of clarity, we suspended this option in favor of an exemplary description of the coding process.

We began our analysis with a close line-by-line reading of the material, during which we developed codes to describe every syntactic unit. In the terms of grounded theory, we broke down the text by developing empirically grounded concepts (Strauss and Corbin 1998, 102). While the codes at first were closely attached to the manifest meaning of a syntactic unit, they quickly became increasingly abstract. We grouped codes that seemed to belong to a category and, if possible, assigned new codes to already established categories. For example, it soon became clear that our codes "attention span problems of security personnel" and "high staff expenses" were framed as dimensions of a bigger problem that we termed "inefficient surveillance strategies". When we found complaints about the poor quality of video footage, we then could assign them as an additional dimension to this category. Problems of unsatisfactory surveillance strategies again referred mainly to one set of proposed solutions, which was the integration of different kinds of smart CCTV components. Thus we developed a category that was called "proposed solutions to inefficient surveillance". We repeated this process, simultaneously grouping and regrouping our codes and categories, until it became apparent that the structure of problems, solutions and respectively accorded actors also fit the logic of other reoccurring themes, as well as enabled the agreement of our other categories. Consequently, we used them as core categories for organizing and comparing the entire data set:

(1) causes attributed to a problem;
(2) actors held responsible as the cause of a problem;
(3) solutions and strategies to a problem proposed;
(4) actors held responsible to solve a problem;
(5) values referenced.

Whenever the content of these categories diverged significantly – for example, when one text fragment framed an institution as the cause of a problem, whereas the same institution was framed to be a solution in another fragment – we interpreted them as respectively belonging to distinct discourses. These distinct orders were not necessarily coherent with the organization of one document: while some documents contained only a single discourse fragment, many contained several fragments belonging to different discourses. By rearranging the material according to the discourses' respective logical structures, we thus obtained different meanings of smart CCTV.

Thus, although our categories are informed by social theory, we did actually develop them from our data. Of course, our reading is not the only possible one; readings obviously differ according to the respective research questions and alternative readings should therefore be encouraged. However, we hope that our mapping can nevertheless provide useful insights into the various issues connected to smart CCTV.

"Smart" CCTV in public discourse

Mapping the controversy

Before we elaborate on our findings in terms of the negotiations of privacy, we briefly outline the various issues that emerged in public discourse. This overview must remain partial owing to the scope of this paper, but it is necessary to understand how negotiations of privacy contribute to the meanings of smart CCTV in public discourse. We distinguished four types of problematizations that reoccurred steadily between 2006 and 2010. They represent the core meanings of smart CCTV available in public discourse, and can be described as the following ideal-type statements:

(1) Crime and terror pose threats to public safety, but can be regulated by developing and employing smart CCTV systems.
(2) Simple CCTV systems are inefficient in terms of resources, but can be improved by developing and employing smart CCTV components.
(3) Mass panic is unpredictable and uncontrollable for human security personnel, but can be predicted and regulated by smart CCTV systems.
(4) Smart CCTV systems pose a threat to personal liberty; therefore, data protection commissioners must control and sanction infringements of laws and guidelines.

The *first discourse* above constitutes smart CCTV as an appropriate and working solution for problems of crime and terrorism. It presumes a very specific model of criminal behavior, as something of natural and evenly patterned appearance, which is a precondition for the functionality of smart CCTV systems. Criminal behavior here is exclusively defined by its consequences, not its causes. The emphasis on the potential harms and dangers of criminal behavior constructs the plausibility that technology could effectively predict and detect these dangers. Thus, the legitimacy of smart CCTV in this context is established by a managerial-regulative definition of crime. The *second discourse* listed above produces the plausibility of smart CCTV systems by contrasting them to simple CCTV systems. It defines smart CCTV's appropriateness by means of managerial arguments as well, but in contrast to the first discourse, the "true" field of intervention is said to be the surveillance practices required by non-computed CCTV. Smart CCTV is hence established as a plausible technology by framing the poor quality of human labor as the main reason for simple CCTV's inefficiency. The *third discourse* also frames smart CCTV as an appropriate solution, yet again for different reasons and in a less elaborated way. Smart CCTV's plausibility here is co-produced by making the irrationality of collective behavior and limited cognitive capacities of humans a mere fact of nature (as opposed to socially shaped). The discourse then rests on contrasting inevitable human failure with the calculative superiority of smart CCTV systems. It is worth mentioning that these three discourses, among other rhetorical strategies, strongly emphasize technological agency over "inferior" human security work. Finally, the *fourth discourse* constitutes smart CCTV as an inappropriate technology. Evoking Orwellian metaphors, this discourse mobilizes privacy and data protection violations to admonish smart CCTV's threats to personal liberty.

Discourses (1), (2) and (4) were reproduced across all media, while discourse (3) remained somewhat fragmented. If these discourses struggled for the legitimate definition of smart CCTV, this took place mainly between discourses (1), (2) and (4). Furthermore, the interpretive stability of the first two discourses refuted our initial assumption that blogs present the topic differently, suggesting that it is a dominant interpretation of smart CCTV.

Personal liberty, privacy and the problem of smart CCTV

According to the data, the core problem of this discourse was that the employment of smart CCTV systems might pose threats to the value of personal liberty (Table 2). Criticism sometimes admonished the compromise between security and personal liberty. Similar criticism again weighed the effectiveness of CCTV systems in terms of crime prevention against constraints of personal liberty. Thus, large parts of this discourse established smart CCTV as an inappropriate technology by stressing the tensions between public safety and personal liberty.

Although the logical structure of this discourse explicitly referenced personal liberty as a value to be protected, descriptions of actual or possible liberty constraints

Table 2.   Problematization of smart CCTV as a threat to personal liberty

Causes attributed to a problem	• Violation of data protection guidelines by employing smart CCTV • Compromise between security and personal liberty
Actors held responsible as the cause of a problem	• Police bureaus (who employ smart CCTV) • Politicians of the governments (who disregard civil rights by introducing smart CCTV) • Researchers and developers of smart CCTV (both universities and corporations)
Solutions and strategies to a problem proposed	• Enforcement of guidelines and sanctioning of data protection infringements • Public supervision of research and development
Actors held responsible to solve a problem	• Data protection commissioners • Germany's Federal Constitutional Court • Political parties (of the opposition)
Values referenced	• Personal liberty as a fundamental right

remained vague. If ever there were descriptions, they predominantly referred to infringements of privacy regulations. Our point here is that there seems to be quite a gap between the idea of personal liberty and privacy regulations. Whereas the broad idea of personal liberty usually denotes the absence of excessive constraints on human action, privacy in Germany is far more specific. Privacy in Germany, which we use synonymously with data protection, is institutionalized as the protection of the right to "informational self-determination". This somewhat unwieldy term means that an individual cannot be coerced to disclose personal information, and can freely decide on its use (Mayer-Schönberger 1997, 229). Accordingly, privacy regulations order the timely deletion of data, provision of information security or signposting of monitored spaces. What privacy regulations protect, then, is only a small fraction of personal liberty: individuals' control over the release and use of their personal data. The important difference is in the range of constraints these concepts encompass: data protection guards personal liberty only by restricting control over personal information, it cannot protect liberties harmed by discrimination, physical assaults or other constrictive actions. Thus, how this discourse defined personal liberty was reduced to infringements of privacy regulations.

A possible consequence of this discourse restricting the meaning of personal liberty to privacy might be that it could have displaced other discourses critical of surveillance technology (for a similar assessment, see Steeves 2009, 192). In fact, infringements of privacy regulations were the only forms of critique. The privacy critique framed smart CCTV as inappropriate, but this was not in relation to the problems that the other discourses posed. For example, the privacy critique did not oppose the proposition of the second discourse, which was to overcome the poor quality of human labor by automating it with smart CCTV. Automation of labor, as Noble (1986) points out, allows for deskilling and reorganization, sometimes disempowering the employees while privileging managerial authority. Because this is not merely an academic concern, we expected criticisms in relation to labor issues to appear in public discourse. Instead, voices of security staff were excluded from public discourse, and their roles were largely defined as an obstacle to greater public safety. Furthermore, the necessity of regulating crime by technical means – the first discourse's central claim – was hardly ever questioned. This is best exemplified by criticisms that referred to simple CCTV's low effectiveness. The argument here was that privacy infringements could not be tolerated, especially when considering the failure of simple CCTV to prevent crime. This argument shows that the privacy discourse did not consider technical regulation of crime as an undesirable aim in itself. In relation to this purpose, it did not question smart CCTV's legitimacy. The relationship between privacy and smart CCTV was thus not defined as mutually exclusive; instead, privacy was framed as a necessary *condition* of its legitimacy. This suggests that, if smart CCTV systems consider privacy regulations, then the privacy discourse would consider them to be legitimate. Finally, the privacy discourse did not refer to the variety of social consequences that surveillance practices might entail for the monitored individuals. For instance, the classification and discrimination of social groups is a major concern among surveillance scholars (e.g. Gandy 1993; Lyon 2001; and the contributions in Lyon 2003b) because of the likelihood that individuals are targeted based on bias. Again, because discrimination based on race, sex or age is not a merely academic concern, we expected it to appear in public discourse. Instead, these concerns were not addressed and targeted individuals were framed in generic terms such as "hooligans" or "terrorists", broadly defining them as potential threats to public safety. In consequence, critiques of social inequality were largely absent, while the public critique of smart CCTV was mainly concerned with infringements of individuals' privacy.

With the emphasis on privacy infringements, it is no surprise that this discourse attributes potential deficits of smart CCTV systems to violations from police bureaus, political actors and smart CCTV developers. Stronger legal control and enforcement of already existing data protection guidelines were deemed the appropriate strategy to regulate the employment of smart CCTV. The roles of data commissioners were thus defined as the main carriers of public accountability, with their trustworthiness based on their legal expertise and affiliation with data protection bureaus. The confidence in expert rationality resonates with Jasanoff's observation that, in Germany, regarding science and technology, public account-ability is understood as a product of trustworthy institutions rather than "proven personal service to citizens or the state" (Jasanoff 2005, 262). Paradoxically, she observes, the strong cultural belief that expert bodies can map the entire terrain of relevant social groups renders the need for additional reasoning unnecessary, thereby potentially excluding additional concerns from the wider public (Jasanoff 2005, 269).

In summary, personal liberty in the context of smart CCTV was discussed in Germany predominantly as a regulative problem of privacy rights. This discourse staged its claim by referring to the expertise of data protection commissioners, whereas references to the potential social consequences of surveillance practices remained mostly excluded. References to public administration's promises of control underlined the project of regulating constraints of liberty through sensible legal instruments. However, by making it a matter of effective bureaucratic control, the privacy discourse, in consequence, did not question the legitimacy of smart CCTV in general; rather, it configured meeting privacy requirements as its major necessary condition.

Preliminary conclusions and suggestions for further research

If public understandings shape technology development, and the privacy discourse framed smart CCTV as inappropriate, then why did the privacy critiques not prevent the emergence of smart CCTV (or other surveillance technology, for that matter)? This is not a trivial question because, as Klein and Kleinman (2002) remind us, success and failure of technology depend not only on their social meanings, but also on structural factors, such as the distribution of power between social groups, the organization of labor, the role of the state, and of course technological preconditions. With these limitations in mind, we can begin to answer this question by pointing to the way in which the public discourse relates privacy to smart CCTV.

First, the privacy discourse interpreted the employment of smart CCTV as a potential threat to privacy requirements, but not as a threat to ideals of social equality. To answer our question, we might thus consider that the privacy critique was not able to create the same political pressure that critiques of social inequality and discrimination possibly would have achieved. At least in present-day Germany, privacy infringements for the sake of public safety seem somewhat compatible with Germany's self-image. This self-image includes political sensitivities about social inequality, which precludes open and public discussions about discrimination. Thus, we might suspect that privacy infringements do have a basic compatibility with Germany's present political culture, and that this might be one reason why the privacy discourse did not prevent the emergence of smart CCTV.

Second, although the privacy discourse defined smart CCTV as a potentially inappropriate technology, it did not define the relationship between privacy and smart CCTV as mutually exclusive. Instead, if smart CCTV systems consider privacy regulations, then the privacy discourse would consider them to be legitimate. This might be an important point in understanding smart CCTV's emergence. As Haggerty (2009) points out, opponents of surveillance technology inadvertently encourage further research and development because their critiques help guide developers toward perceived flaws in the systems. This dynamic of critique and development might also apply to the privacy discourse. Recent German technology policy indicates that the critiques seem to have pressured government into making it obligatory for most projects to include privacy experts in the development process. Privacy regulations again are explicit enough for programmers to integrate into smart CCTV systems. Thus, the participation of these experts might satisfy the privacy critique, especially because the meaning of personal liberty has already been reduced to privacy. Although it may seem paradoxical to privacy advocates who assume that their critique hinders technological development, the privacy critique actually might have contributed to the development of smart CCTV.

Qualitative research always seems to be useful in raising more focused questions, and our preliminary findings call for further comparative and historical empirical research. First, to substantiate our hypothesis concerning the differences between privacy critiques and critiques of social inequality, it would be helpful to compare our findings with the public discourse of alternative surveillance technologies. Although recent research on surveillance discourses in the UK suggests that differences between technologies are of minor importance (Barnard-Wills 2011), the perception of technological differences in Germany may also be influenced by cultural differences. Second, historical research on the German census that was planned for 1981 could prove to be helpful in understanding the cultural transformation of privacy across time. In 1981, privacy issues related to the census led to the formation of massive resistance, but today privacy seems to be regarded as a mere matter of bureaucratic regulation. Third, we encourage research on how privacy issues shape various social worlds relevant to surveillance. This would contribute to understanding the relationship between surveillance technology and its critique. In our opinion, a sociology of knowledge approach is conceptually helpful to accomplish such a disentanglement of historical and institutional configurations regarding new and emerging surveillance technologies.

Acknowledgements

We would like to thank our student assistants Anna Binder, Sophia Gredig and Livia Mattmüller for their invaluable help in organizing the data, Reini Joosten for her support putting together the source material, as well as Maja Apelt and the anonymous reviewer of *Innovation* for helpful comments on earlier drafts of this paper.

Notes

1. Note that we use a specific notion of discourse that differs considerably from other concepts, such as Habermas's discourse ethic, the post-Marxist Essex School (Laclau and Mouffe), critical discourse analysis (Fairclough, Wodak and Jäger), or ethno-methodological discourse analysis (for a discussion see Keller 2011a, pp. 20–62).

2. The first German article that explicitly and prominently discusses a smart CCTV system was published on 17 May 2006, in the electronic newsletter *heise-online* (available from: http://www.heise.de/newsticker/meldung/Flughafen-Helsinki-setzt-Software-fuers-Video-Monitoring-ein-125378.html). Also in 2006, the Bundeskriminalamt (Federal Police Office of Germany) introduced a smart CCTV pilot project that tried to combine a CCTV system with biometric facial recognition software. Because smart CCTV is an emerging technology, it might be necessary to extend the analysis to documents up to the present day.

References

Barnard-Wills, D. 2011. "UK News Media Discourses of Surveillance." *The Sociological Quarterly* 52 (4): 548–567.

Bennett, C. J. 2011. "In Defence of Privacy: The Concept and the Regime." *Surveillance & Society* 8 (4): 485–496.

Berger, P. L., and T. Luckmann. 1966. *The Social Construction of Reality: A Treatise in the Sociology of Knowledge.* Garden City, NY: Doubleday.

Bijker, W. E. 1995. *Of Bicycles, Bakelites, and Bulbs: Toward a Theory of Sociotechnical Change.* Cambridge, MA: MIT Press.

Ferenbok, J., and A. Clement. 2011. "Hidden Changes: From CCTV to 'Smart' Video Surveillance." In *Eyes Everywhere: The Global Growth of Camera Surveillance,* edited by A. Doyle, R. K. Lippert, and D. Lyon, Abingdon: Routledge, 218–233.

Foucault, M. 1972. *The Archeology of Knowledge.* London: Tavistock.

Foucault, M. 1979. *Discipline and Punish: The Birth of the Prison.* New York: Vintage Books.

Foucault, M. 1982. *I, Pierre Rivière, Having Slaughtered My Mother, My Sister, and My Brother: A Case of Parricide in the 19th Century.* Lincoln, NB: University of Nebraska Press.

Gandy, O. H. 1993. *The Panoptic Sort: A Political Economy of Personal Information.* Boulder, CO: Westview.

Gates, K. 2010. "The Tampa 'Smart CCTV' Experiment." *Culture Unbound* 2: 67–89.

Gouallier, V., and A.-E. Fleurant. 2009. *Intelligent Video Surveillance: Promises and Challenges: Technological and Commercial Intelligence Report.* Montréal: Centre de recherche informatique de Montréal.

Haggerty, K. D. 2009. "Methodology as a Knife Fight: The Process, Politics and Paradox of Evaluating Surveillance." *Critical Criminology* 17: 277–291.

Haggerty, K. D., and R. V. Ericson. 2006. *The New Politics of Surveillance and Visibility.* Toronto: University of Toronto Press, 3–25.

Introna, L. D., and D. Wood. 2004. "Picturing Algorithmic Surveillance: The Politics of Facial Recognition Systems." *Surveillance & Society* 2 (2): 177–198.

Jasanoff, S. 2005. *Designs on Nature: Science and Democracy in Europe and the United States.* Princeton, NJ: Princeton University Press.

Keller, R. 2011a. *Diskursforschung: Eine Einführung für SozialwissenschaftlerInnen* [Discourse Analysis: An Introduction for Social Scientists]. 4th ed. Wiesbaden: VS Verlag für Sozialwissenschaften.

Keller, R. 2011b. "The Sociology of Knowledge Approach to Discourse (SKAD)." *Human Studies* 34 (1): 43–65.

Keller, R. 2011c. *Wissenssoziologische Diskursanalyse: Grundlegung eines Forschungsprogramms* [The Sociology of Knowledge Approach to Discourse: Foundations of a Research Perspective]. 3rd ed. Wiesbaden: VS Verlag für Sozialwissenschaften.

Klein, H. K., and D. L. Kleinman. 2002. "The Social Construction of Technology: Structural Considerations." *Science, Technology & Human Values* 27 (1): 28–52.

Kline, R., and T. J. Pinch. 1996. "Users as Agents of Technological Change: The Social Construction of the Automobile in the Rural United States." *Technology and Culture* 37 (4): 763–795.

Lyon, D. 2001. *Surveillance Society: Monitoring Everyday Life.* Buckingham: Open University Press.

Lyon, D. 2003a. "Introduction." In *Surveillance as Social Sorting: Privacy, Risk, and Digital Discrimination,* edited by D. Lyon, 1–9. London: Routledge.

Lyon, D., ed., 2003b. *Surveillance as Social Sorting: Privacy, Risk, and Digital Discrimination*. London: Routledge.

Lyon, D., and E. Zureik. 1996. "Surveillance, Privacy, and the New Technology." In *Computers, Surveillance, and Privacy*, edited by D. Lyon and E. Zureik, 1–18. Minneapolis, MN: University of Minnesota Press.

MacKenzie, D. A., and J. Wajcman. 1999. "Introductory Essay: The Social Shaping of Technology." In *The Social Shaping of Technology*, 2nd ed., edited by A. MacKenzie and J. Wajcman, 3–27. Milton Keynes: Open University Press.

Mayer-Schönberger, V. 1997. "Generational Development of Data Protection in Europe." In *Technology and Privacy: The New Landscape*, edited by P. Agre and M. Rotenberg, 219–241. Cambridge, MA: MIT Press.

Musik, C. 2011. "The Thinking Eye is only Half the Story: High-Level Semantic Video Surveillance." *Information Polity* 16 (4): 339–353.

Noble, D. F. 1986. *Forces of Production: A Social History of Industrial Automation*. New York: Oxford University Press.

Norris, C., and G. Armstrong. 1999. *The Maximum Surveillance Society: The Rise of CCTV*. Oxford: Berg.

Pinch, T. J., and W. E. Bijker. 1984. "The Social Construction of Facts and Artefacts: Or How the Sociology of Science and the Sociology of Technology Might Benefit each Other." *Social Studies of Science* 14 (3): 399–441.

Stalder, F. 2002. "Privacy is not the Antidote to Surveillance." *Surveillance & Society* 1 (1): 120–124.

Steeves, V. M. 2009. "Reclaiming the Social Value of Privacy." In *Lessons from the Identity Trail: Anonymity, Privacy, and Identity in a Networked Society*, edited by I. Kerr, V. M. Steeves, and C. Lucock, 191–208. Oxford: Oxford University Press.

Strauss, A. L. 1987. *Qualitative Analysis for Social Scientists*. Cambridge: Cambridge University Press.

Strauss, A. L., and J. M. Corbin. 1998. *Basics of Qualitative Research: Techniques and Procedures for Developing Grounded Theory*. 2nd ed. Thousand Oaks, CA: Sage.

Surette, R. 2005. "The Thinking Eye: Pros and Cons of Second Generation CCTV Surveillance Systems." *Policing: An International Journal of Police Strategies & Management* 28 (1): 152–173.

van der Ploeg, I. 2003. "Biometrics and the Body as Information: Normative Issues of the Sociotechnical Coding of the Body." In *Surveillance as Social Sorting: Privacy, Risk, and Digital Discrimination*, edited by D. Lyon, 57–73. London: Routledge.

Biocybernetic adaptation and privacy

Knud Böhle, Christopher Coenen, Michael Decker and Michael Rader

Institute for Technology Assessment and Systems Analysis, Karlsruhe Institute of Technology, Karlsruhe, Germany

> Biocybernetic adaptation is a new approach to optimizing human–computer interfaces and human–computer interaction. Bio-signals and, more broadly, vital data of a person are collected and interpreted in real time by a computer in order to trigger its own adaptive processes. The collection of highly sensitive data is thus a necessary condition for the purpose of making the application more user-friendly. Therefore, the most obvious and important social, legal and ethical issues in this kind of application are privacy and data protection. In this research note we report from a technology assessment project for the European Parliament. We provide some conceptual distinctions, highlight the most promising application fields, and discuss privacy challenges and potential regulatory actions to be taken.

Introduction

Project context and project type

The issue of biocybernetic adaptation and privacy was studied in the context of the "Making Perfect Life" project (see information in the box) conducted by the European Technology Assessment Group (ETAG) for the Science and Technology Options Assessment panel of the European Parliament (STOA). The aim of STOA projects is to provide parliamentarians with an overview of important emerging science and technology developments that are not yet in the focus of European legislation. As well as reviewing approaches and the state of the art in technological development, a major task in STOA projects is to highlight issues that might require European regulation in the future and to develop policy options for consideration by parliamentarians.

This project examined the relationship between biology and technology under the headlines "Biology becoming Technology" and "Technology becoming Biology" as an expression of the trend towards the convergence of key technologies (Roco and Bainbridge 2002; High Level Expert Group 2004). Each of the institutes involved worked on a particular field and prepared a case study on a specific policy-relevant topic.

The four areas were (1) *engineering the body* with a case study on *whole genome sequencing*; (2) *engineering the brain* with the *market introduction of neurodevices* as

> The "Making Perfect Life" project (http://www.rathenau.nl/makingperfectlife) was performed by ETAG for the STOA (Science and Technology Options Assessment) panel of the European Parliament, Contract Number IP/A/STOA/FWC/2008-96/SC-1. Parliamentary supervisors were Messrs Malcolm Harbour MEP and Vittorio Prodi MEP. The project ran from August 2009 until December 2011, with a financial budget of €230,000. The project was led by the Rathenau-Instituut, Den Haag, and also involved the Fraunhofer Institute for Systems and Innovation Research, Karlsruhe, and the Institute for Technology Assessment of the Austrian Academy of Sciences, Vienna, in addition to the Institute of Technology Assessment and Systems Analysis of Karlsruhe Institute of Technology, which was responsible for the topics "intelligent artefacts" and "biocybernetic adaptation".

an example; (3) *engineering living artifacts* with the *pursuit of standardization in synthetic biology* as specific topic; and finally (4) *engineering intelligent artifacts* (Böhle et al. 2011) with *biocybernetic adaptation* as the case study in point.

In this case study, work first consisted of a review of existing literature on intelligent artifacts and biocybernetic adaptation. On the basis of the results of this review, a questionnaire addressing future developments and related concerns was drafted (available from the authors). It was used for a consultation of experts active in the field concerned, including various types of expertise: technology developers, data protection experts and ethicists. The questionnaire was sent to 20 experts of whom 50% replied. As a further step, the responses to the questionnaire were used, together with other material, as input for a project workshop. Participants in this workshop were again mainly experts on the subjects already mentioned and helped to complement and refine the results of the literature review and the questionnaire.

Definitions and guiding visions

Until recently, all adaptation efforts linked with technology have been by human users. Adaptation to technology is tedious and the more machines and devices are available in everyday life and the more rapidly models and versions are changing, the more time-consuming and boring it is to adapt technology and to adapt to it. This is especially true for information and communication technologies (ICT). In cases where ICT systems are indispensable, it is not even possible to restrict their use to the knowledgeable and savvy individuals willing and able to adapt. Often even people with reduced capabilities must be able to use these technologies – consider driver assistance systems in the individual transportation sector or elderly care (ambient assisted living, care robotics). Generally speaking, the aim of endeavors in this field is to make the use of technology simpler for the average user. This can mean that the user is freed from the effort needed to operate technology (the disappearing computer: DU 2003; Streitz, Kameas, and Mavrommati 2007). Hence more attention is drawn to the requirement for ICT systems able to adapt to users and their contexts (for an overview see Sheridan 2011). Adaptivity of the technological system is becoming a necessary condition in terms of usability and acceptance (Broadbent, Stafford, and MacDonald 2009; Sharkey and Sharkey 2012). One way to increase the adaptivity of ICT systems is to dynamically feed the computer application with certain kinds of sensitive personal data, thus establishing a cybernetic loop between the performance of the user and the system. More precisely we define a computer system or application as a *biocybernetically adaptive artifact*, if it uses data about the changing affective, physiological or neuro-physiological state of a person, usually the user, in order to trigger its own adaptive processes to then instantaneously change its interface, functionality or behavior. For this purpose, bio-signals or, more broadly, vital data of a person must be sensed, measured, collected and interpreted, often in real time, by a computer.

There is little doubt among experts that the major goals of biocybernetic adaptation will be achieved and that a two-way exchange of information between the user and the system will take place. Computers will no longer respond in a deterministic and totally predictable fashion as they become sensitive to the general context of the user. Pantic et al. (2008) claim that this is "likely to become the single most widespread research topic of AI, if not of computing as a whole" (184). In terms of scientific disciplines, computer science, psychology, physiology and neuro-physiology are fundamental, with further disciplines, expertise required when it comes to specific application areas. The CHI conferences on human factors in computing systems are a preferred place to present advances and new perspectives in the field (see Allanson and Wilson 2002 for the first workshop in 2002 and Fairclough et al. 2011 for the most recent one).

Biocybernetic adaptation is closely linked to physiological computing, a term coined in 2001 by Jennifer Allanson (Wilson and Allanson 2001). Many scholars of human factors and ergonomics regard *physiological computing* as a promising approach to optimizing human–computer interfaces and human–computer interactions: "Physiological computing has the potential to provide a new paradigm for HCI by allowing a computer system to develop and access a dynamic representation of the cognitions, emotions and motivation of the user" (Fairclough 2009).

Physiological computing (including neuro-physiological computing) relies on measurement that exploits the fact that the human body is chemical, electrical, mechanical, thermal and magnetic in nature (Allanson and Fairclough 2004). A person's physiological state is sensed and measured (e.g. temperature, blood pressure, electroencephalograms, electromyograms, electrodermal activities, pupillometry) in order to improve the adaptation capabilities of computing systems. The underlying assumption is that it is possible to derive information about psychological states from physiological data. *Neuro-physiological computing* goes beyond outward evidence of emotion and attempts to identify concealed emotions through the visualization of patterns of brain activity which have been experimentally matched with emotions.

A complementary concept is *affective computing*, defined first by Rosalind Picard (1995, 1) as computing that relates to, arises from or influences emotions. Affective computing as generally understood relies mainly on observations and measurement with respect to the outer appearance and audiovisual expressions of a person's emotions or psychological states (e.g. voice, facial expression, gesture, posture or body language). How emotions and affects are expressed and observed is of course strongly influenced by cultural and social patterns. In contrast, physiological and neuro-physiological computing mainly measures and interprets body data that is not visible and less dependent on the cultural context. In the context of biocybernetic adaptation physiological and affective computing are complementary as both sense and measure data from the human body and apply psychological interpretations of these data.

Biocybernetic technology is designed to "tap private psycho-physiological events" (Fairclough 2009) for use in dynamic human–computer interfaces. In all applications of this type, extremely sensitive and often intimate data on human users is collected, such as data related to the user's health or emotional state. To incorporate knowledge about a user – in general unnoticed and not even transparent to him or her – into a computing system is one of the basic ideas of biocybernetically adaptive computing systems. The more or less unconscious processes of the human body that "produce" vital data have usually been measured and revealed in medical settings only (a patient and a trustworthy physician). Now they are used to increase the adaptability of computing (Allanson and Fairclough 2004, 858ff.). This is ostensibly for the purpose of making the application more user-friendly.

It is obvious that such data can easily be misused or used for other purposes than those for which it was originally collected. Therefore the most important social, legal and ethical issue in this kind of application is privacy and data protection. In the following the most promising types and fields of application are presented, before the privacy issues and the need for regulation are discussed.

Application areas

Computers as companions and interaction partners

Health care is a major application field being specifically targeted by developers. Examples include the MIT "Interactive Social–Emotional Toolkit", designed to help children with disorders linked to sensory processing, such as autism, understand emotions in other people (Sharry, McDermott, and Condron 2003; Hudlicka et al. 2008; Khandaker 2009) and for biofeedback games to treat children diagnosed with Attention Deficit and Hyperactivity Disorder. Playing such games motivates children by rewarding desirable patterns of brain activity.

Brain–computer interfaces were originally developed for use by persons with disabilities and are being modified for healthy users "in order to enhance productivity or to deliver new forms of gaming experience" (www.physiological-computing.net/). Experiments with computer input via EEG also fall into this category: the human concentrates on a word or phrase that is identified by the system as matching a specific pattern and can be used as a command for the system.

Games and interactive media are another important application field: an FAQ on physiological computing (www.physiologicalcomputing.net/) describes the Wii and Kinect gaming consoles as, in a way, being examples of physiological computing as they monitor overt and observable behavior. Although they do not tap a data source directly, they provide the possibility to infer covert psychological states from movement (Choi 2010). Brain–computer interfaces are currently being developed for gaming (Plass-Oude Bos et al. 2010a, 2010b) and helmets with small numbers of electrodes as sensors are already being sold commercially. Research is also being conducted on the development of emotionally adaptive games, e.g. to avoid boredom and frustration by increasing or lowering challenge levels according to the current state of the gamer (Tijs, Brokken, and Jesellsteijn 2009).

In *e-learning*, affective computing can be used to adapt the presentation of a teacher avatar when the student is frustrated, pleased or bored. In some cases, applications of biocybernetic computing function as an "intelligent mirror", which allows the user to learn about him or herself and to adjust performance according to requirements.

Assistance systems for safety-critical applications

An important motive for the development of direct brain–machine interfaces is the reduction of reaction times in critical applications, such as piloting aircraft, "learning and training, automobile control, air traffic control, decision-making, remote sensing of stress, and entertainment" (Asher 2002, 357). Systems incorporating input on the (psycho-)physiological state of drivers could be used to reduce car-to-car spacing on otherwise congested highways. Daimler is already equipping cars with "attention assist", a drowsiness-detection system to warn drivers from falling momentarily asleep (Taylor 2008).

Ambient assisted living is an application of the broader field of ambient intelligence, which is typically intended to be unobtrusive, personalized, adaptive and anticipatory (Gill 2008, 5). In the case of ambient assisted living, an important element is the monitoring of critical body and mental functions, the system being prepared to take measures if any of these are abnormal. The system either takes action of its own accord or calls in a professional expert in cases for which it has not been sufficiently programmed.

Findings on privacy problems

Applications of biocybernetic computing require the collection, storage and processing of immense amounts of sensitive personal data, particularly if the systems are to be fine-tuned and refined to become ever more adaptive. Hence privacy is the major concern linked with this technological development. Privacy-related issues can be summarized in a number of points, each of which is a topic deserving more detailed research.

(1) *Highly sensitive and even intimate data as a new quality*: applications of the kind described previously involve the collection and storage of highly sensitive and even intimate data. This raises the question of how much personal data is really needed to modify human–computer interfaces in the desired way and how long this data needs to be stored.

(2) *Data protection requires extension to responsibility for the interpretation of highly sensitive personal data*: biocybernetically adaptive systems may often not inform the user about the data sensed, its interpretation and its use to adjust machines, partly since unobtrusiveness of the interface is regarded as a desirable property in such applications as ambient assisted living. However, such interpretations are questionable on two levels: first the underlying assumptions of the relation between physiology and psychology may be wrong; and second the technical response derived from the former relation may be inappropriate since computers always work with classifications and models and cannot consider all relevant individual features. Data protection thus extends to responsibility for the interpretation of data.

PRIVACY AND SECURITY IN THE DIGITAL AGE

(3) *Highly sensitive data leave the laboratory and enter everyday life*: the data involved is of different nature than that conventionally regulated by data protection. In earlier times this kind of data was mainly collected in a clinical setting in the course of medical treatment. Now this kind of data can find further use in daily life. Sensitive data is increasingly becoming available to non-professional actors and this is an area not sufficiently covered by existing regulations (with respect especially to neuro-data; Hallinan, Schütz, and Friedewald 2012).

(4) *Cheap and portable computer technology will lead to widespread use*: this applies especially to ambient assisted living, but owing to the availability of cheap sensor technology and portable or even wearable computers (e.g. watches with ambient temperature sensors, heart straps for joggers, pedometers for dieters and so on; Teller 2004, 917ff.), it is likely to become a broader phenomenon in everyday life.

(5) *Highly sensitive personal data will become publicly exposed and available*: in addition, the data obtained will not only be interpreted by non-professionals – they can also be easily shared in the public sphere, e.g. on social networking sites (Gilleade and Lee 2011).

(6) *Highly sensitive personal data can be used for highly exploitable body profiles*: even further, physiological and psycho-physiological data can potentially be used by computers to create virtual images of the bodies of patients or healthy persons for further use without their knowledge or consent. To give an example, a US patent application describes a generator of avatars that reflect a wide range of physical characteristics and psychological traits of the user – including hidden characteristics such as allergies or chronic conditions (US Patent & Trademark Office 2009).

(7) *There is a conflict between unobtrusiveness and personal autonomy*: as well as the lack of opportunity to give consent to data use owing to the desired unobtrusiveness, there is additionally the problem that the users of biocybernetically adaptive systems are frequently persons who are unable to take autonomous decisions on data use. This leads to a need to involve proxies (relatives or other authorized persons). As a result data protection is frequently simply ignored.

(8) "Biocybernetic adaptation" can also be employed to deliberately make the computer appear as an interaction partner able to "understand" or even "anticipate" user needs. An ethical problem accrues, if for example a patient or elderly person is no longer able to distinguish human communication and affection from that of artifacts. Benyon and Mival (2008, 3658, 3661), members of the EC-funded COMPANIONS project, claim that it is possible to design artifacts that will enable people to develop relationships with them. They are further described as believable, intuitive, autonomous, personality-rich and convivial conversational partners sensitive to emotion and capable of demonstrating emotional/affective behavior.

(9) *Implants providing more and continuous biosignals are on the horizon*: a step beyond wearables are implants. As Rogers (2009, 1) states "even the human body (is) now being experimented with as (a) potential place ... to embed computational devices, even to the extent of invading previously private and taboo aspects of our lives". The potential privacy and data protection problems of such implants are continually raising concerns and are meanwhile increasingly becoming a subject of research (Theißen 2009).

(10) *"Mind reading" is no short-term privacy issue*: although current technology is still far removed from being able to "read minds", "mind reading" is a concern strongly linked with new ICTs, especially neuroelectronics, by the general public (Wakunuma et al. 2010). This implies a need for transparency on the true potential of such technologies if society is not to waste resources on what has been termed, in another context, "speculative ethics" (Nordmann and Rip 2009).

(11) Surveillance of public spaces to ensure greater public safety is an area being discussed in connection with practically all technologies with potential in this respect. There is much demand for greater public security and experts claim that acceptance is increasing (Waugh 2010), so that promising technologies would probably find a market. However, the validation problem looms large, since this would require the collection of data from subjects with, for example, genuine criminal intent, and not simply simulating such intent. The potential for the use of these technologies for surveillance purposes is problematic from the viewpoint of data protection both if they fail to fulfil their promise and if they do realize the expected potential.

Conclusion regarding policy relevance and regulatory action

Owing to the early state of most research and development in biocybernetic adaptation, its policy relevance in a narrow sense is still low, and it is difficult to identify if and where regulatory action will eventually be necessary. This applies also to privacy issues, although they are arguably the politically most relevant aspect of biocybernetic adaptation at present. Against this background, political activities at the EU level currently appear to be most needed in terms of funding of relevant research and development.

EU-funded research and other activities that are dedicated to supporting "responsible research and innovation" in the area of privacy-sensitive medical and biometric applications (von Schomberg 2011), or to the development of privacy-enhancing technologies, could more strongly take into account tendencies that signal growing challenges to "biological privacy" outside the medical context. In line with recent conceptualizations of responsible research and innovation, "collective co-responsibility" (von Schomberg 2011) for innovation processes needs to be extended beyond the science system in a narrow sense. In this context it could be fruitful to explore and exploit the potential of "privacy by design" as a means of incorporating data protection concerns in the development of design instead of having to adjust technologies after they have entered routine application. The recommendations of the ETICA project include incorporation of ethical concerns into the process of evaluation of ICT research proposals (Stahl 2011) and the European Data Protection Supervisor offers assistance to projects seeking to incorporate privacy by design (European Data Protection Supervisor 2008).

Furthermore, more funding could be provided for basic research on the relevant technologies, and studies into the various aspects of their use, including ethical, legal, social and economic ones. This could include research on cultural and generational changes with regard to attitudes towards privacy, as well as efforts to define the limits of acceptable research and applications in cases where the developers and service providers rely on deliberate disclosure of personal information on users. As a preventive and proactive measure, an observatory of emerging technologies with an early warning function could be set up at EU or international levels. Furthermore, the results of past and the design of ongoing efforts to develop or refine Codes of Conduct concerning the handling of physiological data (Menevidis, Swartzman, and Stylianidis 2011) could be adapted to handle new technological developments and extended to such players as the entertainment industry, if necessary developing new codes especially for these players.

With regard to regulatory action in the narrow sense (as opposed to soft law and governance activities), areas that will probably be most affected by a further rise of biocybernetic adaptation and a number of general challenges can be identified. In this context it is of special interest how the proposed Data Protection Regulation will define and specify what constitutes "personal data" and "sensitive data", and to what extent the different types of behavioral, physiological and neuro-physiological data will be covered. This still seems to be an open issue (de Hert and Papakonstantinou 2012, 132ff.).

It might still be too early to make detailed proposals concerning more specific legal regulations, although experts sometimes make such proposals. In the health care system, regulatory measures might be needed concerning the growing number of actors who are not health care professionals, such as care-givers and family members. For instance, for users entering spaces monitored by closed-circuit TV, there might be a need to alert visitors to the fact that they are entering ambient intelligence spaces. The creation and use of bio-signal-based data in entertainment contexts (e.g. computer games) may make it necessary to not only promote soft law and governance activities in and for the relevant industries, but also to implement some hard regulation.

Acknowledgements

The authors thank the parliamentary supervisors of the "Making Perfect Life" project, Malcolm Harbour MEP and Vittorio Prodi MEP, for their support and comments. They also thank the members of the "Making Perfect Life" project team for discussions and comments. Most particularly, we wish to thank the participants in the Expert Workshop and the questionnaire survey for their valuable information and input.

References

Allanson, J., and S. Fairclough. 2004. "A Research Agenda for Physiological Computing." *Interacting with Computers* 16: 857–878.

Allanson, J., and G. M. Wilson. 2002. "Physiological Computing." In *Proceedings of the Workshop on Physiological Computing, CHI 2002*, Minneapolis, MN, April 20–25, 2002 [Online]. Accessed October 31, 2011. http://physiologicalcomputing.net/chi2002/proceedings.html

Asher, R. 2002. "Brain–machine Interface." In *Converging Technologies for Improving Human Performance. Nanotechnology, Biotechnology, Information Technology and Cognitive Science*, edited by M. Roco and W. S. Bainbridge, 357–358. Arlington, VA: NSF.

Benyon, D., and O. Mival. 2008. "Landscaping Personification Technologies: From Interactions to Relationships." In *Proceedings of Conference on Human Factors in Computing Systems*, Florence, April 5–10, 2008. New York: ACM, 3657–3662.

Böhle, K., Chr. Coenen, M. Decker, and M. Rader, 2011. "Engineering of Intelligent Artefacts." In *Making Perfect Life. Bio-engineering (in) the 21st Century*, edited by European Parliament – STOA, 136–176. Brussels: European Parliament, [Online]. Accessed April 25, 2012. http://www.itas.fzk.de/deu/lit/2011/boua11a.pdf

Broadbent, E., R. Stafford, and B. MacDonald. 2009. "Acceptance of Healthcare Robots for the Older Population: Review and Future Directions." *International Journal of Social Robotics* 1: 319–330.

Choi, C. Q. 2010. "How Wii and Kinect Hack into Your Emotions". *Wired Science*, November 16 [Online]. Accessed October 31, 2011. http://www.wired.com/wiredscience/2010/11/wii-emotion/

de Hert, P., and V. Papakonstantinou. 2012. "The Proposed Data Protection Regulation Replacing Directive 95/46/EC: A Sound System for the Protection of Individuals." *Computer Law and Security Review* 28: 130–142.

DU. 2003. *The Disappearing Computer* [Online]. Accessed October 31, 2011. http://www.disappearing-computer.net/

European Data Protection Supervisor. 2008. *The EDPS and EU Research and Technological Development. Policy Paper* [Online]. Accessed October 31, 2011. http://www.edps.europa.eu/EDPSWEB/webdav/shared/Documents/EDPS/Publications/Papers/PolicyP/08-04-28_PP_RTD_EN.pdf

Fairclough, S. H. 2009. "Fundamentals of Physiological Computing." *Interacting with Computers* 21: 133–145.

Fairclough, S. H., K. Gilleade, L. E. Nacke, and R. L. Mandryk. 2011. "Brain and Body Interfaces: Designing for Meaningful Interaction." In *Proceedings of the Workshop on Brain and Body Interfaces: Designing for Meaningful Interaction, CHI 2011*, May 7–12, 2011, Vancouver [Online]. Accessed October 31. http://www.physiologicalcomputing.net/wordpress/wp-content/uploads/2010/11/bbiCHI2011-Extended-Abstract.pdf

Gill, J., ed. 2008. *Ambient Intelligence – Paving the Way* [Online]. COST. Accessed October 31, 2011. http://www.tiresias.org/cost219ter/ambient_intelligence/index.htm

Gilleade, K., and K. Lee. 2011. "Issues Inherent in Controlling the Interpretation of the Physiological Cloud." In *Proceedings of the Workshop on Brain and Body Interfaces: Designing for Meaningful Interaction, CHI 2011*, May 7–12, 2011 [Online]. Accessed October 31. http://physiologicalcomputing.net/bbichi2011/Issues inherent in controlling the interpretation of the Physiological Cloud.pdf

Hallinan, D., P. Schütz, and M. Friedewald. 2012. "Neurodata-based Devices and Data Protection." Paper presented at the 5th Bi-annual surveillance and society conference, Sheffield, April 2012.

High Level Expert Group. 2004. *Foresighting the New Technology Wave. Converging Technologies – Shaping the Future of European Societies*. Brussels: European Commission DG Research [Online]. Accessed October 31, 2011. http://ec.europa.eu/research/conferences/2004/ntw/pdf/final_report_en.pdf

Hudlicka, E., C. Lisetti, D. Hodge, A. Paiva, A. Rizzo, and E. Wagner. 2008. "Panel on 'Artificial Agents for Psychotherapy'." AAAI Spring Symposium – Technical Report SS-08-04, 60–64.

Khandaker, M. 2009. "Designing Affective Video Games to Support the Social–emotional Development of Teenagers with Autism Spectrum Disorders." *Studies in Health Technology and Informatics* 144: 37–39.

Menevidis, Z., S. Swartzman, and E. Stylianidis. 2011. "Code of Conduct for FP7 Researchers on Medical and Biometric Data Privacy." In *Towards Responsible Research and Innovation in the Information and Communication Technologies and Security Technologies Fields*, edited by R. von Schomberg, 115–132. Luxembourg: Publications Office of the European Union.

Nordmann, A., and A. Rip. 2009. "Mind the Gap Revisited." *Nature Nanotechnology* 4: 273–274.

Pantic, M., A. Nijholt, A. Pentland, and T. S. Huang. 2008. "Human-centred Intelligent Human–computer Interaction (HCI²): How Far Are We From Attaining It?" *Journal of Autonomous and Adaptive Communications Systems* 1 (2): 168–187.

Picard, R. W. 1995. *Affective Computing*. MIT Media Laboratory Perceptual Computing Section Technical Report no. 321. Boston, MA: MIT.

Plass-Oude Bos, D., B. Reuderink, B. L. A. van de Laar, H. Gürkök, C. Mühl, M. Poel, D. K. J. Heylen, and A. Nijholt. 2010a. Human–computer Interaction for BCI Games: Usability and User Experience. In *Proceedings of the International Conference on CYBER-WORLDS 2010*, edited by A. Sourin, 277–281. Los Alamitos, CA: IEEE Computer Society.

Plass-Oude Bos, D., B. Reuderink, B. L. A. van de Laar, H. Gürkök, C. Mühl, M. Poel, A. Niholt, and D. K. J. Heylen. 2010b. Brain–Computer Interfacing and Games. In *Brain–computer Interfaces. Applying our Minds to Human–computer Interaction*, edited by D. S. Tan and A. Nijholt, 149–178. London: Springer.

Roco, M., and W. S. Bainbridge, eds. 2002. *Converging Technologies for Improving Human Performance. Nanotechnology, Biotechnology, Information Technology and Cognitive Science.* Arlington, VA: NSF.

Rogers, Y. 2009. "The Changing Face of Human–computer Interaction in the Age of Ubiquitous Computing." In *USAB 2009, LNCS 5889*, edited by A. Holzinger and K. Miesenberger, 1–19. Berlin: Springer.

Sharkey, A., and N. Sharkey. 2012. "Granny and the Robots: Ethical Issues in Robot Care for the Elderly." *Ethics and Information Technology* 14 (1): 27–40.

Sharry, J., M. McDermott, and J. S. Condron. 2003. *Relax to Win – Treating Children with Anxiety Problems with a Biofeedback Videogame* [Online]. Accessed October 31, 2011. http://medialabeurope.org/research/library/Sharry_Relax_2003.pdf.

Sheridan, T. 2011. "Adaptive Automation, Level of Automation, Allocation Authority, Supervisory Control, and Adaptive Control: Distinctions and Modes of Adaptation." *IEEE Transactions on Systems, Man, and Cybernetics – Part A: Systems and Humans* 41 (4): 662–667.

Stahl, B. 2011. *Pathways Towards Responsible ICT Innovation*. Policy Brief. EP Science and Technology Options Assessment PE 460.346. [Online]. Accessed October 31. http://ethics.ccsr.cse.dmu.ac.uk/etica/ETICASTOApolicybrieffinal.pdf

Streitz, N., A. Kameas, and I. Mavrommati, eds. 2007. *The Disappearing Computer. Interaction Design, System Infrastructures and Applications for Smart Environments.* Lecture Notes in Computer Science. Vol. 4500. Heidelberg: Springer.

Taylor, D. 2008. "No Doze: Mercedes E-Class Alerts Drowsy Drivers." *Autoweek Daily Drive*, December 24 [Online]. Accessed October 31, 2011 http://www.autoweek.com/article/20081224/FREE/812249991

Teller, A. 2004. "A Platform for Wearable Physiological Computing." *Interacting via Computers* 16: 917–937.

Theißen, S. 2009. *Risiken informations- und kommunikationstechnischer (IKT-) Implantate im Hinblick auf Datenschutz und Datensicherheit* [Risks of information and communication technology (ICT-)implants with respect to privacy and data security]. Karlsruhe: Universitätsverlag Karlsruhe [Online]. Accessed April 25, 2012. http://digbib.ubka.uni-karlsruhe.de/volltexte/documents/728483

Tijs, T., D. Brokken, and W. I. Jesellsteijn. 2009. "Creating an Emotionally Adaptive Game." In *ICEC '08: Proceedings of the 7th International Conference on Entertainment Computing.* Berlin: Springer.

US Patent & Trademark Office. 2009. Avatar individualized by physical characteristics. United States patent application no. 20090309891 (by Karkanias, C. D. *et al.*), filed December 17.

von Schomberg, R., ed., 2011. *Towards Responsible Research and Innovation in the Information and Communication Technologies and Security Technologies Fields.* Luxembourg: Publications Office of the European Union.

Wakunuma, K., V. Ikonen, M. Kanerva, and M. Alaoja. 2010. *Ethical Issues of Future and Emerging Technologies* [Online]. Accessed October 31, 2011. http://ethics.ccsr.cse.dmu.ac.uk/etica/deliverables/D.5.7b2ndFocusGroupReport.pdf.

Waugh, J. 2010. *Biometric Face Detection System – Face Detection is a Reliable Technology* [Online]. Accessed October 31, 2011. http://EzineArticles.com/?expert=Waugh_John.

Wilson, G., and J. Allanson. 2001. "The Role of Electrophysiology in Human–Computer Interaction." In *Proceedings of IHM–HCI Conference*, Lille, September 2001, 251–254.

Generational views of information privacy?

Priscilla M. Regan, Gerald FitzGerald and Peter Balint

Department of Public and International Affairs, George Mason University MSN 3F4, Fairfax, VA 22030, United States

This article investigates whether there are different attitudes about information and communication technologies and information privacy among members of different generations. Specifically we consider: do different generations experience information and communication technology-mediated environments in the same way or not? Are there disjunctures or continuities in the experience of privacy across one generation? Do different generations have dissimilar attitudes about what constitutes a privacy invasion and different levels of concern about such invasions? Or is privacy a concern that develops as one ages through her life cycle and becomes more invested in the social and economic world? In other words, is information privacy, instead, something of a middle-age concern? To answer these questions, we first review the literature on generational differences, as well as the literature on privacy attitudes and introduce a number of hypotheses. We then analyze responses to two survey questions that have been asked periodically over the last 30 years to determine whether there are age cohort and/or generational differences. From the data examined, it is difficult to speak with any authority on the question of whether familiarity with technology means that younger generations or age cohorts are less concerned about technology or whether as all generations and age groups become familiar with technology privacy concerns decrease over time. However we do identify some interesting patterns.

Introduction

It has long been widely recognized that information and communication technologies (ICTs) expose users to myriad information collection and surveillance practices, which have traditionally raised concerns about privacy, civil liberties and organizational accountability. Indeed information privacy and technology issues have been topics of public deliberation and policy action since the late 1960s (Westin 1967; Rule 1973; Flaherty 1989; Regan 1995, Nissenbaum 1998). Yet the cultural, technological and social landscape has undergone a significant transformation since the 1960s – and a number of generations have experienced their social and personal spaces in quite different ways as ICTs have continued to change, become ubiquitous, and seamlessly traverse offline and online experiences.

The purpose of this article is to explore whether there are different generational attitudes with respect to information privacy concerns raised by ICTs. We examine both how generations differ in their attitudes toward ICT concerns at any given time, and how a given generation's attitudes change over time as it ages. To do so, we consider the following questions: do different generations experience ICT-mediated environments in the same way or not? Are there disjunctures or continuities in the experience of privacy across one generation? Do different generations have dissimilar attitudes about what constitutes a privacy invasion and different levels of concern about such invasions? Or is privacy a concern that develops as one ages through her life cycle and becomes more invested in the social and economic world? In other words, is information privacy, instead, something of a middle-age concern?

There is an enormous body of survey and social science research about information privacy and a growing body of social science research about the behavior and attitudes of young people online (Valentine and Halloway 2002; Livingstone and Bober 2003; Steeves 2006), especially in social-networking sites such as Facebook (boyd 2006). This paper will expand on the more recent research involving young people in several ways: it will focus on information privacy rather than on a larger set of values; it will examine attitudes rather than behavior; and it will compare attitudes across age groups, as well as within-generation and within-age group changes over time. Specifically, we present the findings from generational and age cohort analyses of responses to a number of public opinion questions about information privacy and technology. The goal is to determine if there are indeed generational patterns in concerns about privacy, to identify consistencies and disjunctures among generational and/or age cohort attitudes, and to explore how these patterns have emerged over time. Although scholars have analyzed changes in concern about information privacy over time (Gandy 2003), no one has examined how generational or age cohorts' views of privacy are different or similar and how those generational and age cohorts' views change or endure over time.

The paper proceeds in four major parts. The first explores the claims that are being made about the younger tech-savvy generation, often now termed the "Millennials" (Howe and Strauss 2000), and places these claims within the larger framework of social science thinking about generational change and analyses. The second part reviews privacy attitudes in the United States over the last 30 years, with particular attention to findings related to age differences in privacy attitudes. Based on these two parts, we then introduce our hypotheses. The third section of the paper presents our analysis of responses to two survey questions that have been asked periodically over the last 30 years to determine whether there are age cohort and/or generational differences. Our goal here is to see if privacy attitudes change systematically for age and generational groups. For example, do the privacy attitudes of an age cohort and/or generation change over time? Finally, we close with a discussion of our findings and their implications.

Generational and age-cohort differences

Recent generations have grown up with ICTs such as social networking sites and cell phones, prompting some to refer to those born after 1980 as "digital natives" (Palfrey and Gasser 2008) and a recent Pew Research Report to term them "history's first 'always connected' generation" (Pew Research Center 2010, 1).

Interest in the inner workings of the new "digital natives" has sparked something of a boom in social science research and popular culture commentaries on generational attitudes and behaviors, and the concomitant cultural changes that may be taking place. Many social commentators have expressed the belief that "young people don't care about privacy" and this sentiment appears to have caught in the popular culture and as a way of interpreting young people's willingness to post vast quantities of information on social networking sites and to conduct much of their lives in this relatively public space. However, social science studies and analyses of just what behaviors are occurring and just what young people believe are only now beginning.

In the United States, the Pew Internet and American Life Project has conducted a number of surveys and focus groups over recent years to identify the privacy attitudes of young people especially in term of new ICTs. In an April 2007 report, Pew concluded that there is variation among teens about privacy and disclosure of personal information with many teens well aware of the risks of posting information online where that information will be public and long-lasting (Lenhart and Madden 2007). They also found that girls and younger teens were more cautious about revealing information online. A student survey of young Canadians in November 2005 found that "protecting privacy online is a real issue to today's youth" (ERIN Research 2005, 42), that a majority are interested in learning how to protect their privacy, and that a majority of girls (and 47% of boys) "always" or "sometimes" read privacy policies.

In addition to studies of young people with respect to new ICTs and privacy, social scientists are also comparing attitudes and behaviors across age groups. In an April 2010 study specifically examining privacy attitudes among young adults and older adults, Hoofnagle et al. (2010, 20) concluded that, contrary to popular folklore, young adults do care about privacy and that young and older adults are actually quite alike on many privacy topics; indeed their similarities are greater than their differences. In February 2010, the Pew Research Center issued a major report on the "Millennials" (aged 18–29) in which it not only categorized this young generation but also compared it with earlier generations on a number of dimensions, including technology and social media, work and education, and politics and civic engagement. Noting that the Millennials are the first "always connected" generation, the Pew study reported that three-quarters of them have a profile on a social networking site in comparison to 50% of those 30–45, 30% of those 46–64, and 6% of those over 65 (Pew Research Center 2010, 1). Reflecting broad social science and political interest in this topic, the theme of the 2010 Annual Data Protection and Privacy Commissioner Conference focused on this perception of a growing privacy divide between generations, with older and younger age groups appearing to hold different views on the importance of privacy. However, caution in terms of drawing stark conclusions about young people's views was voiced at the conference as it has been in the reports noted above.

Although studies, conferences and the popular press have generated much speculation about generational differences, most analyses do not seriously critically engage the concept of generation, instead using its more popular or cultural interpretation. However, to use the term "generation", some attention to its meaning and implications is necessary; as one commentator noted, "its slippery, ambiguous usage blurs distinctions which should be clarified" (Spitzer 1973, 1354). A generation is thought of as a group that was born within a roughly 20-year time period and thus experiences cultural, social and political events at similar times in their developmental stages (Smola and Sutton 2002). Karl Mannheim's 1923 seminal essay "The Problem of Generations" is the most influential treatment of the concept and how it might be employed in social science analysis. Mannheim sees individuals who are the same age at the same time and who participate in the same social and historical circumstances as sharing a view of the world – and hence being a generation in a sociologically meaningful sense (Mannheim 1952, 298). Members of a generation have a "concrete bond" because they have been exposed to and participated in the "social and intellectual symptoms of a process", usually one of "destabilization" (Mannheim 1952, 303). Additionally, these events must occur during their formative adult years or their youth (Mannheim 1952, 304). They are contemporaries not because they were born between certain dates but as "a subjective condition of having experienced the same dominant influence" (Pilcher 1994, 486).

Although Mannheim did not engage the question of how to empirically demarcate generations, others have referred to generations, as well as more informal age groupings, by a number of different labels. Additionally, not all authors agree what years should be included in the various generations. For example, with respect to the older generation, Howe and Strauss (2000) refer to it as the Silent Generation (1925–1943), Lancaster and Stillman (2002) as Traditionalists (1900–1945), Oblinger and Oblinger (2005) as Matures (born before 1946), and Zemke, Raines and Filipczak (2000) as Veterans (1922–1943). For the purposes of this study, which focuses on the United States, we use the Pew delineation of generations as falling into the following five groups:

- "Greatest Generation" – those born before 1928, who often immigrated to the United States from Europe, came of age during World War II, raised families in the 1950s, and retired in the 1970s. Tom Brokaw's book of the same name memorialized this generation.
- "Silent Generation" – those born from 1928 to 1945, who tended to conform to the ways of their parents and as a group did not experience any profound "coming of age" event.
- "Baby Boomers" – those born from 1946 to 1964, who compose one of the largest age cohorts in history and experienced the cultural changes of the Civil Rights Movement and the Vietnam War during their formative ages.
- "Generation X" – those born from 1965 to 1980, who are often described as entrepreneurial and loners.
- "Millennial" – those born after 1980, who came of age during the new millennium of 2000 (Pew Research Center 2010, 4).

The fundamental idea behind generational differences is that as a generation experiences its lifecycle and seminal events in that lifecycle, that generation develops certain attitudes particular to that generation and these attitudes hold for the generation as a group. Thus any change in attitudes within a generation should change in tandem for members of the generation. Intergeneration discontinuity is the result of different generations' interpretation of the same event and becomes a source of intergenerational conflict and change (Demartini 1985, 2–3).

Others are somewhat more skeptical of painting with such a broad brush as generations represent, preferring instead to analyze a more narrowly defined age segment and dispensing with theories of generational identities (Jobs 2007). The focus then is on what we term age cohorts,[1] divided generally into 10-year segments, as seen more generally in survey research (Mason and Wolfinger 2001).

In our analysis, we use both generational cohorts and decadal age cohorts to see if we can tease out any differing effect of generational views as distinct from views that change as a result of lifecycle aging more generally. Our dependent variable is attitude towards information privacy (measured by responses to two questions), and the independent variables are age groups (measured as both generations and decadal age cohorts) and gender. Before proceeding with our analysis of generational and/or age cohort information privacy attitudes, however, it may be instructive to review privacy attitudes over time in order to identify trends and variables that have been found to be important.

Information privacy attitudes over time

Over the last 30-plus years, there has been a series of public opinion surveys that have queried respondents' attitudes about privacy generally and privacy in the context of threats from computers or new information technologies. Some of these surveys, such as the Roper surveys and General Social Surveys, have been broadly focused on a range of different attitudes, while others, such as the Gallup and ACLU polls, have been focused on civil liberties attitudes, and still others, such as the Privacy and American Business surveys, have been focused on information privacy quite

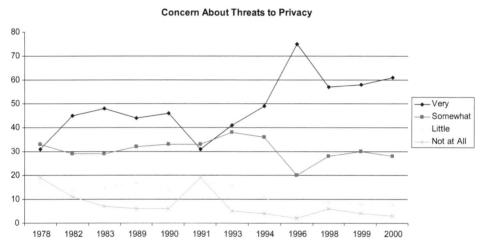

Figure 1. Concern about threats to privacy. Data points are from the following surveys identified in the Roper Center for Public Opinion databases: Dimensions of Privacy Survey by Sentry Insurance (Louis Harris & Associates, 30 November to 10 1978); General Social Survey by National Opinion Research Center (February 1982); Road After 1984: The Impact of Technology on Society Survey by Sothern New England Telephone (Louis Harris & Associates, 1–11 September 1983); Cambridge Reports National Omnibus Survey (Cambridge Reports/Research International, January 1989); Consumers in the Information Age by Equifax (Louis Harris & Associates, 11 January to 11 February 1990); Consumer Privacy Survey by Equifax (Louis Harris & Associates, 1–8 July 1991); Workplace Privacy Survey by Educational Film Center (Louis Harris & Associates, 31 March to 28 April 1993); ABC News Poll (ABC News, 7–8 June 1994); Privacy and Intelligent Transportation Systems by George Mason University and USDOT (Northern Virginia Survey Research Center, 16 January to 20 February 1996); E-Commerce & Privacy by Privacy and American Business (Louis Harris & Associates, 16–27 April 1998); Consumers and the 21st Century by National Consumers League (Louis Harris & Associates, 22 April to 3 May 1999); Freedom of Information in the Digital Age by Freedom Forum, American Society of Newspaper Editors (Center for Survey Research and Analysis, UCONN, 9–19 November 2000).

specifically. Although almost all these surveys have been conducted by major polling firms, following standard practices to derive a sample of the US population, some of these surveys have been funded by interest groups or those who have a stake in the findings of the survey. This is particularly true, as others have also pointed out (Gandy, EPIC), of the surveys funded by Privacy and American Business or specific corporations, including Equifax and Sentry Insurance.

Before discussing the findings of these polls, a number of cautions about reading the results are in order. First, given the nature of the value itself, those who are most concerned about privacy or most sensitive to possible privacy invasions are less likely to be willing to respond to public opinion surveys (Gandy 1993, 125; Katz and Tassone 1990, 126; Regan 1995, 49). Second, in surveys that ask only about privacy, respondents' concerns may be exaggerated; this is also somewhat true about surveys asking about civil liberties. In such surveys, respondents may create an attitude in order to respond to the question asked (Gandy 1993, 127; Regan 1995, 49–50). Third, because privacy is such a multi-faceted concept, respondents may be using different constructs for privacy and thus actually referencing quite different types of concerns (Gandy 1993, 135; Gandy 2003; Katz and Hyman 1993: Regan 1995, 51) and thus surveys may be conflating a number of different concerns in responses to one question. Finally, question wording, as is true for polling generally, does affect respondents' answers. For example, in a January 1989 Cambridge Reports National Omnibus Survey a very similar question was asked two different ways, yielding quite different responses. The first question asked: "As computer usage increases in business and the general society, more and more information on individual consumers is being acquired and stored in computers. How serious a threat to your personal privacy is this development? Is it a serious threat, somewhat serious, only slightly serious, or not a serious threat to your privacy at all?" In response, 22% responded that such computer usage was a "very serious threat". The second question asked more simply: "How concerned are you about safeguarding the privacy of information about you that is stored in computers? Are you very concerned, somewhat concerned, not too concerned, or not concerned at all?" In response, 35% responded that they were "very concerned".

In terms of examining privacy attitudes over time, there are two questions that have been asked with nearly the same question wording over roughly a 30-year timeframe. The first question is quite general, asking: "How concerned are you about the invasion of [threat to] your personal privacy in the United States today? Are you very concerned, somewhat concerned, only a little concerned, or not concerned at all?" In some periods the responses show year-to-year consistency, while in other periods they show substantial year-to-year variation. In looking at longer-term patterns, however, we observe that privacy concerns appear to have increased over the past quarter-century. The gap between those saying they are "very concerned" about threats to privacy and those saying they are "not at all concerned" has widened from under 15 percentage points to more than 55 percentage points. This increase is particularly apparent since 1991.

The second question is asked in slightly different language, depending on the survey, but basically queries the level of respondents' concern that computers are being used to "threaten" or "invade" privacy. As indicated in Figure 2, responses to this question over time follow a somewhat different pattern. That is, annual variations are more striking, and long-term trends are harder to discern. Despite quite a bit of

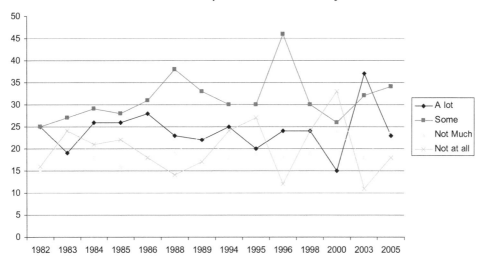

Figure 2. Concern that computer is threat to privacy. Sources from Roper Center for Public Opinion databases: Cambridge Reports National Omnibus Survey (Cambridge Reports/Research International, January 1982); Cambridge Reports National Omnibus Survey (Cambridge Reports/Research International, January 1983); Cambridge Reports National Omnibus Survey (Cambridge Reports/Research International, January 1984); Cambridge Reports National Omnibus Survey (Cambridge Reports/Research International, January 1985); Cambridge Reports National Omnibus Survey (Cambridge Reports/Research International, January 1986); Cambridge Reports National Omnibus Survey (Cambridge Reports/Research International, January 1988); Cambridge Reports National Omnibus Survey (Cambridge Reports/Research International, January 1989); Technology in the American Household by Times Mirror (Princeton Survey Research Associates, 4 January to 17 February 1994); Technology and Online Use Survey by Times Mirror (Princeton Survey Research Associates, 25 May to 22 June 1995); Public Attitudes on Science and Technology by National Science and Technology Medals Foundation (Institute for Social Inquiry/Roper Center UCONN, 31 May to 14 June 1996); Pew Research Center for the People and the Press Technology Survey (Princeton Survey Research Associates, 26 October to 1 December 1998); ABC News Poll (ABC News, 21–26 January 2000); Pew Research Center for the People and the Press Methodology Survey (Princeton Survey Research Associates International, 4 June to 30 October 2003); ABC News/Washington Post Poll (10–13 March 2005).

variation over time, the percentage of respondents expressing "a lot" of concern that computers can be used to threaten privacy is about the same in 2005 as it was in 1982.

The next question then is what the characteristics are of people who are concerned and whether those characteristics have changed over time. For this particular analysis, we are most interested in the effects of age on privacy opinions, but begin with a broader look at factors that seem to play a role in privacy opinion.

The results of these individual polls have often been accompanied by analyses of the factors affecting the results and the meaning of the results. Additionally there have been two summary analyses of trends in privacy concerns, especially of these concerns in the context of new information and communication technologies. Dutton and Meadow (1985) reviewed public opinion surveys on privacy and information technologies conducted between 1936 and 1984 and found generally that:

- people of higher socio-economic status are less concerned and threatened by new technologies than those lower in socio-economic status;
- self-identified Democrats and liberals are more concerned about privacy and civil liberties;
- business and government elites are less concerned with privacy and civil liberties issues of computing and new technology than non-elites.

With respect to specific demographic factors, Dutton and Meadow found a complex picture that in part depended upon the specifics of question wording, the context of the question, and the technology being queried. In terms of specific demographic variables, they found that:

- neither regional nor urban-suburban-rural cultures are important factors;
- women are somewhat more likely to be concerned about privacy and civil liberty threats from new technologies than are men;
- white people tend to be less concerned over privacy and civil liberty threats of new technology than are black people and, to a lesser extent, Hispanics;
- respondents with less education tend to feel more threatened by governmental use of new technology;
- higher-income respondents are less concerned over privacy invasions;
- age is often related to opinion about privacy but the relationships are too complex and inconsistent across studies to reveal a clear pattern (Dutton and Meadow 1985, 48–50).

Dutton and Meadow suggested that the age variable should be explored more fully using multivariate analysis. Cantril and Cantril conducted a series of multiple regression analyses for a 1994 benchmark survey on privacy and found that age was an important factor in explaining attitudes about employee privacy, gay and lesbian rights, and privacy and drug testing – with younger respondents being more privacy conscious. They also found that age was not a factor in attitudes about secondary uses of personal information, covert monitoring in the workplace, gay and lesbian privacy, and reproductive choice. Moreover, in general demographic variables were not significant in the regression analyses, and Cantril and Cantril concluded that it was necessary to explore non-demographic variables for a more complete explanation.

In an analysis of the 1991 Harris–Equifax Consumer Privacy Survey, Alan Westin noted that privacy surveys since 1978 had shown age to be a more important factor in explaining attitudes towards privacy than other demographic characteristics, including race, gender, income, political philosophy, education or region (Westin 1991, 9). His analysis indicated that young people (18–29) were least concerned about threats to privacy, while older people (50+) were the most concerned about threats to privacy; mid-life respondents (20–49) were in the middle in their level of concern (Westin 1991, 9–10). Westin points out that how age is actually affecting privacy attitudes is complex – possibly being accounted for by generational imprinting, life stage changes and/or experience with institutions. He also acknowledges that more complete analyses of the role age plays are necessary.

Hypotheses/expectations

Based on previous analyses of public opinion data and on social science research about generational and age cohort identities, we might expect that views about privacy would differ for different generations and age cohorts. Specifically, we might expect that:

- Based on "generational imprinting", the Greatest Generation and Silent Generation would be least concerned about privacy as those generations came of age during times of high levels of trust in organizations, including government, and little social and political unrest, and the Baby Boomers would be most concerned about privacy as that generation grew up during a time of cultural change and questioning of authority. Generation Xers would be more similar to the earlier generations than to Baby Boomers while the Millennials would be less concerned about privacy as they constitute the first-born digital generation.
- Based on life stage changes, all generations will become most concerned about individual privacy during their middle years, when they are most concerned with the stability and integrity of their social and economic lives, with lower levels of concern during their younger and older years; we would thus see a similar bell-shaped curve regarding privacy attitudes across all generations.
- Based on experience with technology, the younger generations who have grown up with technology will be more trusting of the technology and less concerned about privacy, regardless of the point in their lifecycle. Alternatively, as technology has become a more mainstream component of social and economic life, everyone is become more experienced with technology, and we should see concern about privacy decrease over time regardless of age.

Additionally, based on previous studies of survey data and on social science research about gender differences regarding civil liberties, we might expect that:

- women in all generations and age cohorts will express more concern about privacy than their male counterparts.

Generational and age differences in views of privacy

To determine whether there are generational and/or age cohort differences in views of privacy, we examined responses over a period of roughly 20 years for two questions: (1) approval or disapproval of wiretapping; and (2) whether federal government use of computer data is a serious threat to individual privacy.[2] To try to mitigate some of the concerns discussed above about accurately interpreting public opinion polling regarding privacy, we use responses to questions that were asked as part of a larger survey of public attitudes, rather than surveys specific to privacy, and we use responses to questions that are concrete in the privacy construct that is being referenced. Although our original intent was to analyze responses to a number of information privacy questions, we found that there were very few questions that were repeated in several surveys over a large number of years, thus permitting analyses of age or generational groups over time. We also were limited in that we needed the survey data in a form so that we could recode age and generational groupings for our analysis. We found only two questions, both recurring in the highly regarded General Social Survey, that we use in this analysis.

In each case, we analyze responses both by generational and 10-year age cohorts. We then examine responses separated by gender for the generational cohorts. Our analysis is exploratory to determine what the broad patterns are and to assess the value and direction of further research. In this study, we did a relatively straightforward analysis exploring patterns involving respondents' privacy concerns and generational and decadal age cohorts, first in bivariate cross-tabulations and then in layered cross-tabs also accounting for gender. Accordingly, each of the tables presented below displays the results of several cross-tabulations of General Social Survey data.

Wiretapping as a threat to privacy

Our first analysis utilizes responses to a question asked 14 times[3] in the General Social Survey between 1974 and 1994. Specifically respondents are asked: "Everything considered, would you say that, in general, you approve or disapprove of wiretapping?" Because the survey includes a question on age, we are also able to categorize respondents by generational and decadal age cohorts. In our study, we focus on responses from 1974, 1983 and 1993 to analyze the effects of generational cohorts and age cohorts on privacy concerns over the 20-year period.[4] We then separately examine the effects of gender within these cohorts.

Table 1 presents the results of several cross-tabulations, with approval or disapproval of wiretapping for a given generation across years presented horizontally and approval or disapproval of wiretapping in a given year across generations presented vertically. Analysis of generational cohorts reveals that, in 1974, the vast majority of Baby Boomers, Silent Generation and Greatest Generationers disapproved of wiretapping (see Table 1). In 1983, a trend emerges with older generation cohorts being more likely to approve of wiretapping. That is, significantly more of the Greatest Generation approve of wiretapping than the Silent Generation, and significantly more of the Silent Generation approve than Baby Boomers. In 1993, the vast majority of respondents again disapproved of wiretapping, but the intergenerational differences were not significant.

Table 1. Approval or disapproval of wiretapping by generation over time

Generation	Percentage who "approve/disapprove" of wiretapping		
	1974	1983*	1993
Greatest	18.2%/81.8%	23.5%/76.5%	27.1%/72.9%
Silent	18.7%/81.3%	21.7%/78.3%	25.2%/74.8%
Baby Boomers	13.6%/86.4%	15.6%/84.4%	22.7%/77.3%
Generation X	—	—	22.8%/77.2%

Source: General Social Survey for 1974, 1983 and 1993.
Notes: sample sizes for those answering the wiretapping question are as follows. For the Greatest Generation in 1974 $n = 604$, in 1983 $n = 447$, in 1993 $n = 181$; for the Silent Generation in 1974 $n = 476$, in 1983 $n = 383$, in 1993 $n = 218$; for the Baby Boomer Generation in 1974 $n = 338$, in 1983 $n = 688$, in 1993 $n = 431$; and for Generation X in 1993 $n = 180$.
*$p < 0.05$ for a given year across generations.

We note that the percentage of respondents who approved of wiretapping grew across the three decades for all generations. The percentage of respondents who approved of wiretapping increased by about 9 percentage points for the Greatest Generation, by 6.5 percentage points for the Silent Generation, and by about 9 percentage points for the Baby Boomer Generation. Since the response options to this question are "approve" or "disapprove", the percentages of respondents who disapproved of wiretapping declined by the same amounts. Thus while majorities in all three generations continued to oppose wiretapping across the period, these majorities shrunk over time while the minorities who approved of wiretapping grew.

Looking across Table 1, over a two-decade timeframe, we observe that the Greatest ($p = 0.016$) and Baby Boomer ($p = 0.001$) generations show significant variations in their attitudes towards wiretapping. While the vast majority of Baby Boomers disapproved of wiretapping in 1974, 1983 and 1993, we observe that they became significantly less averse to wiretapping over time. In other words, as we move between 1974 and 1993, Baby Boomers are increasingly likely to approve of wiretapping. We observe a similar trend in the case of the Silent Generation, but these results are not statistically significant. Similarly, while the vast majority of the Greatest Generation disapproved of wiretapping in all the years observed, the Greatest Generation also became significantly less averse to wiretapping over time.

The results in Table 1 also indicate that respondents from older generations appeared to be more likely to support wiretapping than those from younger generations across all the time periods. That is, the minorities supporting wiretapping for the Baby Boomer generation were smaller in all three time periods than those for the Greatest and Silent generations. The gap between the Baby Boomers and the Greatest Generation was 4.6 percentage points in 1974, 7.9 percentage points in 1983 and 4.4 percentage points in 1993. We also note that, for the one year we have data, 1993, the responses of Generation Xers were similar to those of the Baby Boomers.

In addition to the comparison of generational cohorts, we also conducted an analysis of the responses to the same wiretapping question of four 10-year age cohorts, with respondents categorized into decadal cohorts by birth year. As indicated in Table 2, results are similar to those reported earlier for the generational cohorts. That is, strong majorities from all four 10-year age cohorts disapproved of wiretapping across the 20-year period, but in each subsequent decade from 1974 to 1993 those majorities became smaller as a higher percentage of respondents from

Table 2.   Approval or disapproval of wiretapping by decadal age cohort over time

| | Percentage who "approve/disapprove" of wiretapping | | |
Decadal age cohort	1974	1983*	1993
1915–1924	19.7%/80.3%	22.8%/77.2%	24.5%75.5%
1925–1934	18.8%/81.2%	23.5%/76.5%	27.7%/72.3%
1935–1944	18.4%/81.6%	22.9%/77.1%	28.0%/72.0%
1945–1954	14.7%/85.3%	14.2%/85.8%	23.9%/76.1%

Source: General Social Survey for 1974, 1983 and 1993.
Notes: sample sizes for those answering the wiretapping question are as follows. For the 1915–1924 cohort in 1974 $n = 229$, in 1983 $n = 352$, in 1993 $n = 106$; for the 1925–1934 cohort in 1974 $n = 229$, in 1983 $n = 204$, in 1993 $n = 101$; for the 1935–1944 cohort in 1974 $n = 277$, in 1983 $n = 218$, in 1993 $n = 132$; and for the 1945–1954 cohort in 1974 $n = 368$, in 1983 $n = 352$, in 1993 $n = 201$.
*$p < 0.05$ for a given age cohort across years.

PRIVACY AND SECURITY IN THE DIGITAL AGE

each cohort expressed approval for wiretapping. Moreover, the youngest 10-year cohort had lower percentages approving wiretapping than did the older cohorts across the three decades. As expected, given that the birth years for the youngest cohort were from 1945–1954, this matches the finding for Baby Boomers reported in Table 1.

Some of the differences among age cohorts are noteworthy. While the vast majority of the oldest age cohort (born between 1915 and 1924) disapproved of wiretapping in all three years surveyed, the variations across survey years are not significant. The vast majority of the second oldest cohort (born between 1925 and 1934) also disapproved of wiretapping and the trends across survey years are similar to those for the oldest generation and also not significant. While the vast majority of the second youngest cohort (those born between 1935 and 1944) disapproved of wiretapping in all three years surveyed, we find significant (at the $p < 0.10$ level, $p = 0.083$) variations across the three survey years with this age cohort becoming less averse to wiretapping over time. In other words, we can say that respondents born between 1935 and 1944 became significantly more likely to approve of wiretapping over the timeframe observed. For the youngest cohort (born between 1945 and 1956), we find a significant ($p = 0.006$) trend across the three survey years with this age cohort also becoming less averse to wiretapping overtime. That is, we can say that respondents born between 1945 and 1956 became significantly more likely to approve of wiretapping over the timeframe observed.

Next we examined whether there were gender differences in the responses to the wiretapping question within and across generations. As indicated in Table 3, we found for both genders in all generations the same general pattern over time of increasing (although still relatively small) minorities favoring wiretapping. We found that, in 1983, significantly more males than females approved of wiretapping. This general trend is the same in 1974 and 1993 but is not significant. We also observed

Table 3. Approval or disapproval of wiretapping by gender and generation over time

Generation	Percentage who "approve/disapprove" of wiretapping		
	1974	1983*	1993
Greatest			
Male	21.4%/76.8%	28.9%/71.1%	31.5%/68.5%
Female	14.8%/85.2%	19.6%/80.4%	24.1%/75.9%
Silent			
Male	25.3%/74.7%	29.8%/70.2%	33.0%/67.0%
Female	14.2%/85.8%	15.3%/84.7%	19.4%/80.6%
Baby Boomers			
Male	17.9%/82.1%	18.6%/81.4%	22.3%/77.7%
Female	9.7%/90.3%	13.0%/87.0%	23.2%/76.8%

Source: General Social Survey for 1974, 1983 and 1993.
Notes: sample sizes for those answering the wiretapping question are as follows. For the Greatest Generation in 1974 $n = 313$ for males and $n = 291$ for females, in 1983 $n = 187$ for males and $n = 260$ for females, in 1993 $n = 73$ for males and $n = 108$ for females; for the Silent Generation in 1974 $n = 194$ for males and $n = 282$ for females, in 1983 $n = 168$ for males and $n = 215$ for females, in 1993 $n = 94$ for males and $n = 124$ for females; for the Baby Boomer Generation in 1974 $n = 162$ for males and $n = 176$ for females, in 1983 $n = 311$ for males and $n = 377$ for females, in 1993 $n = 211$ for males and $n = 220$ for females.
*$p < 0.05$.

the same general pattern for both genders of younger generations tending to have lower levels of support for wiretapping. Yet the results in Table 3 also generally indicate that lower percentages of women approved of wiretapping than men, suggesting greater privacy concerns among women than among men in all generations. These patterns hold for all generations over the time period with the exception of female Baby Boomers in 1993. Indeed, looking only at female Baby Boomers, we found that on average the vast majority (84.7%) disapproved of wiretapping in all three years. However, we see a significant decline ($p \approx 0$) in disapproval rates from 90.3% in 1974 to 76.8% in 2006. There is also a statistically significant difference between female and male Baby Boomers. The reason for this is unclear and demands further research.

To summarize our findings for the wiretapping question, we found generally high levels of disapproval across the 20-year period. Moreover we found that levels of disapproval, and thus privacy concerns, were generally higher for Baby Boomers compared with older generations, and for women compared with men. However, we also found that the strength of the disapproval appeared to soften over time as the percentages of respondents approving wiretapping in each group tended to increase from 1974 to 1993. This suggests that privacy concerns related to government wiretapping, while remaining high, may have moderated somewhat during this period.

Government computer data as a threat to privacy

Our second analysis utilizes responses to a question asked in the General Social Survey three times, in 1985, 1996 and 2006. Respondents were asked: "The federal government has a lot of different pieces of information about people which computers can bring together very quickly. Is this a very serious threat to individual privacy, a fairly serious threat, not a serious threat, or not a threat at all to individual privacy?" We examine the responses of the generational and decadal age cohorts to this question, following the same approach we used for the wiretapping question.

In Table 4, we present the percentages of respondents from the generational cohorts who answered that government computer data is a "very serious" threat to privacy. These results do not show the consistent pattern of moderating privacy

Table 4. Concern for government computer data by generation over time

Generation	Percentage responding that government computer data is a "very serious" threat to individual privacy		
	1985	1996	2006
Greatest	40.3%	51.5%	27.5%
Silent	33.1%	51.1%	31.4%
Baby Boomers	24.6%	34.9%	29.5%
Generation X	—	33.2%	21.7%
Millennials	—	—	21.8%

Source: General Social Survey for 1985, 1996 and 2006.
Notes: sample sizes for those answering the computer data question are as follows. For the Greatest Generation in 1985 $n = 181$, in 1996 $n = 132$, in 2006 $n = 69$; for the Silent Generation in 1985 $n = 172$, in 1996 $n = 233$, in 2006 $n = 239$; for the Baby Boomer generation in 1985 $n = 256$, in 1996 $n = 538$, in 2006 $n = 569$; for Generation X in 1996 $n = 307$, in 2006 $n = 483$; and for Millennials in 2006 $n = 124$.

concerns noted for the wiretapping question. Instead we see that the percentage of respondents indicating that government computer data is a "very serious" threat to privacy generally increased from 1985 to 1996 and then declined again by 2006.

In these results, as with the wiretapping results, however, we continue to see a pattern of younger generations having responses that differ from those of their older counterparts. In this case, the Baby Boomers, Generation Xers and Millennials appear less likely to rate government computer data as a "very serious" threat, although this distinction largely disappears for Baby Boomers by 2006.

As indicated in Table 4, between 1985 and 1996, we observe significant increases in the percentages of Greatest ($p = 0.002$), Silent ($p \approx 0$) and Baby Boomer ($p \approx 0$) generations who view computer data as a very serious threat to individual privacy. Over the same time period, we also see significant decreases in the percentages of the Greatest, Silent, and Baby Boomer generations who view computer data as not posing a serious threat to individual privacy. However, between 1996 and 2006, we see a significant declines in the percentages of the Greatest ($p = 0.002$), Silent ($p \approx 0$) and Baby Boomer ($p \approx 0$) generations who view computer data as a very serious threat to individual privacy. This decline is particularly marked in the cases of the Greatest and Silent generations. The reasons for this are unclear and will require further research.

Therefore, in terms of privacy concerns, the difference between older and younger generations seems to go in opposite directions for the wiretapping question and the computer data question. The results in Table 1 indicate that younger generations were more likely to disapprove of wiretapping, thus suggesting higher privacy concerns regarding wiretapping when compared with older generations. In contrast, the results in Table 4 indicate that younger generations were generally less likely to rate government computer data as a "very serious threat", thus suggesting lower privacy concerns for computer data when compared with older generations. We discuss these apparently contradictory results below.

We also examined responses to the computer data question for four decadal age cohorts. Because the years when this question was asked on the survey are more recent, we used relatively younger age cohorts for the computer data threat question than for the wiretapping question.

Results for the first three decadal age cohorts presented in Table 5 reflect patterns similar to those reported for generational cohorts in Table 4. That is, the percentage

Table 5. Concern for government computer data by decadal age cohort over time

Decadal age cohort	Percentage responding that government computer data is a "very serious" threat to individual privacy		
	1985	1996	2006
1926–1935	39.6%	50.0%	27.8%
1936–1945	32.4%	52.0%	32.9%
1946–1955	28.5%	40.4%	28.5%
1956–1965	17.8%	29.4%	30.8%

Source: General Social Survey for 1985, 1996 and 2006.
Notes: sample sizes for those answering the computer data question are as follows. For the 1926–1935 cohort in 1985 $n = 91$, in 1996 $n = 106$, in 2006 $n = 97$; for the 1936–1945 cohort in 1985 $n = 102$, in 1996 $n = 148$, in 2006 $n = 161$; for the 1946–1955 cohort in 1985 $n = 142$, in 1996 $n = 267$, in 2006 $n = 263$; and for the 1956–1965 cohort in 1985 $n = 118$, in 1996 $n = 299$, in 2006 $n = 344$.

of respondents in each of these cohorts responding that computer data kept by the government is a "very serious" threat generally increased from 1985 to 1996 and then declined again by 2006. This pattern does not hold for the youngest decadal cohort, however. For that group, the level of concern rose from 1985 to 1996, and then held relatively steady at the new higher level in 2006. This result suggests that the pattern noted for Baby Boomers in Table 4 – that the decline in concern from 1996 to 2006 was less steep than for the older generations – was largely driven by the younger cohort of Baby Boomers, those born between 1956 and 1965. For this younger group of Baby Boomers, the level of concern for government computer data was relatively low in 1996, but then remained steady from that point, bringing it into line with the other cohorts by 2006.

A comparison of results in Tables 4 and 5 also reinforces the point we made above regarding the differences in computer data privacy concerns across generations. Results from both tables suggest that the Baby Boomers had less concern for this issue than the older generations in 1985 and 1996, but that these differences had dissipated by 2006. Yet Table 4 indicates that, by 2006, the two younger generations now first appearing in the survey – Generation Xers and Millennials – show the reduced level of concern that Baby Boomers expressed in earlier years.

As before, we also examined whether there were gender differences in the responses to the computer data question within and across generations. As indicated in Table 6, we found for both genders in all generations the same general patterns indicated in Table 4. That is, the percentages of respondents identifying government computer data as a "very serious" threat to privacy generally increased from 1985 to 1996 and declined from 1996 to 2006. And as in Table 4, Baby Boomers were generally less likely than older generations to consider government computer data a "very serious" threat in 1985 and 1996 but about equally likely to do so by 2006.

Table 6. Concern for government computer data by gender and generation over time

Generation	Percentage responding that government computer data is a "very serious" threat to individual privacy		
	1985	1996	2006
Greatest			
Male	31.7%	42.9%	24.0%
Female	51.9%	55.6%	29.5%
Silent			
Male	31.1%	50.9%	27.6%
Female	36.4%	51.3%	34.0%
Baby Boomers			
Male	23.7%	35.2%	27.2%
Female	26.0%	34.7%	31.6%

Source: General Social Survey for 1985, 1996 and 2006.
Notes: sample sizes for those answering the computer data question are as follows. For the Greatest Generation in 1985 $n = 104$ for males and $n = 77$ for females, in 1996 $n = 42$ for males and $n = 90$ for females, in 2006 $n = 25$ for males and $n = 44$ for females; for the Silent Generation in 1985 $n = 106$ for males and $n = 66$ for females, in 1996 $n = 114$ for males and $n = 119$ for females, in 2006 $n = 98$ for males and $n = 141$ for females; for the Baby Boomer Generation in 1985 $n = 156$ for males and $n = 100$ for females, in 1996 $n = 247$ for males and $n = 291$ for females, in 2006 $n = 272$ for males and $n = 297$ for females.

Yet the results in Table 6 also reveal some differences between men and women within and across generations. Women in the Greatest Generation, for example are more likely than men to identify computer data as a "very serious" threat to privacy. The gaps of 20.2 percentage points in 1985 and 12.7 percentage points in 1996 are particularly wide. Even in 2006 – by which time our earlier analysis indicated a narrowing of differences among the Greatest, Silent and Baby Boomer generations – Table 6 indicates that women in all three groups were more likely than men to identify computer data as a "very serious" concern, by 5.5, 6.4 and 4.4 percentage points, respectively.

To summarize our findings for the computer data question, we did not observe any consistent pattern of increasing or decreasing level of concern over time. With some exceptions, respondents across generations and gender tended to express relatively less concern in 1985, more concern in 1996, and again lower concern in 2006. We did find, however, that women tended to have higher levels of concern for the computer data issue than men. This matches the findings for the wiretapping question, which also showed greater privacy concerns for women.

However, looking at generations, the results for the computer data question appear contrary to the results for the wiretapping question. For the wiretapping question, Baby Boomers tended to have higher levels of disapproval than the older generations, indicating higher levels of privacy concerns. On the other hand for the computer data question, Baby Boomers tended to be less likely than older generations to consider government computer data collection a "very serious" threat, suggesting lower levels of privacy concerns, although these differences did appear diminished as Baby Boomers aged.

Discussion

There are two important limitations of our data that need mention before we discuss our findings. The first is likely to occur in any generational or age cohort analysis in that the number of members of the younger generations is very small in more recent surveys and therefore cannot be fully analyzed. However, as time allows more analysis of the younger generations, the number of members of the older generations and age cohorts will similarly decrease. This seems to be an inherent problem in longitudinal analysis of generational attitudes. The second limitation is more peculiar to our data. Our analysis of attitudes to wiretapping is for 1974, 1983 and 1993, whereas our analysis of computer data as a threat to privacy is for 1985, 1996 and 2006. Therefore, our generations and age cohorts are being queried about their attitudes at different points in time, thus limiting our comparisons across the two questions. Unfortunately we could not find similar questions asked during the same years.

Despite these limitations, we see interesting patterns in these analyses that indicate that there may indeed be generational differences and patterns in some attitudes towards privacy. With respect to wiretapping, we find that all generations become more approving of wiretapping over time. In all three decades, Baby Boomers are less likely to approve, and thus more likely to be concerned about privacy, than both the Silent and Greatest generations. With respect to whether computer data are a threat to privacy, we do not find a simple trend line for any generation. Instead concern about computer data as a threat to privacy is greatest for all generations in 1996 and is lower in 1985 and 2006. In contrast to response about wiretapping, interestingly, in each of the three years fewer Baby Boomers see computer data as a privacy threat than either the Silent or Greatest generations. Thus our analysis finds support for our hypothesis regarding the Silent and Greatest generations being less concerned about privacy with respect to wiretapping but not with respect to government computer data. Baby Boomers, on the other hand, voice more concern about privacy with respect to wiretapping than older generations but less concern about privacy with respect to government computer data. Unfortunately it is too early to have sufficient survey data to analyze change in attitudes over time for Generation Xers and Millennials, but our data for 2006 do indicate that these generations show less concern about computer data than older generations.

Our findings here, however, do seem to indicate that there is similar movement of attitudes within the Greatest, Silent and Baby Boomer generations over time, and consistent patterns of differences in response to the two questions analyzed. Interestingly the patterns are different for the two questions, which we suggest has to do with the differences in privacy concern elicited by the question. The wiretapping question queries attitudes toward government activities in law enforcement, something that is quite specific and generally regarded as a legitimate government function, while the question about government computer data is more open-ended and more directly related to a technological innovation. If this is a plausible explanation, then younger generations may indeed be more comfortable with the technology and less concerned about its privacy implications.

We find similar patterns for our age cohort analyses. With respect to wiretapping, we find that all age cohorts generally become more approving of wiretapping – except for a slight decline in support for wiretapping in 1983 for the youngest (born 1945–1956). The youngest age cohort has the lowest approval of wiretapping across all three survey years. The age cohort pattern for whether computer data are a threat to privacy is similar to the pattern for generations with the oldest age cohort (1926–1935) seeing computer data as more serious than other age cohorts in 1985, but the second oldest (1936–1945) seeing it as more serious than other cohorts in 1996 and 2006. The youngest age cohort (1956–1965) views it least seriously across the three survey years. For all four age cohorts, we observe a startling increase in viewing computer data as a very serious threat from 1985 to 1996 and then a decline across all age groups in 2006. With respect to both questions, our analysis does not appear to support the hypothesis that concern about privacy raises during the middle years and declines in the older years.

From the data examined, it is difficult to speak with any authority to the question of whether familiarity with technology means that younger generations or age cohorts are less concerned about technology or whether as all generations and age groups become familiar with technology privacy concerns decreases over time. However we do identify some interesting patterns. As noted above, we believe that the wiretapping question speaks less directly to technology than the government computer data question. If that is the case, then the spike in those viewing computer data as a very serious threat in 1996 for all age groups may be the result of the rise of email and online transactions, which by 2006 are then more familiar to all age cohorts and thus perceived as a less serious threat.

Finally our data indicate that there are interesting differences between men and women in all generations regarding both approval of wiretapping and attitudes regarding whether computer data are a threat to privacy. Generally it can be said that women across generations and across years are more concerned about privacy with lower percentages of women than men in all generations approving of wiretapping (except female Baby Boomers in 1993) and women in all generations more likely than men to identify computer data as a "very serious" concern (except female Baby Boomers in 1996). Based on this rather limited data, it appears that female Baby Boomers between the mid-1980s to mid-1990s may have become less privacy conscious than women of other generations.

This exploratory analysis indicates that further research in this area seems warranted. Specifically we believe that multivariate analyses of income, familiarity with technology and gender might enable us to better understand the underlying explanations for generational variations. For both the wiretapping approval question and the computer threat to individual privacy, we analyzed a number of demographic variables – including income, education, political party and gender – across the three time surveys examined and found that gender yielded significant differences in two years. However, our preliminary analysis indicates that more sophisticated multivariate analysis could reveal some interesting results.

Additionally identification of additional questions that have been asked over time in other surveys might be analyzed in ways similar to what we have done here. However, it is important to recognize that none of the questions asked on public opinion surveys accurately and fully captures concern about privacy. As we noted initially, privacy is an enormously complicated and broad concept, and it is nearly impossible to phrase a question to capture its nuances. Additionally, many specific questions about privacy have not been consistently asked on general public opinion surveys. For example, the more general questions about "concern about the invasion of [threat to] your personal privacy" and "concern that computers are being used to threaten [or invade] privacy" might be appropriate for more detailed analysis but are most often asked in surveys that are specific to privacy rather than general social surveys.

Notes

1. We recognize that there is discussion in sociological theory about the overlap in meaning between the terms "generation" and "age cohort" with some scholars, such as Rosow (1978), pointing out that Mannheim's concept of "generation" is a "cohort". In our analysis we use age cohort to delineate defined 10-year time periods and generation to represent Mannheim's broader sociological concept.
2. Given that our analysis only involves privacy issues related to government intrusions, we investigated whether attitudes toward wiretapping might be driven by levels of confidence in the federal government. However, while confidence in the federal government has fallen over time, our findings indicate that all generational cohorts have become more likely to approve of wiretapping over time.
3. In 1974, 1975, 1977, 1978, 1982, 1983, 1985, 1986, 1988, 1989, 1990, 1991, 1993, 1994.
4. As indicated in note 3, the question was not asked in 1984.

References

boyd, D. 2006. "Friends, Friendsters, and Fop 8: Writing Community into Being on Social Network Sites." *First Monday.* http://firstmonday.org/issues/issue11_12/boyd/index.html
Demartini, J. R. 1985. "Change Agents and Generational Relationships: A Reevaluation of Mannheim's Problem of Generations." *Social Forces* 64 (1): 1–16.
Dutton, W. H. and R. G. Meadow. 1985. "Public Perspectives on Government Information Technology: A Review of Survey Research on Privacy, Civil Liberties and the Democratic Process". Unpublished report for the Office of Technology Assessment, US Congress.

PRIVACY AND SECURITY IN THE DIGITAL AGE

ERIN, Research Inc. 2005. "Young Canadians in a Wired World. Phase II: Student Survey" (November). http://mediasmarts.ca/research-policy

Flaherty, D. H. 1989. *Protecting Privacy in Surveillance Societies: The Federal republic of Germany, Sweden, France, Canada, and the United States.* Chapel Hill, NC: University of North Carolina Press.

Gandy, O. H. Jr. 1993. *The Panoptic Sort: A Political Economy of Personal Information.* Boulder, CO: Westview Press.

Gandy, O. H. Jr. 2003. "Public Opinion Surveys and the Formation of Privacy Policy." *Journal of Social Issues* 59 (2): 283–299.

Hoofnagle, C., J. King, S. Li, and J. Turow, J. 2010. "How Different are Young Adults From Older Americans When it Comes to Information Privacy Attitudes and Policies?" (April 14). http://papers.ssrn.com/sol3/papers.cfm?abstract_id=1589864

Howe, N., and W. Strauss. 2000. *Millennials Rising: The Next Great Generation.* New York: Vintage Books.

Jobs, R. I. 2007. *Riding the New Wave.* Stanford, CA: Stanford University Press.

Katz, J. E., and M. M. Hyman. 1993. "Dimensions of Concern over Telecommunications Policy in the United States." *Information Society* 9 (2): 251–275.

Katz, J. E., and A. R. Tassone. 1990. "Public Opinion Trends: Privacy and Information Technology." *Public Opinion Quarterly* 54: 125–143.

Lancaster, L. C., and D. Stillman. 2002. *When Generations Collide: Who They Are, Why They Clash, How to Solve the Generational Puzzle at Work.* New York: Collins Business.

Lenhart, A. and M. Madden. 2007. *Teens, Privacy & Online Social Networks.* Pew Internet & American Life Project, April 18.

Livingstone, S., and M. Bober. 2003. *UK Children go Online: Listening to Young People's Experiences.* London: Economic and Social Research Council.

Mannheim, K. 1952. "The Problem of Generations." In *Essays on the Sociology of Knowledge.* London: RKP (originally published 1923).

Mason, W. M. and N. H. Wolfinger. 2001. *Cohort Analysis.* California Center for Population Research, On-Line Working Papers Series (April). http://escholarship.org/uc/item/8wc8v8cv

Nissenbaum, H. 1998. "Protecting Privacy in an Information Age: The Problem of Privacy in Public." *Law and Philosophy* 17: 559–596.

Oblinger, D. G. and J. L. Oblinger, eds. 2005. *Educating the Net Gen.* Washington, DC: EDUCASE.

Palfrey, J., and U. Gasser. 2008. *Born Digital: Understanding the First Generation of Digital Natives.* New York: Basic Books.

Pew Research Center. 2010. "The Millennials: Confident. Connected. Open to Change." http://www.pewresearch.org/millennials

Pilcher, J. 1994. "Mannheim's Sociology of Generations: An Undervalued Legacy." *The British Journal of Sociology* 45 (3): 481–495.

Regan, P. M. 1995. *Legislating Privacy: Technology, Social Values, and Public Policy.* Chapel Hill. NC: University of North Carolina Press.

Rosow, I. 1978. "What is a Cohort and Why?" *Human Development* 21: 65–75.

Rule, J. B. 1973. *Private Lives and Public Surveillance: Social Control in the Computer Age.* London: Allen Lane.

Smola, K. W., and C. D. Sutton. 2002. "Generational Differences: Revisiting Generational Work Values for the new Millennium." *Journal of Organizational Behavior* 23 (4): 363–382.

Spitzer, A. B. 1973. "The Historical Problem of Generations." *The American Historical Review* 78 (5): 1353–1385.

Steeves, V. 2006. "It's No Child's Play: The Online Invasion of Children's Privacy." *University of Ottawa Law and Technology Journal* 3 (1): 169–188.

Valentine, G., and S. L. Holloway. 2002. "Cyberkids? Exploring Children's Identities and Social Networks in On-Line and Off-Line Worlds." *Annals of the Association of American Geographers* 92 (2): 302–319.

Westin, A. F. 1967. *Privacy and Freedom.* New York: Atheneum.

Westin, A.F. 1991. "Introduction and Analysis." In *Harris-Equifax Consumer Privacy Survey,* edited by L. Harris and Alan F. Westin, 6–12. Atlanta, GA: Equifax.

Zemke, R., C. Raines, and B. Filipczak. 2000. *Generations at Work: Managing the Class of Veterans, Boomers, X-ers, and Nexters in Your Workplace.* New York: Amacon.

Public attitudes towards privacy and surveillance in Croatia[1]

Jelena Budak, Ivan-Damir Anić and Edo Rajh

Institute of Economics, Zagreb, Trg J. F. Kennedyja 7, 10000, Zagreb, Croatia

> This paper investigates public attitudes towards privacy, data protection, surveillance and security in Croatia. The public opinion survey assesses the value privacy may have for the individuals and if privacy is recognized as a social and political value. Four principal groups of privacy violations are covered in the survey: information collection, information processing, information dissemination and invasion. Citizens' awareness of the data protection issues and related confidence in government and business practices are examined as well. Furthermore, this paper investigates if public attitudes towards surveillance in Croatia are in favor of the "nothing to hide" argument. Based on empirical data, the findings indicate that there are three groups of Croatian citizens with different opinions: "pro-surveillance" oriented citizens; citizens concerned about being surveilled; and citizens concerned about data and privacy protection. Identified groups of citizens differ in demographics. Policy implications of the research results are discussed in the paper.

Introduction

Issues relating to privacy and surveillance are gaining in importance across disciplines and have become hotly contested political issues (Haggerty and Ericson 2006). Security issues and the associated necessity of enhanced surveillance are subjects of debates among scholars and practitioners (Dinev et al. 2005). New technology-based surveillance practices are being developed to meet demands for safety and security, efficiency and coordination in the society, but also introduce certain threats. Many people have become deeply concerned about the spread of surveillance (Dinev et al. 2005; Goold 2009). In a "surveillance society" institutions and government might gain too much power over individuals. Data protection, which is closely related to privacy and surveillance, has also become one of the major concerns of modern society (Solove 2008a). Not only can awareness of surveillance, security and data protection issues make a person feel uncomfortable, it can also cause people to alter their behavior (Solove 2006). Understanding the effects of privacy concern and the issues of surveillance, security and data protection, as well as addressing the multidimensional impacts they have on individuals and society have become part of the research agenda in many countries.

Past research examines privacy from various perspectives, including the meaning of privacy, general privacy concern, public opinion trends, the impact of surveillance technologies, causes and consequences of privacy protection, consumers' responses to privacy concern, and the need for government surveillance and privacy regulation (e.g. Patton 2000; Kumaraguru and Cranor 2005; Wirtz, Lwin, and Williams 2007; Goold 2009). Previous studies indicate that there are differences in information privacy concerns across cultures (Dinev et al. 2005), and that different groups of people share different views on surveillance and privacy (Haggerty and Gazso 2005; Wirtz, Lwin, and Williams 2007). Citizens' attitudes towards privacy and data protection also vary according to demographic characteristics (e.g. European Commission 2011). Additional attitudinal studies of privacy, data protection, surveillance and security would help to understand people's behavior, and different behavior requires different policy approaches (Wirtz, Lwin, and Williams 2007).

This paper explores whether Croatian citizens are concerned about privacy and data protection, whether citizens are concerned about being surveilled, and whether some population groups would opt for more enforced surveillance, for example to prevent crime. This study aims to answer two main research questions: (1) what is the Croatian public opinion on surveillance, data protection and privacy; and (2) which population groups share similar attitudes, and can these groups be differentiated in terms of demographic characteristics?

The study builds on the existing literature on privacy, data protection and surveillance, and contributes to that research area by making the following advances. We develop the privacy and surveillance measurement instrument and apply it in the Croatian environment. The study develops the typology of citizens according to their attitudes towards privacy, surveillance, data protection and security. Furthermore, the empirical research aims to identify and classify citizens according to their attitudes. The underlying assumption is that there are few groups of citizens who share similar attitudes and that those groups differ according to demographic characteristics. Finally, many privacy surveys have been conducted in the United States, Europe, Australia and Canada (Kumaraguru and Cranor 2005), but little information is available for Croatia. Taking into consideration the paucity of research on privacy, surveillance, data protection and security issues in Croatia, it would be necessary to get additional insight into those issues in this country too. From a policy angle, such public opinion survey about privacy, surveillance, data protection and security might play an important role in framing the public debate.

The next section elaborates the situation in Croatia and the rationale for the national study. Theoretical underpinnings for this study are presented in the third section, followed by sections on the methodology applied and the results of the empirical analysis. The concluding section provides preliminary policy recommendations and indicates lines of future research.

Rationale for exploring privacy issues in Croatia

Croatia was one of the republics of former Yugoslavia that gained independence in 1991. At the time, Yugoslavia was a socialist country with a rather unique political system that was quite different from the authoritarian communist regimes prevalent in other East European countries. However, to ensure political and social stability and discipline, some mechanisms of social and political control were put in place. In the new era of independent Croatia, the whole social set-up radically changed. Particularly, transition and the European Union (EU) accession process which started in 2001 raised questions about government openness and transparency over and above concerns regarding privacy protection, and political control in democracy became rather irrelevant.

In the process of accession to the EU, Croatia has harmonized its legislation to the *acquis communautaire*. *Acquis communautaire*, also called the *Community acquis*, is the accumulated legislation and case law of the EU Court of Justice, as well as the declarations and resolutions adopted by the EU. It constitutes the body of common rights and obligations binding all the Member States together within the EU. All Member States are bound to comply with the *acquis communautaire*, and countries joining the EU (such as Croatia) must have implemented the existing *acquis communautaire* by the time of accession. Croatia is due to become the 28th Member state of the EU on 1 July 2013.

The legal framework defining personal data protection and supervision over collecting, processing and use of personal data in the Republic of Croatia is accordingly regulated by the Act on Personal Data Protection.[2] The Croatian Personal Data Protection Agency has been established by the Act as an independent and autonomous body for the purpose of supervising the work of personal data processing in the Republic of Croatia. Personal data protection is guaranteed by the Constitution to every person in order to protect the privacy of individuals and other human rights and fundamental freedoms in the process of collecting, processing and use of personal data. Personal data protection guaranteed by the law comprises information on an individual's health data, personal identification number, data on earnings, school grades, bank accounts, tax refunds, biometrical data, passport or ID card number, and so on.[3]

Despite the existing legislation, the privacy protection is often seen as insufficient owing to the poor implementation of the law and weak control mechanisms. As one of the interviewees in the qualitative part of our research pointed out, Croatian citizens witnessed a situation in which banks would not allow them to open a bank account without providing a valid personal ID number (the so-called JMBG) even after the JMBG had become a legally protected confidential personal ID number. Interestingly, most citizens were willing to provide it without reporting such misbehavior of private companies. There may be various reasons for this kind of practice, including pragmatic ones (e.g. speeding up the bank procedure). The imbalance of power between service providers (corporations, state institutions) and individuals (citizens) might also be significant. One could also argue that some Croatian citizens do not quite understand why they should protect their own privacy. As privacy is a vague concept of personal space under the control of the individual (Stalder 2002), the notion of privacy and privacy protection is ambiguous: some people would voluntarily provide personal information and data to literally anyone, but would become very sensitive if disturbed in their "private time" (e.g. official calls on private cell phones over the weekends are often seen as intrusions on privacy). A vague understanding of privacy and surveillance might arise from Croatian language specifics (e.g. the terms "safety" and "security" are translated with the same word in Croatian, while surveillance could be interpreted as control[4]), but it can also be attributed to the public mindset inherited from the past regime. Croatian citizens are still used to being asked to identify themselves by any person in uniform: security personnel, public transport inspectors, phone service provider clerks, etc. On the other hand, during the past regime, citizens were more aware of the necessity to hide some things from others. However, since it was all happening in an environment of institutional repression, this should not be attributed to better awareness but rather to the survival instinct.

As the civil sector and democracy developed in Croatia, the role of the state and government services changed. Regarding the collection and exchange of information among state/government services, there are some services that take the issue of accessing data very seriously (e.g. the Ministry of the Interior), but there are other services whose employees are not even aware that some of the data they are working with are of a private nature. Although keeping records and procedures for storage of personal data are also regulated by legal acts,[5] there is a problem of access to data, because many data are sensitive but not perceived as such. Generally speaking, public employees are not educated about data privacy and data protection. Added to the poor control of data collection and storage, in these conditions information leakage is quite possible, intentionally or not. One could suppose that the same is true for private companies and employers in general: some (large) companies have implemented corporate procedures to keep personal data and information about employees personal and confidential, while small private firms probably would not invest resources to enforce privacy protection practices.

Finally, the new era of reality shows, personalized marketing campaigns and CCTV cameras has spread so fast in Croatia that it remains unclear if and how public attitudes towards them have been formed. The concept of our research was initially based on these intriguing questions. Focusing the research on public opinion, we do not discuss the different motives and interests of various stakeholders in implementing surveillance and data collection policies. For example, private companies collect personal data to maximize profits. Their clients and consumers often voluntarily provide personal data in exchange for "special offers" and there is some research on consumer information privacy concerns (e.g. Dolnicar and Jordaan 2007). State institutions collect information about citizens to ensure the functioning of the state, from national security to providing public services. The latter role of the state has been of the utmost public interest. Croatian citizens and the business sector are asking for consolidation and better utilization of various government databases to enable efficient control of public funding, limiting the grey economy and improve access to public services.

Theoretical background

Privacy exists as a concept at the interface of surveillance, security and data protection. A precise definition of privacy does not exist. Warren and Brandeis (1890) offered one of the first definitions of privacy in discussing the invasion of privacy by media at the turn of nineteenth century. They broadly defined privacy as a right to be "let alone" in the sense of one's right to "keep his private life". One of the most cited definitions of privacy was provided by Alan Westin (1970): "Privacy is the claim of individuals, groups, or institutions to determine for themselves when, how, and to what extent information about them is communicated to others". Some authors conceptualize privacy as a narrow category, such as a concept of privacy defined in terms of intimacy only (Inness 1996), or understand privacy as secrecy (see Raab and Goold 2011). Solove (2008a) offers systematization of research that clusters privacy around six dimensions: the right to be let alone; limited access to the self; secrecy; control of personal information; personhood; and intimacy.

Privacy is recognized as an individual right, but also as a social and political value (Solove 2008a; Goold 2010; Raab and Goold 2011). Solove (2008a) argues that, in the modern society, "the value of privacy must be determined on the basis of its importance to society, not in terms of individual rights". Privacy has a social value because "privacy is ... the protection of the individual based on society's own norms and values" (Solove 2008a). Social privacy includes the individual's ability and effort to control social contacts (Westin 1970). The aspect of social privacy is important in the individual's building of personal relationships, where he or she might want to control the access to intimate information.

Our survey covers four principal groups of "socially recognized privacy violations", yet it is limited to selected sub-groups of privacy violation activities that we have estimated to pose privacy problems in Croatia. Thus we have covered activities within (1) information collection (surveillance); (2) information processing (insecurity, secondary use of information, exclusion); (3) information dissemination (breach of confidentiality)l and (4) invasion (intrusion) (Solove 2006). Although subjective perceptions of privacy violations are hard to adequately legislate, policy-makers and legislators are recognizing the social value of privacy (Benett 2011). The efficacy of privacy protection legislation in Croatia is therefore questioned in the survey.

Concepts of privacy are not mutually exclusive, but keeping the focus on one particular privacy value determines expectations of potential threats to privacy and the level of legal privacy protection. Raab and Goold (2011) provide an example showing that, if privacy is recognized as ability to control information, then (un)fair information practices will be seen as a major privacy concern. Informational privacy relates to an individual's right to determine how, when and to what extent information about the self will be released to another person or organization (Westin 1970). This concept of privacy as control over (private) information is prevalent in European privacy policy. Information privacy served as a basis to establish so called "fair information practices" and was used in designing data protection legislation in a number of countries. Privacy rights should be balanced with the state's legitimate need for information. However, personal information collected by the state and private companies is shared beyond the knowledge and control of individuals concerned. Increased demand for information and the spread of new technologies such as surveillance cameras indeed limit the purely private spaces. Our research interest is in whether Croatian citizens are concerned about privacy protection and data protection, that is, two components of the protection of personal information.

The expansion of information technologies and the growing use of computers have placed increasing demands on data protection. The main concern is with access to data, with what its contents should include and how it should be protected. Data protection is closely related to information privacy and encompasses the rules that regulate the collection, maintenance, use and disclosure of personal information (Flaherty 1989).

Data protection and fundamental safeguarding of privacy rights of EU citizens is of great importance to the European Commission (European Commission 2011). Since 1991, the European Commission has been monitoring the perceptions, attitudes and views of the EU's citizens on data protection and privacy. The surveys showed that a majority of EU citizens showed concern about their privacy and data protection.

For the data protection part of the survey we have used the data abuse pyramid concept developed by Solove (2008b). Abuse of personal information is ubiquitous in the digital age, but Solove argues that the problem does not stem from the technology but from government and business practices. Therefore, in our survey we asked about (1) the misuse of personal information; (2) leaks of personal information from the company or organization databases or improper access; and (3) insecurity on how well the data are protected. These questions relate to both public and private sector practices.

Surveillance is defined as the collection and analysis of information about individuals or groups of people in order to govern their activity. Personal and mass surveillance denotes supervision, observation or oversight of behavior through the use of personal data and data systems (*dataveillance*), by means of physical surveillance, communications surveillance or combined, electronic surveillance (Clarke 2006). Public opinion on surveillance may vary depending on the surveillance instruments employed, and these potential differences have been captured in our survey as well.

Surveillance is a tool of social control over (unwanted) human behavior. Although there is consensus that every society needs some kind of social control, the boundaries of acceptable social control are debatable. As the level of surveillance in society increases, it becomes difficult for individuals to maintain identities and many people are deeply concerned about the spread of surveillance. Surveillance is criticized for its chilling effect on people's behavior and too much social control can adversely impact freedom, creativity and self-development (Solove 2006). In discussing the level of public tolerance to surveillance, Goold (2010) argues that citizens would demand less surveillance when experiencing state surveillance as a threat to political rights and democracy. Otherwise some would opt in favor of surveillance as an effective deterrent to crime, which makes it more socially acceptable. The "nothing to hide argument" is a widespread popular discourse when discussing government surveillance and data mining as a threat to privacy (Solove 2007). We tested whether public attitudes towards surveillance in Croatia are in favor of this argument.

In designing policies towards the privacy, surveillance, data protection and security, the private and public institutions should take into consideration demographic differences. Past research indicates that there are several groups of citizens who share similar interests towards surveillance. Haggerty and Gazso (2005) discussed two groups of citizens: individuals concerned about increasing surveillance or reduced privacy rights and individuals who might be characterized as being "pro-surveillance oriented". Similarly, there are groups of people who have different attitudes towards privacy issues. Wirtz, Lwin, and Williams (2007) indicate that citizens who show less concern for internet privacy are those individuals who perceive that corporations are acting responsibly in terms of their privacy policies, and that sufficient legal regulation is in place to protect their privacy and have greater trust and confidence in these power-holders. On the other hand, if those in power positions (regulators and firms) are not seen to be responsible, consumer concern is likely to increase, and thus would lead to defensive measures to reduce dependence on these power-holders. In 1991, an Equifax public opinion survey on privacy in the United States (Gandy 2003) identified the following groups of citizens: a highly concerned group of respondents was named "privacy fundamentalists"; moderates were named "the pragmatic majority"; and the low concern group was named "the unconcerned". The European survey on online activities identified two types of citizens with different degree of privacy concern and behavior: "digital natives" and "digital initiates" (European Commission 2011). A socio-demographic breakdown also revealed some differences among citizens. Furthermore, the study of McCahill and Finn (2010) showed how children's experience and response to surveillance varies across social positions of class and gender. Finally, a cross-national study of privacy explored, among other research questions, whether public attitudes are shaped by unique historical experience and whether they are affected by demographic variables (Zureik 2004). Based on the past research, we also expect to find in Croatia groups of citizens who are pro-surveillance-oriented and those concerned about surveillance, privacy and data protection. In our sample there should be also demographic differences among those segments of citizens.

Methodology

This research is primarily based on a quantitative survey, although exploratory research qualitative methodology was also used. The qualitative research as the exploratory study consisted of interviewing two Croatian experts in the area of data protection, internet security and privacy perceptions. Semi-structured interviews were conducted according to the guidelines developed to assess six research topics: the estimated level of privacy protection in Croatia; efficiency of the legal framework; companies' attitudes and practices in data protection; surveillance mechanisms employed; internet security; and education on security standards. From the methodological perspective, this approach contributes to the quality of the survey and its methodological rigor. It is quite common to employ qualitative research as an exploratory study in order to design a quantitative survey (Silverman 2006). Interviews other than face-to-face are adequate in cases of semi-structured interviews (Berg 1995). One expert preferred to answer in written form, and the other one responded in a face-to face interview. The insights generated by the exploratory research were used for the country-specific survey design and for the interpretation of quantitative research results. Some empirical studies on public attitudes towards the use of CCTV in public spaces (Philips 1999; Slobogin 2002), as well as public attitudes towards providing personal data to the government (e.g. Singer, Van Hoewyk, and Neugebauer 2003) or to businesses (Taylor 2003; Nam et al. 2006), the perceived importance of privacy (Katz and Tassone 1990) and privacy concerns (Okazaki, Li, and Hirose 2009) gave us useful guidelines for survey design. A review of relevant literature, including borrowing from the marketing consumer research relevant literature (Dolnicar and Jordaan 2007; Okazaki, Li, and Hirose 2009), was used to develop measures for variables applied in this study. The final questionnaire was then supplemented and adapted to the study context.

After developing the questionnaire, a pilot survey was conducted to test the questionnaire structure and question formulation as well as the interview length. The pilot testing was conducted in the City of Zagreb area and the pilot sample size was 3% of the survey sample size. Printed versions of questionnaires were distributed to adult respondents of various gender, age and education. After making slight changes to the wording and structure, the final questionnaire was created.

The survey covered the territory of the Republic of Croatia. The target sample includes 500 respondents, which gives a standard error of around 2.2%. The nationally representative sample is based on a two-way stratification in terms of regions (counties) and the population size by gender and age. The sample allocated to each stratum is proportional to the population living in each stratum (Census 2001, total population of 4.4 million). The sample characteristics by counties (administrative regions in Croatia) are shown in Table 1.

Data were collected by using a telephone survey in February and March 2011. A multistage design was used in developing the sample. The total population was stratified by 21 counties and four types of settlement according to settlement size. After that, for each stratum pages in the telephone book containing names and addresses of potential respondents were selected using systematic sampling procedure, while a simple random sampling technique was employed to choose potential respondents within the selected telephone book pages. Finally, gender and age of the respondents were used as stratifying variables in post-stratification in order to achieve a sample structure that is proportional to the population structure with regard to gender and age. The required time to complete an interview was less than 20 minutes. The net sample size contained 506 respondents of age 18–70. The summary statistics on sampled respondents is presented in Table 2.

The respondents were 50.4% males and 49.6% females. The average age of respondents was 46 years. The respondents reported an average household net monthly income of 7508 HRK (approximately 1000 EUR). The majority of respondents had completed secondary school (62%). The sample is to a large extent representative of the population in the Republic of Croatia on all demographic characteristics, except for education.

The measurement instrument included 43 questions (see Appendix). The survey included questions about the public opinion on data collection conducted by private companies and institutions, data storage and security, data usage, data disclosure

Table 1.   Survey sample by Croatian counties, $n = 506$.

	County	n	%
1	County of Zagreb	35	6.92
2	County of Krapina–Zagorje	17	3.36
3	County of Sisak–Moslavina	22	4.35
4	County of Karlovac	16	3.16
5	County of Varaždin	21	4.15
6	County of Koprivnica–Križevci	14	2.77
7	County of Bjelovar–Bilogora	15	2.96
8	County of Primorje–Gorski Kotar	34	6.72
9	County of Lika–Senj	6	1.19
10	County of Virovitica–Podravina	11	2.17
11	County of Požega–Slavonia	10	1.98
12	County of Slavonski Brod–Posavina	20	3.95
13	County of Zadar	18	3.56
14	County of Osijek–Baranja	37	7.31
15	County of Šibenik–Knin	13	2.57
16	County of Vukovar–Sirmium	24	4.74
17	County of Split–Dalmatia	53	10.47
18	County of Istria	24	4.74
19	County of Dubrovnik–Neretva	14	2.77
20	County of Medimurje	14	2.77
21	City of Zagreb	88	17.39

PRIVACY AND SECURITY IN THE DIGITAL AGE

Table 2. Summary statistics of sampled respondents, $n = 506$.

Respondent profile	Sample	Population[a]
1 Gender (%)		
1.1 Male	50.4	48.2
1.2 Female	49.6	51.8
2 Average age (in years)	46.4	42.9
3 Average number of people in a household	3.2	3.0
4 Educational level (%)		
4.1 Primary school	6.9	38.9
4.2 Secondary school	61.5	48.8
4.3 University and higher education	31.4	12.3
5 Average household net monthly income (in HRK[b])	7508	7951
6 Employment status (%)		
6.1 Employed	49.4	49.2
6.2 Non-employment status	50.6	50.8

[a] Population includes citizens ranging from 18 to 70 years of age. [b] 1 Euro = 7.4 HRK.
Sources: Croatian Bureau of Statistics, www.dzs.hr; Croatian National Bank, www.hnb.hr

and dissemination done by private companies and institutions, privacy protection policies, legislation and government protection, citizens' privacy concern, effectiveness of CCTV and other methods of surveillance, as well as citizens' patterns of behavior. Each item in the questionnaire was measured by Likert-scaled items, ranging from 1 (strongly disagree) to 5 (strongly agree).

Demographic variables include gender, age, household size, household income, education and employment status. The gender of the respondent was coded as 1 for male and 2 for female. The respondents reported their age in years, number of persons in the household (household size), household income (in local currency HRK) and the county of residence. Education was coded as follows: (1) primary school or less; (2) secondary school; and (3) university or higher degree of education. Regarding employment, the respondents were asked whether they were employed or not.

The collected data were first analyzed in a descriptive manner to determine the public opinion on privacy and surveillance in Croatia. Cronbach α coefficients were calculated to quantify the scale reliabilities. For the second step, exploratory factor analysis was used to identify the factors of surveillance/privacy concern. Then, K-means cluster analysis was employed to determine the segments of population with similar attitudes, while differences in respondents' attitudes towards privacy and surveillance between segments were analyzed using the χ^2-square test.

Results

The first step in the analysis was the assessment of construct validity and reliability of scales. The initial measurement instrument of 43 questions was tested by using exploratory factor analysis in order to explore the underlying structure among analyzed variables and to identify sets of variables that were highly interrelated, that is, factors. Principal components analysis was employed to extract the factors. This factor extraction method was used in order to summarize most of the original variance in a minimum number of factors because data reduction was a primary concern in our research. The Kaiser–Guttman rule was used to determine the number of factors to extract. The first run of exploratory factor analysis indicated that there were 21 items that have low factor loading on the respective factor, low factor loadings on all factors and high factor loading on some other factor (i1, i2, i4, i8, i9, i11, i12, i13, i15, i17, i18, i20, i22, i26, i27, i30, i31, i33, i40, i42 and i43). These items were excluded from further analysis. In the second run, the exploratory factor analysis indicated six distinct factors explaining 63.8% of the total variance. The factor loadings are greater than 0.50, which is considered sufficient (Bagozzi and Yi 1988). Factors were labeled according to dominant variables in the factor as follows: factor 1 (i32, i34, i35), perceived surveillance effectiveness; factor 2 (i36, i37, i38, i39), concern about being surveilled; factor 3 (i3, i5, i6, i7, i10), trust in privacy protection procedures; factor 4 (i14, i16, i19, i21), concern about CCTV privacy intrusion; factor 5 (i28, i29, i41), concern about personal data manipulation; and factor 6 (i23, i24, i25), need for surveillance enforcement (Table 3).

Reliability of scales was assessed using Cronbach α coefficients, which represent a measure of internal consistency of a set of items. Following the standard procedure recommended by Churchill (1979), the items that decreased Cronbach α coefficients of respective scales were deleted from further analysis (i3, i23, i29), in order to

Table 3. Factor analysis results, factor loadings.

Items	Factor 1 Perceived surveillance effectiveness	Factor 2 Concern about being surveilled	Factor 3 Trust in privacy protection procedures	Factor 4 Concern about CCTV privacy intrusion	Factor 5 Concern about personal data manipulation	Factor 6 Need for surveillance enforcement
i3			0.51			
i5			0.73			
i6			0.84			
i7			0.78			
i10			0.64			
i14				0.73		
i16				0.79		
i19				0.74		
i21				0.63		
i23						0.59
i24						0.81
i25						0.75
i28					0.71	
i29					0.60	
i32	0.78					
i34	0.84					
i35	0.77					
i36		0.98				
i37		0.98				
i38		0.96				
i39		0.64				
i41					0.68	

improve the Cronbach's α coefficients. Final Cronbach's α coefficients were in the range 0.52–0.92 and indicate an acceptable level of reliability.

Confirmatory factor analysis was performed to test the convergent and discriminant validity of measures and to detect the unidimensionality of each construct. With confirmatory factor analysis the extent to which the *a priori* pattern of factor loadings represents the actual empirical data is tested. Uni-dimensionality is evidence that a single trait or construct underlies a set of measures (Gerbing and Anderson 1988). The specified measurement model included six uncorrelated factors with uncorrelated measurement errors. The goodness-of-fit index and adjusted goodness-of-fit index were 0.904 and 0.881, respectively. The normed fit index, non-normed fit index, comparative fit index and root mean square error of approximation (RMSEA) were 0.923, 0.939, 0.946, and 0.066, respectively. Although the χ^2 test was significant, it is important to note that it is sensitive to the sample size. Other model fit indices indicated a reasonable level of fit of the model (Hu and Bentler 1999). The values of fit indices obtained from the six-factor model represent a substantial improvement over the values obtained from a one-factor model. The results of confirmatory factor analysis indicate an acceptable level of convergent and discriminant validity, as well as unidimensionality (Table 4).

K-Means cluster analysis was employed to classify citizens according to their attitudes towards surveillance and privacy issues. The Hartigan index was used as a criterion for determining the number of clusters in a data set. Mean values were calculated for each factor using only the items that remained after the reliability and construct validity assessment. These mean values were taken as an input in the K-means cluster analysis. The K-means cluster analysis indicated three homogeneous segments of citizens (Figure 1).

On average, citizens in Croatia show a high level of concern about personal data manipulation (mean $= 3.9$). They seem to be cautious regarding the effectiveness of surveillance (mean $= 3.0$) and privacy concern procedures (mean $= 2.9$). The respondents were not concerned about CCTV privacy intrusion (mean $= 2.3$) and about being surveilled (mean $= 2.2$). The rather low rating of their concern about CCTV privacy intrusion and about being surveilled can be explained by the fact that citizens are often not fully aware of the risk associated with growing surveillance. However, the data support the notion that citizens are more aware of the risk associated with private data manipulation.

The differences between the groups in the analyzed factors were significant at the 0.01 level. The groups were labeled according to the cluster means, as follows: segment 1, "pro-surveillance" oriented citizens; segment 2, citizens concerned about

Table 4. Confirmatory factor analysis results.

Fit Indices	Six-factor model	One-factor model
Goodness-of-fit index	0.904	0.590
Adjusted goodness-of-fit index	0.881	0.503
Normed fit index	0.923	0.627
Non-normed fit index	0.939	0.608
Comparative fit index	0.946	0.646
RMSEA	0.066	0.186
Chi-square (degrees of freedom), *p*-level	641.61 (209), 0.000	2509.78 (209), 0.000

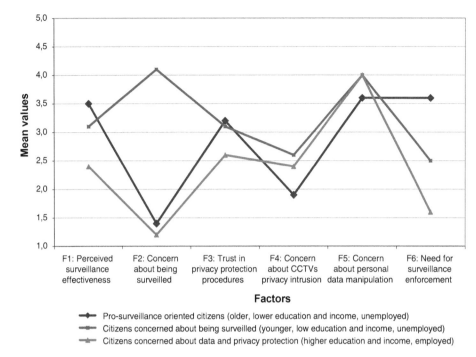

Figure 1. K-Means cluster results. Notes: Items were measured on the scale ranging from 1 (strongly disagree) to 5 (strongly agree). Differences are significant at $p < 0.01$ level.

being surveilled; and segment 3, citizens concerned about data and privacy protection. "Pro-surveillance" oriented individuals think that surveillance should be enforced, since it prevents terrorism, crime and corruption effectively. They trust privacy protection procedures more than the other groups of citizens. At the same time, they are not concerned about being surveilled or about CCTV privacy intrusion. Segments 2 and 3 include the individuals who are more "anti-surveillance" oriented than citizens in segment 1, since they disagree with the enforcement of surveillance in schools, by the police and national security services. Segment 2 contains citizens who are concerned about being surveilled, and segment 3 comprises individuals who are most concerned about data and privacy protection. The identification of "pro-surveillance" and "anti-surveillance" oriented citizens is in line with the existing literature (Haggerty and Gazso 2005).

Cross tabulation analysis (χ^2 test) was used to determine differences between segments of citizens in terms of gender, age, education, employment status and household income. Chi-square test results are presented in Table 5.

Chi-square test results show significant differences in age ($p < 0.05$) and education ($p < 0.01$) between the groups of citizens. There are no significant differences between the groups in gender, employment status and household income.

Older individuals prevailed in segment 1, while younger citizens prevailed in segments 2 and 3. Accordingly, younger individuals tend to be more cautious and more concerned about being surveilled, as well as about data and privacy protection, than older individuals. On the other hand, older citizens seem to be more "pro-surveillance" oriented.

PRIVACY AND SECURITY IN THE DIGITAL AGE

Table 5. Demographic differences and Pearson χ^2 test.

Demographics	Segment 1: pro-surveillance oriented citizens ($n = 172$)	Segment 2: citizens concerned about being surveilled ($n = 156$)	Segment 3: citizens concerned about data and privacy protection ($n = 178$)
Gender (Pearson χ^2 1.14, d.f. $=2$, $p = 0.565$) (%)			
Male	47.1	51.9	52.3
Female	52.9	48.1	47.7
Age (Pearson χ^2 6.96, d.f. $=2$, $p = 0.031$) (%)			
18–46	40.1	53.2	51.7
47–70	59.9	46.8	48.3
Education (Pearson χ^2 21.25, d.f. $=4$, $p = 0.000$) (%)			
Primary school or less	7.6	12.2	1.7
Secondary school	67.3	59.0	58.4
Higher education	25.2	28.9	39.9
Employment status (Pearson χ^2 0.91, d.f. $=2$, $p = 0.635$) (%)			
Employed	48.3	47.4	52.3
Unemployed	51.7	52.6	47.8
Household income (Pearson χ^2 3.74, d.f. $=2$, $p = 0.154$) (%)			
$= 7000$ HRK	52.4	56.2	45.7
> 7000 HRK	47.6	43.8	54.3

d.f., Degrees of freedom.

The groups of citizens also differ significantly in education level. In the overall sample, the largest share of highly educated citizens is found in segment 3. The highest percentage of citizens with secondary school education is found in segment 1, while the percentage of citizens with primary school or less was found in the segment 2. Accordingly, citizens with higher education are more concerned about data and privacy protection, while those with primary school or less are more concerned about being surveilled. Most of the respondents with secondary education are "pro-surveillance" oriented. With a higher level of education, individuals become more concerned about data and privacy protection. People with a higher education level have more knowledge about the potential risks of increasing surveillance and manipulation of the data.

Discussion and conclusions

This paper has examined public attitudes towards privacy and surveillance in Croatia. The factor analysis produced six distinct factors: (1) perceived surveillance effectiveness; (2) concern about being surveilled; (3) trust in privacy protection procedures; (4) concern about CCTV privacy intrusion; (5) concern about personal data manipulation; and (6) the need for surveillance enforcement. The findings indicate that citizens in Croatia show the highest concern about personal data manipulation, and are more cautious about the effectiveness of surveillance, privacy concern procedures and the need for surveillance enforcement. However, they do not seem to be concerned about CCTV privacy intrusion and about being surveilled.

112

An important implication of the study's results is that it reveals differential public attitudes towards privacy and surveillance. Cluster analysis identified three groups of citizens: "pro-surveillance" oriented citizens; citizens concerned about being surveilled; and citizens concerned about data and privacy protection. Groups of citizens differ significantly in age and education, but no significant differences among groups were found in gender, employment status and household income.

Both "pro-surveillance" citizens and citizens concerned about being surveilled believe that enforced surveillance prevents crime, terrorism and corruption quite effectively. However, the two groups will behave in exactly opposite ways when talking over the phone, when they are in public places or when sending emails. The citizens concerned about being surveilled are cautious because of their belief that they might be wiretapped and their mails intercepted. The "pro-surveillance" oriented citizens are not worried at all about being tapped, nor do they feel that CCTVs are threatening their or anyone else's privacy. This is probably because the "pro-surveillance" oriented group sees enforced surveillance as necessary but lacking in Croatia, in particular to control potential criminal activities. This cluster, unlike the other two, opts for empowering the police and other officials to search people, collect data and employ more surveillance instruments. The demographic characteristics of the "pro-surveillance" group are quite different from the other two clusters. Namely, 60% of the "pro-surveillance" oriented citizens are 47 and older, while 75% of them have secondary or lower education. Furthermore, women, the unemployed and those with lower income slightly prevail in this cluster.

Those citizens who are concerned about being surveilled share high concerns about personal data manipulation, but they would oppose the need for enforced surveillance. Similar to the "pro-surveillance" cluster, this group consists of citizens with a low education level and low income, and the unemployed. On the other hand, the younger population and men prevail in this group. Although all three groups exhibit low CCTV intrusiveness ratings, which is in line with the findings of Slobogin (2002), this cluster is the one most concerned about it.

The "modern generation" of highly educated citizens, who are employed and have higher household income, regardless of gender, believe that surveillance methods are not efficient in preventing crime and would strongly oppose any further empowerment of authorities in this sense. However, this group is concerned about privacy intrusion and personal information misuse, by both private and government agencies. In general, while Croatian citizens are not much concerned about CCTV monitoring in shops, banks and other business facilities, sharing and using their personal information for marketing purposes bothers them considerably.

The main findings of this study revealed interesting public attitudes towards privacy and surveillance. Croatian citizens strongly agree that protecting personal privacy is very important to them. However, they only partially agree that personal privacy is invaded and inadequately ensured by the existing legislation. Citizens believe that, compared with a decade ago, their privacy is less respected and protected, which indicates a derogation of privacy protection. Citizens firmly stated that, if they knew about a misuse of personal data, they would report it immediately, but they also claimed not to know who to report it to. This calls for a re-consideration of current government policy on privacy protection.

The common Western practice of using public opinion surveys in policy-making (despite the problem of misinterpretations driven by particular interests; see Gandy 2003) is rarely used in the Western Balkans region. By this study we wanted to ensure the highest visibility of our research and to encourage privacy and data protection policy-makers to benefit from our findings.

Several practical implications might derive from this study. Both government and private companies should not expect much public criticism if more CCTVs are introduced, especially in areas potentially exposed to vandalism and crime. This is particularly true considering that, out of all items in the questionnaire, citizens most strongly disagree with the statement "I feel uncomfortable in space under the CCTV supervision". Also, they do not think that CCTV cameras in public spaces threaten civil rights and liberties. These findings are in line with the suggestions of Goold (2010) that citizens would oppose surveillance at the point of experiencing surveillance as a threat to political rights and democracy. It seems that Croatian citizens support the "nothing to hide" argument when expressing their views in favor of more surveillance cameras as an effective tool to prevent crime.

The private sector is considered to be better at protecting information than government institutions. Therefore government should pay more attention to establishing procedures that would reinforce public trust in institutions and information security policies. Finally, the observed relation between information concerns and personal characteristics of the three groups could encourage the private sector to develop effective and responsible direct marketing strategies.

Furthermore, citizens mostly agree that introducing stricter control in schools could contribute to the ongoing debate on student violence and drug prevention in schools, and encourage government authorities to change the related regulations. The risk awareness regarding the misuse of data is higher among the younger population. Younger people are using more technology and might be better informed and more aware of data protection risks. The perceptions of surveillance and behavioral responses of the young population might vary across class and gender (as shown in McCahill and Finn 2010). However this is still an under-researched area.

Although this study produced interesting and comprehensive findings, some limitations need to be pointed out. First, there is a difference between the sample and the general population with regard to education level, and this difference in sample composition could influence research results to some extent. Also, the survey provides a kind of a "snapshot" of citizens' attitudes at one point in time, while new insights could be attained by regularly surveying public attitudes towards privacy and surveillance. It would be interesting to identify the differences in the attitudes of citizens towards privacy and surveillance with respect to their usage of internet and experiences of data misuse in Croatia as well.

The results indicate a distinction between citizens concerned about privacy and those concerned about data protection. Croatian citizens are not homogenous and it has been evidenced that those groups have different social and demographic characteristics. It would be interesting to further explore the related social context and the new surveillance and data protection policy. The government will have to take into account different public opinions when shaping new surveillance and data collection and data protection policies.

Finally, one could presume that similar public perceptions and opinions exist in other countries of Western Balkans region; or that the public attitudes in other post-socialist societies and EU New Member States follow a rather similar pattern. However, these research questions remain to be explored in comparative case studies.

Acknowledgement

We appreciate the useful comments of the anonymous reviewers and of Paul Stubbs, which helped us to improve the paper.

Notes

1. A preliminary version of this study was presented at the LiSS Annual Conference II held in Iasi, Romania, 3–5 May 2011 and published in EIZ Working Papers Series, EIZ-WP-1101 (http://www.eizg.hr/hr-HR/Stavovi-javnosti-o-nadzoru-i-privatnosti-u-Hrvatskoj-698.aspx).
2. Official Gazette no. 103/03, 118/06 and 41/08.
3. Detailed information provided by the Croatian Personal Data Protection Agency, www.azop.hr.
4. There is an initiative raised by some researchers within the international research network COST Action LiSS (Living in Surveillance Societies) to explore semantic issues of "surveillance".
5. Regulation on the manner of keeping the records of personal data filing systems and the pertinent records form (Official Gazette no. 105/04) and Regulation on the procedure for storage and special measures relating to the technical protection of special categories of personal data (Official Gazette no. 139/04).

References

Bagozzi, R., and Y. Yi. 1988. "On the Evaluation of Structural Equation Models." *Journal of the Academy of Marketing Science* 16 (1): 74–79.

Benett, C. 2011. "In Defence of Privacy: The Concept and the Regime." *Surveillance & Society* 8 (4): 485–496.

Berg, B. L. 1995. *Qualitative Research Methods for the Social Sciences*. 2nd ed. Boston: Allyn and Bacon.

Churchill, G. A. 1979. "A Paradigm for Developing Better Measures of Marketing Constructs." *Journal of Marketing Research* 16 (1): 64–73.

Clarke, R. 2006. Introduction to Dataveillance and Information Privacy, and Definitions of Terms. Accessed May 24, 2012. http://www.anu.edu.au/people/Roger.Clarke/DV/Intro.html

Dinev, T., M. Bellotto, P. Hart, C. Colautti, V. Russo, and I. Serra. 2005. "Internet Users' Privacy Concerns and Attitudes towards Government Surveillance – An Exploratory Study of Cross-Cultural Differences Between Italy and the United States." In *18th Bled Conference, Integration in Action*, Bled, Slovenia, June 6–8.

Dolnicar, S., and Y. Jordaan. 2007. "A Market-Oriented Approach to Responsibly Managing Information Privacy Concerns in Direct Marketing." *Journal of advertising* 36 (2): 123–149.

European Commission. 2011. *Attitudes on Data Protection and Electronic Identity in the European Union*. Special Eurobarometer 359 [online]. Accessed May 20, 2012. http://ec.europa.eu/public_opinion/archives/ebs/ebs_359_en.pdf

Flaherty, D. H. 1989. *Protecting Privacy in Surveillance Societies: The Federal Republic of Germany, Sweden, France, Canada, and the United States*. Chapel Hill: University of North Carolina Press.

Gandy, O. H., Jr. 2003. "Public Opinion Surveys and the Formation of Privacy Policy." *Journal of Social Issues* 59 (2): 283–299.

Gerbing, D. W., and J. C. Anderson. 1988. "An Updated Paradigm for Scale Development Incorporating Unidimensionality and its Assessment." *Journal of Marketing Research* 25 (2): 186–192.

Goold, B. J. 2009. "Surveillance and the Political Value of Privacy." *Amsterdam Law Forum* 1 (4): 3–6.

Goold, B. J. 2010. "How Much Surveillance is too Much? Some Thoughts on Surveillance, Democracy and Political Value of Privacy." In *Overvåkning i en Rettsstat – Surveillance in a Constitutional Government*, edited by D. W. Schartum, 38–48. Bergen: Fagbokforlaget. http://ssrn.com/abstract=1876069

Haggerty, K. D., and R. V. Ericson, eds. 2006. *The New Politics of Surveillance and Visibility.* Toronto: University of Toronto Press.

Haggerty, K. D., and A. Gazso. 2005. "The Public Politics of Opinion Research on Surveillance and Privacy." *Surveillance & Society* 3 (2/3): 173–180.

Hu, L. T., and P. M. Bentler. 1999. "Cutoff Criteria for Fit Indexes in Covariance Structure Analysis: Conventional Criteria versus New Alternatives." *Structural Equation Modeling* 6 (1): 1–55.

Inness, J. C. 1996. *Privacy, Intimacy, and Isolation.* New York: Oxford University Press.

Katz, J. E., and Tassone, A. R. 1990. "Public Opinion Trends: Privacy and Information Technology." *Public Opinion Quarterly* 54 (1): 125–143.

Kumaraguru, P., and L. Cranor. 2005. "Privacy in India: Attitudes and Awareness." In *Proceedings of Workshop on Privacy Enhancing Technologies (PET2005)*, Dubrovnik, Croatia, May 30–June 1, 2005. http://www-2.cs.cmu.edu/~ponguru/PET_2005.pdf

McCahill, M., and R. Finn. 2010. "The Social Impact of Surveillance in Three UK schools: 'Angels', Devils' and 'Teen Mums'." *Surveillance & Society* 7 (3/4): 273–289.

Nam, C., C. Song, E. Lee, and C. I. Park. 2006. "Consumer's Privacy Concerns and Willingness to Provide Marketing-Related Personal Information Online." *Advances in Consumer Research* 33: 212–217.

Okazaki, S., H. Li, and M. Hirose. 2009. "Consumer Privacy Concerns and Preference for Degree of Regulatory Control." *Journal of Advertising* 38 (4): 63–77.

Patton, J. W. 2000. "Protecting Privacy in Public? Surveillance Technologies and the Value of Public Places." *Ethics and Information Technology* 2: 181–187.

Philips, C. 1999. "A Review of CCTV Evaluations: Crime Reduction Effects and Attitudes Towards its use." *Crime Prevention Studies* 10: 123–155.

Raab, C., and B. J. Goold. 2011. *Protecting Information Privacy.* Equality and Human Rights Commission Research Report 69.

Silverman, D. 2006. *Interpreting Qualitative Data.* 3rd ed. London: Sage Publications.

Singer, E., J. Van Hoewyk, and R. J. Neugebauer. 2003. "Attitudes and Behaviour: the Impact of Privacy and Confidentiality Concerns on Participation in the 2000 Census." *Public Opinion Quarterly* 67 (3): 368–384.

Slobogin, C. 2002. "Public Privacy: Camera Surveillance of Public Places and the Right to Anonymity." *Mississippi Law Journal* 72: 213–299.

Solove, D. J. 2006. "A Taxonomy of Privacy." *University of Pennsylvania Law Review* 154 (3): 477–560.

Solove, D. J. 2007. "'I've Got Nothing to Hide' and Other Misunderstandings of Privacy." In *San Diego Law Review*, 44, GWU Law School Public Law Research Paper No. 289 [online]. http://ssrn.com/abstract=0998565

Solove, D. J. 2008a. "Understanding Privacy." In *The George Washington University Law School, Public Law and Legal Theory Working Paper, 420, Legal Studies Research Paper.*

Solove, D. J. 2008b. "The New Vulnerability: Data Security and Personal Information." In *Securing Privacy in the Internet Age*, edited by A. Chander, L. Gelman, and M. J. Radin, Stanford University Press; GWU Law School Public Law Research Paper no. 102 [online]. Accessed August 9, 2011. http://ssrn.com/abstract=583483

Stalder, F. 2002. "Opinion. Privacy is not the Antidote to Surveillance." *Surveillance & Society* 1 (1): 120–124.

Taylor, C. R. 2003. "Consumer Privacy and the Market for Customer Information." *Rand Journal of Economics* 35 (4): 631–650.

Warren, S. D., and L. D. Brandeis. 1890. "The Right to Privacy." *Harvard Law Review* 4 (5): 193–220.

Westin, A. F. 1970. *Privacy and Freedom.* 1st ed. 1967. New York: Atheneum.

Wirtz, J., M. O. Lwin, and J. D. Williams. 2007. "Causes and Consequences of Consumer Online Privacy Concern." *International Journal of Service Industry Management* 18 (4): 326–348.

Zureik, E. 2004. "Globalization of Personal Data Project International Survey Concept Paper." In *The Surveillance Project Public Opinion Workshop*, March 3, 2004, Kingston.

PRIVACY AND SECURITY IN THE DIGITAL AGE

Appendix: Surveillance/privacy concern survey – questionnaire

1	Protection of my personal privacy is very important to me.	1	2	3	4	5
2	My personal privacy is invaded in Croatia today.	1	2	3	4	5
3	The privacy of citizens in Croatia is more respected and protected today than ten years ago.	1	2	3	4	5
4	My employer safeguards my personal information.	1	2	3	4	5
5	Banks safeguard confidential information about their clients.	1	2	3	4	5
6	Government institutions safeguard confidentiality and privacy of the data on citizens and firms they collect.	1	2	3	4	5
7	Government institutions take care of the data protection against fraud and misuse.	1	2	3	4	5
8	Government institutions often ask for more personal data than they actually need.	1	2	3	4	5
9	Private companies and agencies often ask for more personal data than they actually need.	1	2	3	4	5
10	Privacy protection and the usage of personal data in Croatia are adequately ensured by the existing legislation.	1	2	3	4	5
11	I am well informed about the risks of misusing my personal data.	1	2	3	4	5
12	Identity theft might happen in Croatia.	1	2	3	4	5
13	Information I send over the Internet (e-mail, Facebook and other) could be misused.	1	2	3	4	5
14	CCTV cameras in public spaces (streets, squares, stadiums) threaten the privacy of citizens.	1	2	3	4	5
15	CCTV cameras in public spaces (streets, squares, stadiums) prevent crime.	1	2	3	4	5
16	CCTV cameras in public spaces should be prohibited because they threaten civil rights and liberties of citizens.	1	2	3	4	5
17	CCTV cameras prevent hooligans and vandalism (at stadiums and in public transport, graffiti, etc.)	1	2	3	4	5
18	CCTV cameras in shops, banks, post offices . . . are needed since they prevent theft.	1	2	3	4	5
19	CCTV cameras in shops, banks, post offices . . . threaten the privacy of shoppers and employees.	1	2	3	4	5
20	There is a well-established control of CCTV records regarding persons who have access to view records and what happens with the records afterwards.	1	2	3	4	5
21	I feel uncomfortable in a space under the CCTV camera supervision.	1	2	3	4	5
22	I would feel safer if I worked and lived in a space under the CCTV camera supervision.	1	2	3	4	5
23	School officials should be entitled to search students and their belongings for stuff not permitted in school.	1	2	3	4	5
24	The police should have unrestricted access to any data on every citizen.	1	2	3	4	5
25	The police and national security services should be entitled to surveil and tap all persons they rate as suspicious without any special warrant (e.g. permission of the court).	1	2	3	4	5
26	I never tell anybody my passwords, PINs and codes.	1	2	3	4	5
27	The use of computers and ICT increases the possibility of personal data manipulation.	1	2	3	4	5
28	I am concerned with the volume of personal information and data stored on computers that might be misused.	1	2	3	4	5

Appendix (*Continued*)

29	Personal medical records, psychological and IQ test results, etc. are not protected enough as private and confidential data.	1	2	3	4	5
30	Croatian citizens are educated enough and are well informed about the risks of unauthorized usage of data and about keeping safe personal data.	1	2	3	4	5
31	There is a lack of citizens' initiative to protect privacy in Croatia.	1	2	3	4	5
32	Enforced surveillance of people effectively prevents terrorism.	1	2	3	4	5
33	There is a need to enforce surveillance of people in Croatia to prevent terrorism and general hazards.	1	2	3	4	5
34	Enforced surveillance of people effectively prevents crime.	1	2	3	4	5
35	Enforced surveillance of people effectively prevents corruption.	1	2	3	4	5
36	I am careful when talking over the telephone because I never know if I've been wiretapped.	1	2	3	4	5
37	I am careful when talking over the mobile phone because I never know if I've been wiretapped.	1	2	3	4	5
38	I am careful when talking in public places because I never know if I've been tapped.	1	2	3	4	5
39	I am careful when writing e-mails because I am not sure if some third person may access my messages.	1	2	3	4	5
40	Private companies and agencies share my personal data and information with each other without my knowledge.	1	2	3	4	5
41	It bothers me when my personal information is shared and used for marketing purposes.	1	2	3	4	5
42	If I knew about the misuse of my personal data, I would report it immediately.	1	2	3	4	5
43	I know who to report the misuse of personal data to.	1	2	3	4	5

Reconciling privacy and security

Marc van Lieshout[a], Michael Friedewald[b], David Wright[c] and Serge Gutwirth[d]

[a]*TNO Information and Communication Technologies, Delft, the Netherlands;* [b]*Fraunhofer Institute for Systems and Innovation Research, Karlsruhe, Germany;* [c]*Trilateral Research & Consulting, London, UK;* [d]*Law Science Technology & Society (LSTS), Vrije Universiteit Brussels, Brussels, Belgium*

This paper considers the relationship between privacy and security and, in particular, the traditional "trade-off" paradigm. The issue is this: how, in a democracy, can one reconcile the trend towards increasing security (for example, as manifested by increasing surveillance) with the fundamental right of privacy? Our political masters justify their intrusions upon our privacy with proclamations of the need to protect the citizenry against further terrorist attacks like those that have already marred the early twenty-first century. The surveillance industry has been quick to exploit this new market opportunity, supported as it is by inexorable technological "progress" in devising new ways to infringe upon our privacy. The trade-off paradigm has troubled academics. While the European Commission has been devoting billions of euro to security research, it too is troubled by the trade-off paradigm. It is funding the PRISMS project, which will undertake a major public opinion survey on privacy and security and which aims to formulate a decision support system that should offer an alternative to the traditional trade-off model.

Introduction

Various governments, and the European Union as a whole, have chosen to invest in new technological devices to foster a proactive attitude against terror (e.g. closed circuit television, passenger scanning, data retention, eavesdropping, biometric passport). Although these technologies are expected to enhance public security, they are subjecting ordinary citizens to an increasing amount of permanent surveillance, potentially causing infringements of privacy and a restriction of fundamental rights.

The relationship between privacy and security has traditionally been seen as a trade-off, whereby any increase in security would inevitably curb the privacy enjoyed by the citizenry. Thus, mainstream literature on the public perception of security technologies generally aims at enquiring how much privacy citizens are willing to trade in exchange for greater security. The trade-off model has, however, been criticized, because it approaches privacy and security in abstract terms, and because it reduces public opinion to one specific attitude, which considers these technologies as useful in terms of security but potentially harmful in terms of privacy.

This paper has two main objectives. First, it considers the right to privacy and the right to security, the relationship between them and the criticism that has been leveled at the traditional trade-off approach. Second, the paper provides the background for a project that aims to devise an alternative to the traditional trade-off model, wherein our political masters, aided and abetted by the security industry, often appear willing to sacrifice some of the citizenry's privacy in order to better secure society against more terrorist attacks such as those that have already marred the early twenty-first century. The paper refers to European policies that support the surveillance and security research funded by the European Commission. In particular, it highlights the PRISMS project, which began in January 2012 and carries on for 42 months. The project aims to conduct a major survey across all EU Member States to gather the views of citizens on privacy and security. It also aims to develop a decision support system for policy-makers and other users of surveillance systems that will help them understand the ramifications of prospective investments in surveillance systems and avoid jeopardizing the European fundamental right to privacy.

The right to privacy

Although the concept of privacy is hard to define precisely, some common understanding of various components of privacy exists. Privacy can be understood as a social value and public good as well as an individual value (Regan 1995; Gutwirth 2002; Bennett and Raab 2006; Solove 2008). Following Solove, Zureik et al. (2010) discern six dimensions of privacy: (1) the right to be let alone; (2) limited access to the self; (3) secrecy; (4) control of personal information; (5) personhood; and (6) intimacy. This is an extension of the distinction made by Alan Westin (1967), differentiating between solitude, intimacy, anonymity and reserve as leading principles indicating the relevance of privacy for individuals. Echoing these multi-dimensional conceptualizations of privacy, the European Court of Human Rights has ruled that it is neither possible nor necessary to determine the content of privacy in an exhaustive way (*Niemietz v. Germany* 1992; *Pretty v. United Kingdom* 2002),[1] and it can thus cover a wide range of issues such as integrity, access to information and public documents, secrecy of correspondence and communication, protection of the domicile, protection of personal data, wiretapping, gender, health, identity, sexual orientation, protection against environmental nuisances, and so on; the list is, of course, not exhaustive (Gutwirth 2002; Sudre et al. 2003; Sudre 2005).

However, and in spite of the fact that privacy entails some informational control, not all issues of information control pertain to the privacy of individuals (De Hert and Gutwirth 2009). That is the reason why the European legal framework is composed of both a right to privacy and of a right to the protection of personal data, as embodied by the 2000 EU Charter of Fundamental Rights in its Articles 7 and 8. Therefore, the European regulatory framework is composed of a right centered on the protection of citizens' personal data, and a right protecting the privacy of citizens. Having two separate rights is no coincidence. Indeed, both of them aim at the protection of privacy as a political value, that is, the political private sphere. Yet, they do so by obeying two different constitutional logics, respectively a prohibitive or "opacity" logic, and a regulatory or "transparency" logic. By default, privacy proscribes interferences with one's autonomy, while data protection, by default, acknowledges that the processing of personal data is legitimate if a number of conditions are met. Privacy shields the citizens and protects their opacity, while data protection accepts the processing of personal data and aims at rendering it transparent (De Hert and Gutwirth 2006). In other words, privacy as a political value is legally embodied in two different rights that both aim at protecting it, although through different means.

The increasing impact of technology on privacy is obvious. Since the first famous incident with privacy intrusion owing to a "mobile camera", eloquently described by Warren and Brandeis (1890), the emergence of ever more intrusive technologies has altered the discourse on privacy fundamentally. People's perception of privacy and the differentiation that can be made between so-called fundamentalist, pragmatic and unconcerned citizens shows change over time but shows some consistency in the distribution among these three groups as well (Kumaraguru and Cranor 2005; similar in Murphy 2007). Surveys indicate that awareness of privacy intrusion is still high while the precise contexts are relevant for the determination of how people experience the intrusions (Attema and de Nood 2010).

In a European policy context, the focus is more on protection of personal data than on the protection of privacy. The first European data protection directive, originating from 1995 (European Parliament and the Council 1995), incorporates principles promulgated in the 1970s and early 1980s (OECD 1980) and that focus on protection of personal data. Judicial and police affairs have been dealt with in separate European directives, and in some sectors (such as health), specific privacy regulations have come into place as well. However, the Data Protection Directive has held the most relevant privacy principles. From May 2009, the Commission undertook an intense round of consultation with stakeholders about the need to update the data protection framework. This eventually led to its publication of a proposal for a Regulation in late January 2012 (De Hert et al. 2012; European Commission 2012). The Commission has proposed a Regulation of the European Parliament and the Council in place of the Directive that it supersedes because the Regulation will be directly applicable in the Member States, unlike the Directive, which had been transposed by the Member States in somewhat different ways. Thus, the Regulation aims to instil much greater harmonization of the data protection framework in Europe and to avoid the fragmentation, the differing rules that have marked the regime until now.[2]

The proposed Regulation, while building firmly on the foundation of the 95/46/EC Directive, introduces many new changes. It enshrines a right to be forgotten (Article 17). The Regulation envisages greater use of privacy by design (data protection by design, Article 23) and the use of privacy seals (Article 39). It has provisions for mandatory notifications of personal data breaches to the data protection authority (Article 31) and data subjects (Article 32). It would make privacy impact assessments (here termed data protection impact assessments) mandatory (Article 33). Companies with 250 employees or more would be obliged to have a data protection officer (Article 35). The Article 29 Working Party would be replaced by a European Data Protection Board (Article 64). Penalties for violating the Regulation would range up to 2% of turnover (Article 79).

Several elements in the draft Regulation make clear that privacy features must be integrated into the entire development process of a system from its earliest conception onwards. Thus, privacy and data protection will be an indistinguishable part of any system and any perceived system change (Hustinx 2010; van Lieshout et al. 2011). The fact that the European Commission is putting an increasing emphasis upon "privacy-oriented" tools is not a coincidence. Developments in the ICT environment have created new practices that threaten the privacy of individuals without actually processing their personal data. Indeed, when using various ICTs, individuals leave a vast number of electronic traces (e.g. IP addresses) that are not personal data in the sense of the relevant directives, but which nonetheless become the resources of extensive profiling activities that entail several risks for the privacy of the persons concerned (De Hert and Gutwirth 2008). That is the reason why the amended e-privacy directive (European Parliament and the Council 2002) regulates data that are not *stricto sensu* personal data: traffic and location data. It is, therefore, not without dangers, especially in the field of ICTs, to equate privacy and data protection, since this position fails to deal with infringements upon privacy that are not linked to the processing of personal data.

The right to security

The concept of security is at least as difficult to approach as privacy. Different languages have different words and different connotations for the meaning of security. In English, words such as security, safety and continuity are used for different aspects of being and feeling secure (Bauman 1999). The German word *Sicherheit* refers to both security and safety while the Dutch and French use two different words as well (*veiligheid* and *zekerheid*, *sécurité* and *sûreté*). Security implies freedom from risks and dangers. It is used in various contexts, from social security to technologically secure systems. Information security is a distinct branch that refers to secure handling of information, preventing unauthorized access and use of data. Secure communications are communications that function as expected and are robust and vital, able to resist attacks on their functionality. For individual citizens, security is related to the absence of dangers with reference to the external environment but also relates to issues of social comfort (family life, health), financial certainties and personal deployment opportunities.

Within the policy context of the European Union, security relates to the integrity of the European Union as a whole, the protection of its outer borders and the fight against criminality, terrorism, fraud and illegal immigration. This is what the European Commission identifies as belonging to its internal security, and for which it has developed over time a large set of measures and practices (with external security relating to securing the position of Europe vis-à-vis external developments and threats in the external environment). External security relates to maintaining sovereignty in the face of attackers and extends to peace-keeping operations and the like.

With globalization, the rise of new economic superpowers and the accompanying change in power relations, the idea of security in a globalized world is fundamentally more complex and difficult than it used to be. The German sociologist Ulrich Beck points to the detrimental feedback mechanisms that cannot be brought back under control owing to their reflexive characteristics, popping up as unforeseen and unwanted side-effects of previous attempts to control specific societal practices (Beck 1986). The concept present in the work of Beck, Giddens, and Lash (1994) that can serve as a bridge between the concept of privacy and security is the concept of risk. Both privacy and security are related to the notion of risk and risk containment. Containment of risk requires surveillance, directed at natural dangers (e.g. earthquakes) as well as man-made dangers (e.g. nuclear reactors, air traffic). The very moment surveillance relates to individual persons, however, infringement of privacy may be at stake.

The relationship between privacy and security

Privacy and security are problematic because they are open to a variety of social, political and scientific interpretations and explanations. Each concept needs to be considered in a multidisciplinary way in order to grasp the dynamics that determine the interpretation and evaluation of these concepts by various stakeholder communities. Media, politics, technology, criminology and law all present a different perspective on privacy and security. These perspectives contribute in their own manner to the creation and construction of the public's perception of privacy and security. The challenge is to unravel these various dimensions in the construction of these concepts such that the perspectives and attitudes of citizens can be empirically questioned.

No commonly shared definitions of privacy and security exist. These concepts have contested ontological and epistemological backgrounds, although certain similarities in approach can be discerned. The often heard assumption that privacy is an individual value, reflecting liberal principles about role distribution between citizens and the state, is contested on the ground that this lends too much support for a restrictive policy towards privacy, and that especially the social, collective value of privacy is relevant from a societal and political perspective (e.g. Regan 1995). One can find descriptive accounts of privacy, relating to what privacy *is*, to normative accounts that focus on the *value* of privacy and the level of privacy to be protected. Legal accounts focus on the *right* to privacy and to what extent this should be regulated, while sociological accounts focus on the *interests* that people experience in protecting privacy (for a delimitation of the concepts see Gutwirth et al. 2011).

Can privacy and security be reconciled? There is abundant evidence that many technologies aimed at enhancing security are subjecting citizens to an increasing amount of surveillance and, in many cases, causing infringements of privacy and fundamental rights. Scarcely a day goes by without stories in the press about how we are losing our privacy as a result of increasingly stringent security requirements.

The traditional "trade-off" model between privacy and security (presupposing citizens make an informed judgement in trading off the one for the other) can be and has been criticized because it is based upon invalid assumptions about people's attitudes and understanding of privacy and security. Both privacy and security are multidimensional and contextual concepts, which cannot be reduced to simplistic descriptions. The systematic recourse to the notion of "balancing" suggests that privacy and security can only be enforced at each other's expense, while the obvious challenge is inventing a way to enforce both without loss on either side.

The often supposed relationship between security and privacy in terms of a trade-off poses an intellectual and policy challenge: is it possible to empirically contest existing ideas that have dominated national and European policy-making for too long, that having more security leads to less privacy?

Reconciling the right to privacy and the right to security

Privacy has often been pitted against other social values, notably security. Policy-makers may curtail privacy for security reasons. After 9/11 and the bombings in

Madrid in March 2004 and London in July 2005, policy-makers in the United States, the UK, the EU and elsewhere took a number of initiatives, supposedly in the interests of making our society safer against the threats of terrorism. For example, the Bush administration in the United States engaged in warrantless telephone intercepts. The EU introduced the Data Retention Directive whereby electronic communications suppliers were required to retain certain phone call and e-mail information, although not the actual content, for up to two years. Many critics regarded such measures as an infringement of privacy. Our privacy was being traded off against security (or security theater, to use Bruce Schneier's term), the effectiveness of which has been called into question.

It is not just our political leaders who engage in the process of balancing privacy against other values, in this case security. Virtually all stakeholders are engaged in this balancing process, often on a daily basis. Individuals make trade-offs when they consider how much personal data they are willing to give to service providers in exchange for a service. Industry players, concerned about trust and reputation, must balance their desire to collect as much personal data of their customers as possible against the potential reaction of their customers to undue intrusion. The same media who rail against the laxity of governments and companies in not preventing data theft or loss are often engaged in reporting on the "private" lives of public figures, sometimes illegally by intercepting mobile calls (Marsden 2009). Governmental officials share personal data in an effort to counter benefit fraud or to detect children at risk of abuse.

Much has been written in academic journals (and elsewhere) about the trade-offs between privacy and other social values, notably security. Many scholars see the trade-off as problematic because it weighs apples and oranges: how can one weigh one value (privacy) against another value (security), which are two different values? If privacy is regarded as a cornerstone of democracy,[3] then sacrificing privacy in the name of security undermines democracy itself. Do we want to be completely secure in a police state? Lucia Zedner (2009, 135–136) concisely points out the problems with the balancing metaphor.

> First... rebalancing presupposes an existing imbalance that can be calibrated with sufficient precision for it to be possible to say what adjustment is necessary in order to restore security. Yet terrorist attacks create a political climate of fear that is not conducive to sober assessment of the gravity of the threat posed...
>
> A second ground for caution is the question of whose interests lie in the scales when rebalancing is proposed. This issue is generally fudged by the implicit suggestion that security is to be enjoyed by all. In practice the balance is commonly set as between the security interests of the majority and the civil liberties of that small minority of suspects who find themselves subject to state investigation... The purported balance between liberty and security is thus in reality a "proposal to trade off the liberties of a few against the security of the majority"...
>
> Third, claims to rebalance rarely entail a close consideration of what lies in the scales. Any talk of balancing implies commensurability, but... there are at least two grounds for doubting the commensurability of security and liberty interests. The first is that, as we have already observed, we are weighing collective interests against those of small minorities or individuals. The second is what might be called temporal dissonance, namely the fact that we seek to weigh known present interests (in liberty) against future uncertainties (in respect of security risks). Although the certain loss of liberty might be expected to prevail over uncertain future security benefits, future risks tend to outweigh present interests precisely because they are unknowable but potentially catastrophic. Fundamental rights that ought to be considered non-derogable and to be protected are placed in peril by the consequentialist claims of security.

> Together, these concerns should provide a powerful check upon demands to rebalance in the name of security. As Thomas concludes: "the idea of trading off freedom for safety on a sliding scale is a scientific chimera ... Balance should not enter the equation: it is false and misleading" ... Given the powerful political appeal of balancing, the primary challenge is to find an alternative rhetoric with which to frame the debate.

Finding a credible, alternative rhetoric remains a challenge. This perhaps accounts for the somewhat schizophrenic policies that have characterized the approaches adopted by governments and the EU. Policy-makers wish to be seen adopting a tough approach against terrorism – to protect democracy – yet at the same time at least some of them recognize that the measures adopted threaten the very democratic values and fundamental rights, including perhaps especially privacy, they seek to protect. In the next section, we review and discuss the key policies that have framed this debate at the European level.

EU security policies

The European Commission's security strategy has evolved from various programs and actions. Over the past decade, the Tampere program (1999–2004), the Hague program (2005–2009) and most recently the Stockholm program (2010–2014) form the basis of the Commission's internal security strategy. Various events (the attack on the World Trade Center in New York, the bombings in Madrid and London) contributed to the request for new measures to safeguard Europe and its Member States from terrorist attacks and opened the door to a variety of measures that were potentially intrusive on personal privacy (such as CCTV and biometric identification techniques).

The new security threats and challenges after the 9/11 attacks were recognized in December 2003 with the adoption of the EU Security Strategy (Council of the European Union 2003) and the European Commission's decision to establish an EU Security Research Programme (ESRP). As a first step, the European Commission decided to form a "Group of Personalities" (GoP) with members from the Commission, research institutions and the European security and defense industry to oversee the development of the ESRP. In their report, presented in March 2004, the GoP stated that the EU needed to develop capabilities to protect the security of its citizens and that "Europe must take advantage of its technological strengths" to achieve these goals (Group of Personalities in the field of Security Research 2004). The European Commission seized upon these suggestions in its Communication on security research (European Commission 2004b) and the subsequent enhancement of European industrial potential in the field of security research (European Commission 2004a). It specified in its 2006 Security Research Agenda that security research should be aimed at identifying and protecting against unlawful or intentional malicious acts harming European societies (European Security Research Advisory Board 2006). The GoP report makes the point that "technology itself cannot guarantee security, but security without the support of technology is impossible". It provides public authorities with information about threats, which is needed to build effective protection against them.

The European Security Research Advisory Board (ESRAB), which was established to provide advice to the European Commission and to oversee the ESRP, explained in 2006 that

> improving situation awareness and assessment [requires] the capture, fusion, correlation and interpretation of disparate forms of real-time and historical data and their presentation in a clear manner, facilitating effective decision-making and performance in a complex environment. Interoperable databases will be essential to allow surveillance information to be cross-referenced against multiple heterogeneous sources. (European Security Research Advisory Board 2006)

This statement basically says that more security is only possible at the price of collecting more information and increased surveillance, which immediately raises questions of privacy and data protection. Many of the projects funded under the European Commission's Preparatory Action for Security Research and in the first two calls on security research in the EC's Seventh Framework Programme concern this kind of surveillance technology. The necessity of (smart) surveillance is especially stressed for border security, protection against terrorism and organized crime, and critical infrastructure protection (European Security Research Advisory Board 2006).

In its 2010 Communication, the European Commission presents an overview of European initiatives to safeguard the security of its citizens by combating criminal and terrorist behavior and fighting illegal immigration (European Commission 2010b). It identifies 18 different initiatives, some of which were established several years ago (e.g. the Schengen Information System) and others are the result of the heightened threat alerts in recent years. Some are still in the stage of implementation, such as the Registered Travellers Programme (part of the Smart Borders Package) for which legislation is expected in 2012 (European Commission 2011).

In its analysis, the Commission concludes that most systems are functionally separate and have separate legislation covering their operation, thus building in safeguards for function creep, that is, the danger arises when a system can be used for other functions or purposes in addition to those originally envisaged, thereby potentially eroding data protection safeguards. On the other hand, the Commission acknowledges that many systems collect similar data (15 out of 18 collect biometric data) that could be shared to validate, update or complete data sets. Six out of 18 initiatives are centralized systems, and many use the same secured European infrastructure (European Commission 2006). In addition the Commission proposes a centralized IT agency to help improve operating centralized and decentralized data exchange practices.

Regulations concerning data retention vary considerably, from 24 hours for Advanced Passenger Information to 15 years for Passenger Name Records collected by the United States. Although a formal review process for all initiatives is in place, hard evidence for the effectiveness of the initiatives is lacking. For some initiatives, anecdotal evidence is presented that shows beneficial effects of some measures (the Data Retention Directive, Cybercrime Alert Platforms, Europol, Eurojust, Passenger Name Records, Terrorist Finance Tracking Programme) and for other initiatives, figures are presented on assets or items collected, but no systematic appraisal of the effectiveness of surveillance systems is presented. No information is provided about the acceptance of these systems by European citizens nor the extent to which they trust surveillance initiatives for improving their security.

Recognizing this problematic potential of surveillance technologies, the Commission stated as early as 2004 that in security research "individual rights, democratic values, ethics and liberties need to be respected. A balance must be struck between surveillance and control to minimize the potential impact of terrorist action, and respect for human rights, privacy, social and community cohesion and the successful integration of minority communities" (European Commission 2004b). The EC's 2009 Communication on freedom, security and justice reinforced this claim: "The area of freedom, security and justice must above all be a single area in which fundamental rights are protected, and in which respect for the human person and human dignity, and for the other rights enshrined in the Charter of Fundamental Rights, is a core value" (European Commission 2009). The same Communication goes on to state that the EU must be increasingly aware of privacy and data protection issues related to emerging technologies and act accordingly in order to fulfil the above claim.

The Commission seems intent on implementing its security strategy while maintaining a high level of trust by citizens in its activities, by safeguarding individual rights and protecting personal data. As indicated above, the various Communications published in recent years reflect this ambition, although the undertone of the GoP and ESRAB reports and the nature of the technologies funded by the Commissions (European Commission, DG Enterprise and Industry 2009) raise doubts that equal weight is given to privacy and security.

The PRISMS project: a survey on privacy and security

The Commission has questioned the privacy–security trade-off paradigm. In 2010, in a call for proposals in the Security research program under its Seventh Framework Programme, the Commission has posed questions such as:

- Do people actually evaluate the introduction of new security technologies in terms of a trade-off between privacy and security?
- What are the main factors that affect public assessment of the security and privacy implications of given security technology?

Addressing these questions is not simply a matter of gathering data from a public opinion survey, as such questions have intricate conceptual, methodological and empirical dimensions. Citizens are influenced by a multitude of factors. Privacy and security may be experienced differently in different political and socio-cultural contexts. No more than two decades ago Europe was characterized by a political landscape in which different political systems co-existed. This has affected how people perceive concepts such as trust, accountability, concern and the like in relation to the state (Castles 1993), rendering a uniform empirical approach to researching these concepts into a difficult challenge. Socio-cultural differences throughout Europe are such that no uniform empirical approach to researching how people perceive concepts such as privacy, trust, security and concern can be adopted. Until now, no survey or study has yet addressed the facets in a comprehensive way across all Member States.[4]

The Commission also called for development of a decision support system to be provided to users of surveillance systems to help give them insight into the pros and cons of specific security investments compared with a set of alternatives taking into account a wider societal context.

A consortium[5] responded successfully to this call and, accordingly, the Commission is funding the PRISMS (Privacy and Security Mirrors: Towards a European framework for integrated decision making) project, which intends to critically examine the validity of the trade-off concept and to propose an alternative paradigm (e.g. privacy risk management) in order to arrive at a more sophisticated approach to the relationship between privacy and security. The consortium will address the above questions and related questions by means, *inter alia*, of a survey of the European population. The project was launched in February 2012 and goes on for 42 months.

The PRISMS project starts with a multidimensional analysis of the relation between privacy and security from the different perspectives of technology, policy, media, criminology and law. These diverse perspectives offer the analytical background against which perceptions and attitudes of citizens can be studied. The consortium is also determining the factors that affect public assessment of the security and privacy implications of a given security technology. Having analyzed the conceptualizations of and interrelations between privacy and security, the consortium plans to test and validate its analysis in interviews, focus groups and workshops that will bring together various stakeholder groups (citizens, policy advisors, security people, societal organizations, criminologists and techno-political scientists).

The core of PRISMS will be a full-fledged survey that investigates the opinions, attitudes and behavior of a representative sample of 1000 citizens from each of the 27 Member States of the Union on privacy and security. The project will use these results in devising a decision support system providing users (those who deploy and operate security systems) with insight into the pros and cons, constraints and limits of specific security investments compared with alternatives taking into account a wider societal context. The decision support system will need to reconcile the various dimensions such that the results can be understood in terms of discriminating between options for security investments.

There seems to be only one precedent for a cross-national study of citizens' attitudes towards security and privacy, that is, a project organized and led by the Queen's University in Canada (Zureik et al. 2010), which conducted a survey in eight countries. That study noted a clear and striking absence of surveys on attitudes towards privacy and security. It concluded that analyzing attitudes is relevant, given current developments that confront citizens with transborder data flows in everyday situations (e.g. banking, traveling), but it warned against a too simplistic approach of surveying these attitudes. Methodological problems abound and need to be taken into account. Differences may arise in responses owing to the sequence of questions. Having a question on a security incident before a question on privacy may lead to different outcomes than posing the questions the other way around. In addition to these methodological problems, researchers face substantive problems with understanding the concepts of privacy and security. The survey performed by the Queen's University took several years from initiation to completion, and only recently has been finalized in a book providing the main results. The PRISMS consortium will use the expertise built up during the eight-country survey by Queen's University. Indeed, two researchers from that study are also partners in the PRISMS project as well as an affiliate of the organization that conducted the survey.

The PRISMS approach is characterized by a strong emphasis on practical cases, to be used as hypotheses and testing grounds in the survey to be undertaken by the consortium. This is prerequisite to get results that are easily understood and that can be interpreted over various demographic, geo-spatial and socio-cultural clusters existing within Europe. The survey and multidimensional analysis will provide input necessary for the creation of the decision support system. The various analyses will help in the construction of hypotheses that will be tested in the survey, but they also have a value in their own respect. In this manner, the various approaches (technological, policy, criminological, media, legal) will add value to the body of knowledge of the disciplines to which they belong while offering cross-disciplinary results as well.

Throughout the entire project, there will be extensive stakeholder interaction and consultation in various forms. Stakeholders vary from institutional actors and policy-makers to the public at large. In the early phases of the project, interaction with stakeholders will be dedicated to obtaining a better understanding of their perceptions and attitudes vis-à-vis the key concepts and approaches of our project. In the later phases of the project, interaction is dedicated more to arriving at a shared understanding of how stakeholders can profit from the results of the project and what constraints the decision support system might encounter. Throughout the entire project, the consortium will use resources to inform stakeholders and the broader community on the existence of the PRISMS project, the intermediate results and the manner in which one could become more engaged with the project.

The decision support system will support stakeholders in making a decision about security investments to be made. A decision support system might have the connotation of a push-button system that yields specific outcomes based on specific inputs. The consortium considers such a decision support system not to have much practical value given the complexity of the situations for which security investments have to be made. The system is meant to support the decision-making process, and not to be a system that makes the decisions itself. The decision support system will combine substantive principles with process-oriented principles, offering state-of-the-art insights in how to arrive at the most optimal approach and solution. It will help in understanding the consequences of specific decisions and in incorporating insights on perspectives and attitudes of citizens in realizing the best of possible systems needed to assure a secure Europe while maintaining the highest level of privacy and data protection.

Acknowledgment

Among other sources, this paper draws on research carried out in the EC-funded FP7 project PRISMS: The Privacy and Security Mirrors: Towards a European framework for integrated decision making (FP7-SEC-2010-285399).

Notes

1. § 29 of the Niemietz judgment says: "The Court does not consider it possible or necessary to attempt an exhaustive definition of the notion of "private life". However, it would be too restrictive to limit the notion to an "inner circle" in which the individual may live his own personal life as he chooses and to exclude there from entirely the outside world not encompassed within that circle. Respect for private life must also comprise to a certain degree the right to establish and develop relationships with other human beings."
2. In its regulatory reform package officially released on 25 January 2012, the Commission also proposed a Directive "on the protection of individuals with regard to the processing of personal data by competent authorities for the purposes of prevention, investigation, detection or prosecution of criminal offences or the execution of criminal penalties, and the free movement of such data".

PRIVACY AND SECURITY IN THE DIGITAL AGE

3. The Supreme Court of Canada has stated that "society has come to realize that privacy is at the heart of liberty in a modern state ... Grounded in man's physical and moral autonomy, privacy is essential for the well-being of the individual" (*R. v. Dyment* 1988). Goold (2009) states: "Without privacy, it is much harder for dissent to flourish or for democracy to remain healthy and robust. Equally, without privacy the individual is always at the mercy of the state, forced to explain why the government should not know something rather than being in the position to demand why questions are being asked in the first place."
4. The European Commission's (2010a) Internal Security Strategy action plan, released in late November 2010, and its Communication on the Stockholm Programme (European Commission 2009), released in June 2009, are strong indicators of the increasing policy importance attached to security and privacy and of the need to take both into account in decision-making.
5. The PRISMS consortium comprises eight partners: Fraunhofer Institute for Systems and Innovation Research, Karlsruhe, Germany (co-ordinator); Trilateral Research & Consulting LLP, London, UK; Vrije Universiteit Brussels, Research Group on Law Science Technology and Society, Belgium; TNO Information and Communication Technologies, Delft, The Netherlands; the University of Edinburgh, UK; Eötvös Károly Institute, Budapest, Hungary; Zuyd University, Infonomics and New Media Center, Maastricht, The Netherlands; and Ipsos MORI, London, UK.

References

Attema, J., and D. de Nood. 2010. *Over de rolverdeling tussen overheid en burger bij het beschermen van identiteit* [About the roles of government and citizens in the protecting indentity]. Leidschendam: ECP-EPN.

Bauman, Z. 1999. *In Search of Politics.* Cambridge: Polity Press.

Beck, U. 1986. *Risikogesellschaft: Auf dem Weg in eine andere Moderne* [Risk society – towards a new modernity]. Frankfurt am Main: Suhrkamp.

Beck, U., A. Giddens, and S. Lash. 1994. *Reflexive Modernization: Politics, Tradition and Aesthetics in the Modern Social Order.* Stanford, CA: Stanford University Press.

Bennett, C. J., and C. D. Raab. 2006. *The Governance of Privacy: Policy Instruments in Global Perspective.* 2nd ed. Cambridge, MA: MIT Press.

Castles, F. G. 1993. *Families of Nations: Patterns of Public Policy in Western Democracies.* Aldershot: Dartmouth.

Council of the European Union. 2003. "A secure Europe in a better world – the European Security Strategy." Approved by the European Council held in Brussels on 12 December 2003 and drafted under the responsibilities of the EU High Representative Javier Solana, Brussels.

De Hert, P., and S. Gutwirth. 2006. "Privacy, Data Protection and Law Enforcement. Opacity of the Individual and Transparency of Power." In *Privacy and the Criminal Law*, edited by E. Claes, A. Duff, and S. Gutwirth, 61–104. Antwerp: Intersentia.

De Hert, P., and S. Gutwirth. 2008. "Regulating Profiling in a Democratic Constitutional State." In *Profiling the European Citizen: Cross-disciplinary Perspectives*, edited by M. Hildebrandt and S. Gutwirth, 271–291. Dordrecht: Springer.

De Hert, P., and S. Gutwirth. 2009. "Data Protection in the Case Law of Strasbourg and Luxembourg: Constitutionalism in Action." In *Reinventing Data Protection?*, edited by S. Gutwirth, Y. Poullet, P. De Hert, C. de Terwangne, and S. Nouwt, 3–44. Dordrecht: Springer.

De Hert, P., V. Papakonstantinou, D. Wright, and S. Gutwirth. 2012. "Principles and the Proposed New Data Protection Regulation." *Innovation: the European Journal of Social Science Research*, 25 (this issue).

European Commission. 2004a. *On the Implementation of the Preparatory Action on the Enhancement of the European Industrial Potential in the Field of Security Research, Towards a Programme to Advance European Security Through Research and Technology.* COM(2004) 72 final. Brussels European Commission.

European Commission. 2004b. *Security Research: the next steps.* COM(2004) 590 final. Brussels European Commission.

European Commission. 2006. "European Commission Signs 210 Million New Contract to Create Safer EU IT Network." Press release IP/06/1301.

European Commission. 2009. *An Area of Freedom, Security and Justice Serving the Citizen.* COM(2009) 262 final. Brussels: European Commission.

European Commission. 2010a. *The EU Internal Security Strategy in Action: Five Steps Towards a more Secure Europe.* COM(2010) 673 final. Brussels: European Commission.

European Commission. 2010b. *Overview of Information Management in the Area of Freedom, Security and Justice.* COM(2010) 385 final. Brussels: European Commission.

European Commission. 2011. *Smart Borders – Options and the Way Ahead.* COM(2011) 680 final. Brussels: European Commission.

European Commission. 2012. *Proposal for a Regulation of the European Parliament and of the Council on the Protection of Individuals with Regard to the Processing of Personal Data and on the Free Movement of Such Data* (*General Data Protection Regulation*). COM(2012) 11 final. Brussels: European Commission.

European Commission, DG Enterpise and Industry. 2009. *Towards a more Secure Society and Increased Industrial Competitiveness: Security Research Projects Under the 7th Framework Programme for Research.* Brussels: European Commission.

European Parliament and the Council. 1995. "Directive 95/46/EC of 24 October 1995 on the Protection of Individuals with Regard to the Processing of Personal Data on the Free Movement of Such Data." *Offficial Journal* L281: 31–50, November 23.

European Parliament and the Council. 2002. "Directive 2002/58 of 12 July 2002 Concerning the Processing of Personal Data and the Protection of Privacy in the Electronic Communications Sector." *Offficial Journal* L201, 37–47, July 31.

European Security Research Advisory Board. 2006. *Meeting the Challenge: The European Security Research Agenda. A Report from the European Security Research Advisory Board.* Luxembourg: Office for Official Publications of the European Communities.

Goold, B. J. 2009. "Surveillance and the Political Value of Privacy." *Amsterdam Law Forum* 1 (4): 3–6.

Group of Personalities in the Field of Security Research. 2004. *Research for a Secure Europe.* Luxembourg: Office for Official Publications of the European Communities.

Gutwirth, S. 2002. *Privacy and the Information Age.* Lanham, MD: Rowman & Littlefield.

Gutwirth, S., R. Gellert, R. Bellanova, M. Friedewald, P. Schütz, D. Wright, E. Mordini, and S. Venier. 2011. *Legal, Social, Economic and Ethical Conceptualisations of Privacy and Data Protection. Deliverable 1, The Prescient Project* [Online]. Accessed December 12. http://www.prescient-project.eu/prescient/inhalte/download/PRESCIENT-D1---final.pdf

Hustinx, P. 2010. "Privacy by Design: Delivering the Promises." *Identity in the Information Society* 3, 253–255.

Kumaraguru, P., and L. C. Cranor. 2005. *Privacy Indexes: A Survey of Westin's Studies.* CMU-ISRI-05-138. Pittsburgh, PA: Carnegie Mellon University [Online]. Accessed December 12, 2011. http://reports-archive.adm.cs.cmu.edu/anon/isri2005/CMU-ISRI-05-138.pdf

Marsden, S. 2009. "Phone 'blagging' methods exposed." *The Independent*, 9 July [Online]. Accessed December 12, 2011. http://www.independent.co.uk/news/uk/crime/phone-blagging-methods-exposed-1739387.html

Murphy, O. 2007. *A Surveillance Society: Qualitative Research Report.* Wilmslow: ICO.

Niemietz v. Germany. 1992. 72/1991/324/396, December 16. Council of Europe: European Court of Human Rights [online]. Accessed December 12, 2011. http://www.unhcr.org/refworld/docid/3f32560b4.html

OECD. 1980. *Guidelines Governing the Protection of Privacy and Transborder Data Flows of Personal Data.* Paris: Organisation for Economic Co-operation and Development.

Pretty v. United Kingdom. 2002. Application no. 2346/02, 29 April. Council of Europe: European Court of Human Rights [online]. Accessed December 12, 2011. http://www.unhcr.org/refworld/docid/4daee1682.html

R. v. Dyment. 1988. CanLII 10 (SCC), [1988] 2 SCR 417 [online]. Accessed December 12, 2011. http://canlii.ca/t/1ftc6

Regan, P. M. 1995. *Legislating Privacy: Technology, Social Values, and Public Policy.* Chapel Hill, NC: University of North Carolina Press.

Solove, D. J. 2008. *Understanding Privacy.* Cambridge, MA: Harvard University Press.

Sudre, F. 2005. "Rapport introductif: La construction par le juge européen du droit au respect de la vie privée" [The right privacy under the European Convention on Human Rights]. In *Le droit au respect de la vie privée au sens de la Convention européenne des droits de l'homme* [Introductory report: The construction of the right to privacy by the European Courts], edited by F. Sudre. Brussels: Bruylant.

Sudre, F., J.-P. Marguénaud, J. Andriantsimbazovina, A. Gouttenoire, and M. Levinet. 2003. *Les grands arrêts de la Cour Européenne des Droits de l'Homme* [The major judgements of the European Court of Human Rights]. Paris: Presses Universitaires Française.

van Lieshout, M., L. Kool, B. van Schoonhoven, and M. de Jong. 2011. "Privacy by Design: An Alternative to Existing Practice in Safeguarding Privacy." *Info* 13 (6): 55–68.

Warren, S. D., and L. D. Brandeis. 1890. "The Right to Privacy." *Harvard Law Review* 4 (5): 193–220.

Westin, A. F. 1967. *Privacy and Freedom*. New York: Atheneum.

Zedner, L. 2009. *Security. Key Ideas in Criminology*. London: Routledge.

Zureik, E., L. H. Stalker, E. Smith, D. Lyon, and Y. E. Chan. 2010. *Surveillance, Privacy, and the Globalization of Personal Information: International Comparisons*. Montreal: McGill–Queen's University Press.

The proposed Regulation and the construction of a principles-driven system for individual data protection

Paul de Hert[a], Vagelis Papakonstantinou[a], David Wright[b] and Serge Gutwirth[a]

[a]Vrije Universiteit Brussels – Tilburg University (TILT), Brussels, Belgium; [b]Trilateral Research and Consulting, London, UK

> The overhaul of the EU data protection regime is a welcome development for various reasons: the 1995 Directive is largely outdated and cumbersome within an Internet (indeed, Web 2.0) environment. The 2008 Framework Decision is a practically unenforceable instrument, and even harmful in its weakness in protecting personal data. The Commission's proposed Regulation and Directive intended to replace it to improve the data protection afforded to individuals in their respective fields of application across the EU today. This paper considers some of the principles, some new, some old, that underpin the proposed new data protection framework, which was released on 25 January 2012. We offer an analysis of the key principles of lawfulness of the processing, access to justice, transparency and accountability – principles intended to be all-encompassing, abstract and omnipresent. Some of the above principles may appear to be new, but such is not necessarily the case. For instance, the principle of lawfulness is central in the current 1995 Directive, but it reappears in an amended form in the proposed EU data protection framework. On the other hand, the principle of accountability is an addition to the list that will need to prove its value in practice. Regardless of the outcome of the EU data protection framework amendment process and the ultimate wording of the instruments that compose it, the application and visibility of these principles ought to remain unaffected.

Introduction

The Commission initiated the process of amending the EU data protection framework in 2009. After public consultations were held, the Commission released a Communication in late 2010 (European Commission 2010). Subsequently, all major participants in the process published their views (Article 29 Data Protection Working Party 2011; European Council 2011; European Data Protection Supervisor 2011; European Parliament 2011a). Altogether, this documentation creates the institutional and theoretical environment that led to the Commission draft proposals released on 25 January 2012: the proposed General Data Protection Regulation (European Commission 2012b) and the proposed Police and Criminal Justice Data Protection Directive (European Commission 2012a). The former is intended to replace the EU Data Protection Directive (European Parliament and the Council

1995), a document that since its release in 1995 has been the basic reference text for data protection worldwide. The latter intends to replace a specific legal instrument, the 2008 Framework Decision on the processing of data relating to security and criminal justice (European Council 2008).

The Commission proposals for the amendment of the EU data protection framework are not only impressive in volume – both comprise no less than 155 articles (and 172 pages) – but also wide-reaching and ambitious in scope. The Regulation in particular is a detailed document, each provision of which invites discussion in terms of aims, effectiveness and proportionality.

Rather than giving a detailed analysis of the provisions of both texts, which are still drafts, we examine in this paper the principles underlying the proposed new data protection rules. These principles are intended to be all-encompassing, abstract and omnipresent through the amended EU data protection framework, regardless of whether in the proposed Regulation or in the Directive or elsewhere. To this end, an analysis of the principles of lawfulness of the processing, access to justice, transparency and accountability follows. Regardless of the outcome of the EU data protection framework amendment process and the ultimate wording of the instruments that compose it, the application and visibility of these principles ought to remain unaffected.

After presenting in brief the main changes brought by the Commission proposals to the EU data protection framework in effect today, we elaborate the principles of lawfulness of the processing, access to justice, transparency and accountability, and their ramifications for the EU data protection system in the analysis that follows.

Some of the above principles may appear to be new, but such is not necessarily the case. For instance, the principle of lawfulness (discussed below) is central in the current 1995 Directive, but it reappears in an amended form in the proposed EU data protection framework. On the other hand, the principle of accountability (discussed below) is an addition to the list that will need to prove its value in practice.

A brief analysis of some of the new proposed data protection rights

One of the reasons for the change of the 1995 Directive through a Regulation lies in the lack of a sufficient harmonization level in data protection laws across the EU today. The 1995 Directive failed to create a uniform regulatory environment, in which all Member States would abide by (exactly) the same rules. As a rule, a Directive is not supposed to completely harmonize legal systems. Unlike a Regulation, some legal discretion is left to the Member States in its implementation. History has shown, however, that too much discretion was left in the hands of the Member States. Contemporary processing activities, which routinely transcend national borders, have helped to accentuate such disparities (notoriously, Google's Street View was received very differently among Member States). Because the creation of a single regulatory environment is deemed essential and because Member States evidently cannot be trusted to create such an environment through a Directive, the Commission has opted for a Regulation, an EU legal instrument that allows much more detailed and unifying (rather than harmonizing) regulation, which, once adopted, enables direct application into national laws (European Commission 2012b, 5).

In addition to unifying of data protection rules across the Member States, a primary task of the Regulation is to update the 1995 Directive's provisions into the contemporary personal data processing environment. The Directive was drafted at a time when the Internet was little known. Evidently, the same applies to applications such as social networking websites, cloud computing and geo-location services. It is not, however, only a lack of technology updates that plagues the Directive's provisions: its personal data processing model has become out of phase in the meantime. In essence, the 1995 Directive assumed that a single, well-identifiable entity, named the "data controller", would take the initiative and control the circumstances of a single personal data processing operation. At best, such a data controller would be assisted, passively, by a "data processor". In this way, all processing operations could be singled out, and indeed catalogued into a registry held by the controlling mechanism (the Data Protection Authority). As is widely known, practically all of the above assumptions have been overturned in the contemporary processing environment.

Therefore, the proposed Regulation boldly updates the 1995 Directive provisions, reinforcing the mechanisms that seem to be working and deleting those that appear no longer connected to the state of the art. The list of information principles in the Directive that describes how processing should be carried out ("Principles relating to data quality" and "Principles regarding confidentiality and security of processing") continues to hold a central place in personal data processing (in Article 5); to the list is added, under the same Article, the data minimization principle and the "establishment of a comprehensive responsibility and liability of the controller" (European Commission 2012b, 8).

The same is the case with the set of individual data protection rights: the rights to information, access to one's personal data and rectification are substantially reinforced, in order to deal with contemporary complexity (in Articles 14, 15 and 16 respectively). Data exports to third countries continue to require the "adequacy" criterion (in Article 41). On the other hand, the new Regulation will abolish the notification system; it is to be replaced by data controller accountability, a system of prior notifications whenever needed, data protection impact assessments and the establishment of data protection officers in organizations with more than 250 employees.[1]

Replacing the Directive alone would have been a formidable task. However, the Commission chose to go much further than that: in addition to the above, it introduced a series of novelties that have already attracted the public's attention and, if ultimately adopted, are expected to play a significant role in the renewed EU data protection framework.

The introduction of a "right to be forgotten", in Article 17, is probably the best example from this point of view. The Commission decided to include in its proposal an individual's right to order that his or her data on the Internet be deleted, in spite of the strong criticism both from a practical (i.e. its applicability) and a theoretical (i.e. its relation to freedom of expression) perspective. Another novelty is the introduction of mandatory data protection impact assessments, in Article 33, following the example of environmental policy and law. Intended to precede risky processing operations, data protection impact assessments are expected to form yet another tool for the better monitoring of the Regulation's application. Finally, the same applies to "privacy-by-design" implementations (Article 23): by expressly acknowledging them in the proposed Regulation text, the Commission demonstrated that it considers such technical means important parts of the EU data protection model.

The other component in the Commission's proposed overhaul of the data protection framework is a new Police and Criminal Justice Data Protection Directive.

It might appear less ambitious in comparison to the Regulation; however, if ultimately adopted, it will bring substantial improvements in individual rights protection in a field where such progress ought not be taken for granted. The Directive would replace the 2008 Framework Decision. It would make a significant contribution to individual data protection, because the 2008 Framework Decision is ill-suited to serve its declared purposes, that is, to regulate security-related personal data processing in the EU. Such processing increased exponentially in importance after 9/11 and subsequent terrorist attacks in European capitals. However, data protection regulation never really caught up with processing developments in this field. Rather than establishing a coherent regulatory system (the 1995 Directive did not apply, as stated in its Article 3), specific sectors went on by themselves to establish their own data protection regime (for instance, the Schengen Information System, Europol, Eurojust, bilateral Passenger Name Records (PNR) Agreements, etc.). The 2008 Framework Decision was a latecomer in the field that, instead of providing the long-awaited principles and rules by which all other sector-specific instruments should abide, limited its scope to cross-border processing only. In addition, it provides for exemptions from practically every single fair information principle, while also failing to introduce a supervisory or coordinating body at EU level.

The proposed Directive broadly follows the Regulation's structure and wording. Its scope (Article 2) covers domestic data processing as well; the fair information principles and the individual rights of information, access to data and rectification are acknowledged (in Articles 4, 11, 12 and 15, respectively), while space for exemptions is kept at a minimum. On the other hand, differentiations are noted where the Commission considered that security-related processing deserves specialized treatment: data quality requirements are more relaxed (see, for instance, Article 6); profiling is allowed (in Article 9); and other personal data processing instruments relating to the area of freedom, security and justice remain unaffected by its provisions (see Article 59).

The principle of lawfulness: quality and legitimacy as conjunctive requirements

Let us now turn to a discussion of the proposed legal instruments and their underlying basic principles. The principle of lawfulness ought to be listed first among them. We therefore start with a complex message about the principle that processing should show a certain quality and the principle that processing needs to have a solid legal starting point: either consent, or a legal mandate, or any other recognized or legitimate starting point. Together both requirements – quality and legitimacy – create a lawful basis.

Articles 6 and 7 of the 1995 Directive prescribe the conditions under which personal data processing becomes lawful in the EU: the former pertains to the "principles relating to data quality" and the latter to the "criteria for making data processing legitimate". However, no clear guidance is found in the text of the 1995 Directive regarding the relationship between them. In practice, only Recital 30 provides some assistance to this end: Articles 6 and 7 ought to be read conjunctively – both the data quality conditions and the processing legitimacy grounds should concur in order for a specific processing to be lawful. This is of paramount importance to personal data protection. Any processing operation cannot be based on only one of these Articles: a processing operation adhering to all the "principles relating to data quality" may be found unlawful if it is not based on individual consent or the other legal bases laid down in Article 7 of the 1995 Directive. Or a processing operation that is indeed based on individual consent or on any other of the legal bases of Article 7 may be found unlawful if it is not conducted according to all "principles relating to data quality" of Article 6. Application here is conjunctive and not selective.[2]

Nevertheless, the 1995 Directive's lack of a clear and straightforward connection between Articles 6 and 7 allowed data processors to adopt at times an opportunistic approach, whereby they could – erroneously from our point of view – argue that they could choose to apply only Article 7 or only Article 6 in order to justify the legitimacy of their processing (Knyrim and Trieb 2011).

The proposed Regulation does not have an explicit and unequivocal provision requiring both Articles (now, 5 and 6) to apply to any and all personal data processing operation in order for it to be lawful. In addition, the helpful wording of the 1995 Directive Recital 30 has now been replaced, further undermining the above interpretation.[3] Consequently, opportunistic data processor approaches may continue, if not increase, once the new regulatory framework comes into place. Such a change shall gravely worsen individual data protection. The lack of clear guidance as to the exact conditions for the principle of lawfulness to apply to personal data processing is a significant omission by the Commission, which needs to be addressed in the future.

The principle of access to justice and the creation of a "closest to the home" individual redress right

Let us now turn to a second principle: the data subject needs to have good access to the legal system to challenge processing practices. Within a globalized international environment permeated by the Internet, the issue of local jurisdiction appears impossible to resolve. Effectively, it exceeds the data protection boundaries, being ultimately relevant to all fields of law that enable any level of international interaction at individual level without the intervention of intermediaries. However, this issue is increasingly pressing for data protection for two reasons. First, it affects individuals directly: an individual residing in a Member State may have to support her case on the infringement of her data protection rights outside her own country, or even outside the EU itself – an expensive, complex and time-consuming undertaking that is normally not accessible to the majority of the persons concerned. Second, it is sensitive to differences between intra-EU data protection models, impeding adherence to data protection regulations by data controllers with multiple places of residence. Exactly this shortcoming of the 1995 Directive led to the Commission's proposal for a change of instrument in the form of a Regulation.

The distinguishing criteria for the applicable law employed by the 1995 Directive refer primarily to the location of the data controller and, alternatively, to the location of its equipment.[4] The general rule sets out that the Member State's Data Protection Act applicable each time is the one of the residence of the data controller concerned. If the data controller is not established on EU territory, then a specific Member State Data Protection Act may still apply, if the data controller uses equipment located within its territory. The criterion is therefore of a "locality" nature. As such, however, this criterion has proven of limited practical use to individuals, because, even if they are able to establish the whereabouts of either the data controller or its equipment, they will ultimately be forced to get involved in expensive and time-consuming litigation outside their own country of residence.[5]

Nor is the 1995 Directive accommodating with regard to multi-national data controllers' needs. Article 4.1 states that, "when the same controller is established on the territory of several Member States, he must take the necessary measures to ensure that each of these establishments complies with the obligations laid down by the national law applicable". This task has proven quite difficult to accomplish over the years, owing to a lack of harmonization among Member States.

A bold, user-centric approach is admittedly adopted in the text of the proposed Regulation.[6] Abandoning the "chase for the server", a task further complicated in cloud computing and "software-as-a-service" environments (European Data Protection Supervisor 2010), the Regulation is intended to apply to processing of personal data executed not only by data controllers or processors within the EU but also by processors established in third countries, where the processing activities are related to "the offering of goods or services" to data subjects residing in the EU or "serve to monitor their behaviour" (Article 3.2).[7] Whether this provision is kept in the Regulation's final wording remains to be seen, particularly given that it appears to regulate the whole of the Internet (and, perhaps indirectly, the whole of the world).[8]

The user-centric approach is further reinforced by a series of new powers granted to national data protection authorities. Data controllers not established in the Union are expected to appoint representatives, who are obliged to cooperate with the local data protection authorities (Article 29). Supervisory authorities carry a mandate to cooperate and coordinate among themselves, providing, among other things, mutual assistance (Article 55) and carrying our joint operations (Article 56), in order to warrant to individuals an increased level of protection in the contemporary cross-border processing environment.

Nevertheless, resolving jurisdictional issues does not necessarily mean improving individuals' access to justice as well. This is why the draft Regulation, in its Chapter VIII, grants individuals the right to lodge a complaint against a controller or a processor either before the courts of the Member State where the controller or processor has an establishment or before the courts of the Member State where the data subject has its habitual residence.[9] This, "closest to the home" individual redress right, together with the principle of accountability discussed in the next section, is expected to assist individuals to effectively exercise their right to data protection.

The principle of transparency

The principle of transparency is particularly important in the data protection field. Processing operations do not take place in public, nor are their results felt immediately by the individuals concerned, in order for them to respond accordingly. On the contrary, the processing of personal data takes place behind closed doors, or rather within automated systems, without the individuals whose data are being processed being present or even aware that such processing takes place. The knowledge generated about an individual is very often not accessible to her, nor any information about how it was produced. In addition, the results of such processing in the majority of cases do not lead to direct action, positive or negative, towards the individuals concerned, but are rather stored in computer systems for future use. In the real world, individuals come across decisions that affect them (for instance, rejection of a loan or insurance policy, failure to get a job, failure to enter a country) yet are unaware of the automated processing operations the results of which have been used to formulate such decisions. The task of safeguarding their rights is virtually impossible: individuals do not know that their data have been processed unless they are faced with a (negative) decision against them. Only then do they have reason to start inquiring how or why a decision was made. They need all the help they can get to learn what happened.

The principle of transparency is therefore of paramount importance for the creation of an effective data protection regulatory framework: it fosters a personal data processing environment of trust and enables any interested party to enforce effectively data protection rights and obligations. However, its effect may only be fully appreciated when it operates at multiple levels.[10] In particular, the principle of transparency needs to apply to data controllers and data processors alike as well as to the processing operations themselves. It also needs to apply to the data protection enforcement mechanism. An enforcement mechanism must be open and transparent to citizens and to any third party with an interest in inquiring about its operation and effectiveness.

The principle of transparency is acknowledged in the text of the 1995 Directive, albeit not expressly. Instead, its established mechanisms serve its causes indirectly. The notification system is such an example. Transparency within the 1995 Directive framework may also be achieved, from the data subject's point of view, through exercising rights to information and access. It may also be achieved through the obligation of national data protection authorities to submit formal annual reports.

The proposed Regulation places the principle of transparency at its epicenter. With regard to its meaning in the data protection context, "the principle of transparency requires that any information, both of the public and of the data subject should be easily accessible and easy to understand, and that clear and plain language is used" (European Commission 2012b, Recital 39). A new relevant principle is expressly introduced in its list of Fair Information Principles, complementing the fairness and lawfulness of the processing principle: "personal data must be processed lawfully, fairly and in a transparent manner in relation to the data subject". Accordingly, data controllers carry an explicit obligation: Article 11 introduces the obligation for "transparent information and communication".[11] All aforementioned transparency instances in the text of the 1995 Directive (apart from the notification system) are maintained in the draft Regulation.

The proposed Directive on police and justice processing does not seem to follow the Regulation's example with regard to the principle of transparency, restricting it (in fact, the only relevant reference may be found in its Article 10) perhaps according to perceived specialized security-related processing needs. From this point of view, notwithstanding the plausibility of a distinction between the two types of processing, individuals may be surprised when they discover that safeguards afforded to them in general personal data processing are not even remotely applicable in security-related circumstances. Solutions may be sought in trusted third party systems that would provide the controls and checks upon request of a data subject, without passing her substantial information about the processing itself. Data Protection Authorities could act as such trusted third parties.

The principle of accountability: the revolutionary newcomer

The introduction of a principle of accountability for data controllers in the personal data processing context (European Parliament 2011b) is by no means a new idea in the field. Discussions from a legal point of view date as far back as 2009 (Article 29

Data Protection Working Party 2010a, 2011). Its explicit appearance in the text of the draft Regulation should come as no surprise either to data protection proponents or data controllers.

In broad terms, a principle of accountability would place upon data controllers the burden of implementing within their organizations specific measures in order to ensure that data protection requirements are met. Such measures could include anything from the appointment of a data protection officer to implementing data protection impact assessments or employing a privacy-by-design system architecture (European Commission 2010; Article 29 Data Protection Working Party 2011). The Commission, in its Communication on the amendment of the EU data protection framework, perhaps worryingly, connected an introduction of a principle of accountability with a reduction in the data controllers' "administrative formalities".[12] It is exactly at this point where a major concern before the introduction of the draft Regulation lay: what exactly would be the added value of introducing a general principle of accountability into the overall, sound, principles-based environment of the 1995 Directive? Data controllers are anyway responsible for observing the data protection rules. Is a principle of accountability to be perceived as an alternative to certain requirements for compliance with rules? If it means the abolition of administrative procedures regarded as a bureaucratic burden by data controllers, would it not at the same time compromise the level of protection afforded to individuals?

Various views have been expressed on this issue. The principle of accountability would need to address difficult questions, such as how to reconcile the need for specificity with a general nature principle or how to resolve the issue of scalability or proportionality. In other words, which criteria shall decide the adequacy of measures implemented by data controllers?[13] It has also been suggested that the added value of a general principle of accountability lies in the fact that it could function as a general obligation to demonstrate results, while leaving freedom to data controllers as to the means they employ (Hijmans 2011).

The wording of the proposed Regulation attempts to alleviate these data protection concerns. Article 22 "takes account of the debate on a 'principle of accountability' and describes in detail the obligation of responsibility of the controller to comply with this Regulation and to demonstrate this compliance, including by way of adoption of internal policies and mechanisms for ensuring such compliance" (European Commission 2012b, para. 3.4.4). As such, the principle of accountability in the draft Regulation indeed introduces a results-oriented criterion: data controllers are free to decide which policies and measures to introduce in order to achieve verifiable results: "the controller shall adopt policies and implement appropriate measures to ensure and be able to demonstrate that the processing of personal data is performed in compliance with this Regulation" (Article 22.1). However, the draft Regulation does provide further guidance, in the form of minimum requirements for data controllers: these include keeping the required documentation, implementing data security measures, performing data protection impact assessments or prior consultations or designating a data protection officer. Their implementation may be externally audited. Altogether, these minimum requirements admittedly set rather high standards for data controllers.

We can see novelties in the proposed Regulation, such as privacy by design (in Article 23) or personal data breach notifications (in Article 31) in this same quid-pro-quo context. For example, data controllers win the abolition of the notification system and other bureaucratic burdens but in return are expected to act responsibly. Practically, they are left alone to decide upon the circumstances of their personal data processing; unless they are audited and found lacking (or unless the Commission identifies a whole sector in need of intervention and decides to intervene), they are mostly left unhindered in their activities.[14]

Finally, an important consequence of the introduction of the principle of accountability into the data protection field is the reversal of the burden of proof in favor of individuals. Because personal data processing is customarily conducted behind closed doors and individuals only become aware of their data being processed whenever (adverse) results affect them, they are frequently unable to adequately prove their case in courts. Therefore, a reversal of the burden of proof obliges data controllers to demonstrate that they comply with the law, that the various legal prescriptions were applied faultlessly. The data subject does not have to demonstrate exactly where the processing, which they never witness, went wrong. This would substantially increase individual protection. This option would also be in line with fundamental case law by the European Court on Human Rights (2008): in effect, the Court has recognized the inability of an individual to prove his or her case before national courts but has concluded that "to place such a burden of proof on the applicant is to overlook the acknowledged deficiencies in the [data controller]'s record keeping at the material time".

The reversal of the burden of proof is not included in Article 22 of the draft Regulation but is found in various other provisions in its text (for instance, in Articles 7, 12 or even 19). Altogether, particularly if combined with the potential severity of penalties and sanctions suggested in the proposed Regulation, their contribution to personal data protection is expected to be critical.

Conclusion

The overhaul of the EU data protection regime is a welcome development for various reasons: the 1995 Directive is largely outdated and cumbersome within an Internet (indeed, Web 2.0) environment. The 2008 Framework Decision is a practically unenforceable instrument, and even harmful in its weakness in protecting personal data. The Commission's proposed Regulation and Directive intended to replace them and improve data protection afforded to individuals in their respective fields of application across the EU today.

This, however, is most likely the only statement that would equally apply to both sets of regulatory texts under discussion.[15] Once it is agreed that the instruments in effect today are in dire need of replacement, and new rules have been released to this end, each process goes its own separate and distinct way. While the proposed Regulation in its current wording appears to make positive contributions to individual data protection (De Hert and Papakonstantinou 2012), the same cannot always be held for the proposed Directive. Practically, of the four identified system-guiding principles above, whose efficient implementation offers an increased level of data protection, two are completely missing from the text of the Directive (the principles of transparency and accountability) and one is more or less inapplicable (the principle of access to justice). Concerns about the Directive's proposed provisions are thus justified.

The above differentiation is probably the inevitable result of a distinction made at an earlier stage by the Commission: that general-purpose and security-related personal data processing are and should be distinguished, each deserving separate rules and regulations. However, this distinction is artificial and impossible to apply in an increasingly interconnected, processing-intensive environment.[16] Also, one can challenge the assumption that security-processing of personal data merits a substantially and fundamentally different treatment than general-purpose processing.[17]

The construction of a principles-driven system for individual data protection is the obvious option in view of contemporary data processing complexity. Personal data processing has become an economic, social and political phenomenon, whose exact circumstances are in constant flux. Attempting to predict, in order to regulate, its future forms or regulate in detail its contemporary appearances is a futile law-making pursuit. Instead, encompassing principles that remain broad in scope and technological specifications could provide the necessary guidance as to the applicable rules and regulations each time a processing operation appears to transcend existing models and schemes. To this end, the principles of lawfulness of processing, access to justice, transparency and accountability constitute the bases upon which the new EU data protection framework needs to build.

Notes

1. Admittedly, however, this is a considerable step backwards for those Member States that already have rules requiring significantly lower numbers.
2. This has important drawbacks with regards to the role of the data subject's consent in data protection. If one takes seriously the interplay between Article 6 and 7 of the 1995 Directive, it is not clear at all – in the general rules, and thus not for sensitive data – when a consent is really needed, and how it can contribute to "lawfulness". Consent is always additional, and thus per se superfluous. Hence there is no "principle of consent" in data protection and it should be avoided that consent be (ab)used for legitimizing processings that do not meet the other conditions spelled out in Article 6 and 7 (Gutwirth 2012).
3. The same appears to be the case with the proposed Justice and Police Directive (the respective Articles are 4 and 7).
4. See its Article 4. The Article 29 Working Party (2010b) made concrete recommendations for the amendments required to further enforce the relevant Directive provisions; its suggestions seem to have been adopted (European Commission 2010, section 2.2.3).
5. See European Commission (2010, section 2.2.3).
6. The Article 29 Working Party (2002) has already attempted to introduce similarly protective criteria since 2002, admittedly adopting a rather creative reasoning (see Moerel 2011).
7. See also the draft Regulation's Article 22, and on "national targeting", see Article 29 Data Protection Working Party (2010b, p. 31). On the other hand, the proposed Directive contains no extra-territorial effect.
8. This option may not be as burdensome, or even unrealistic, as one might imagine. When data controllers are powerful multinational organizations, as is often the case (for instance, search engines, social network websites, Web 2.0 providers), they can evidently cope with the costs of international litigation much more easily than individuals. In the same context, when "national targeting" may be established (for instance, web pages of country-specific interest or translated into the local language), then it is only reasonable that sales within such territory also include some (litigation) risks. Ultimately, if service providers are unwilling to undertake the risk of international litigation, they may very well refuse to provide services to individuals trying to connect from third countries (through their IP addresses); after all, this is a business policy frequently implemented in order to maximize international profits or to control international distribution channels and it would therefore be feasible for it to expand in order to minimize international exposure as well.

9. This option does not seem to be available to individuals in the proposed Directive.
10. The principle of transparency discussed here is broader than the "increasing transparency for data subjects" analysis included in the Commission Communication (section 2.1.2), in that the principle elaborated here is intended to operate at multiple levels, and addresses all data protection participants, rather than placing specific obligations upon data controllers only (thus, expanding the individual right to information).
11. As expressly inspired by the Madrid Resolution on international standards on the protection of personal data and privacy (European Commission 2012b, para. 3.4).
12. "This [principle of accountability] would not aim to increase the administrative burden on data controllers, since such measures would rather focus on establishing safeguards and mechanisms which make data protection compliance more effective while at the same time reducing and simplifying certain administrative formalities, such as notifications" (section 2.2.4).
13. A point favored by the Council (Győző 2011).
14. The proposed Directive does not appear to acknowledge application of a principle of accountability in the security processing field.
15. See also the European Data Protection Supervisor (2012b), in which the lack of comprehensiveness of the proposed regulatory framework is identified as its main weakness.
16. Distinguishing in practice between commercial and security personal data processing is extremely difficult. Apart from clear-cut cases whereby, for instance, data is collected by the police and kept in its systems, or data collected by commercial data controllers in the course of their duties may be used by law enforcement agencies and vice versa (see, for instance, Article 60 of the proposed Directive), case law provides little assistance to this end: although PNR processing was ultimately considered security-related, electronic communications processing was considered commercial processing (on PNR-related processing, which was found to be security-related in spite of the fact that data are collected by airline carriers for commercial purposes; see, for instance, Papakonstantinou and de Hert 2009). On the other hand, the retention of telecommunications data, collected by telecommunications providers for commercial purposes, has been judged as commercial processing (as established by the European Court of Justice in its Case C-301/06, Ireland v. Parliament and Council).
17. See, for instance, the EDPS Press Release on the proposed EU data protection framework (European Data Protection Supervisor 2012a).

References

Article 29 Data Protection Working Party. 2002. *Working Document on Determining the International Application of EU Data Protection Law to Personal Data Processing on the Internet by non-EU Based Websites*, WP 56. Brussels, May 30.
Article 29 Data Protection Working Party. 2010a. *Opinion 3/2010 on the Principle of Accountability*, WP 173. Brussels, July 13.
Article 29 Data Protection Working Party. 2010b. *Opinion 8/2010 on Applicable Law*, WP 179. Brussels, December 16.
Article 29 Data Protection Working Party. 2011. *Letter to Vice-President Reading Regarding the Article 29 Data Protection Working Party's Reaction to the Commission Communication, "A Comprehensive Approach to Personal Data Protection in the EU"*. Brussels, January 14.
De Hert, P., and V. Papakonstantinou. 2012. "The Proposed Data Protection Regulation Replacing Directive 95/46/EC: A Sound System for the Protection of Individuals." *Computer Law and Security Review* 28 (2): 1–13.
European Commission. 2010. *Communication to the European Parliament, the Council, the Economic and Social Committee and the Committee of the Regions, A Comprehensive Approach on Personal Data Protection in the European Union*, COM(2010) 609 final. Brussels: European Commission, November 4.
European Commission. 2012a. *Proposal for a Directive of the European Parliament and of the Council on the Protection of Individuals with Regard to the Processing of Personal Data by Competent Authorities for the Purposes of Prevention, Investigation, Detection or Prosecution*

of Criminal Offences or the Execution of Criminal Penalties, and the Free Movement of Such Data, COM(2012) 10 final. Brussels: European Commission.

European Commission. 2012b. *Proposal for a Regulation of the European Parliament and of the Council on the Protection of Individuals with Regard to the Processing of Personal Data and on the Free Movement of Such Data (General Data Protection Regulation)*, COM(2012) 11 final. Brussels: European Commission.

European Council. 2008. *Framework Decision 2008/977/JHA of 27 November 2008 on the Protection of Personal Data Processed in the Framework of Police and Judicial Cooperation in Criminal Matters.* Brussels: European Council.

European Council. 2011. *Conclusions on the Communication from the Commission to the European Parliament and the Council – A Comprehensive Approach on Personal Data Protection in the European Union, 3071st Justice and Home Affairs Council Meeting.* Brussels: European Council, February 24 and 25.

European Court on Human Rights. 2008. *K.U. vs. Finland*, Judgment of 2 December.

European Data Protection Supervisor. 2010. *"Data Protection and Cloud Computing under EU law"*, Third European Cyber Security Awareness Day. Brussels: European Parliament, April 13.

European Data Protection Supervisor. 2011. *Opinion on the Communication from the Commission on "A Comprehensive Approach on Personal Data Protection in the European Union."* Brussels: European Data Protection Supervisor, January 14.

European Data Protection Supervisor. 2012a. *EDPS Welcomes a "Huge Step Forward for Data Protection in Europe", but Regrets Inadequate Rules for the Police and Justice Area*, EDPS/02/12. Brussels: European Data Protection Supervisor, January 25.

European Data Protection Supervisor. 2012b. *Opinion on the Data Protection Reform Package.* Brussels: European Data Protection Supervisor, March 7.

European Parliament. 2011a. *Committee on Civil Liberties, Justice and Home Affairs, Working Document (1 and 2) on a Comprehensive Approach on Personal Data Protection in the European Union.* Brussels: European Parliament, March 15.

European Parliament. 2011b. *Towards a New EU Legal Framework for Data Protection and Privacy, Committee on Civil Liberties, Justice and Home Affairs.* Brussels: European Parliament.

European Parliament and the Council. 1995. *Directive 95/46/EC of 24 October 1995 on the Protection of Individuals with Regard to the Processing of Personal Data and on the Free Movement of such Data.* Brussels: European Parliament and the Council. Accessed April 14 2012. http://eur-lex.europa.eu/LexUriServ/LexUriServ.do?uri=CELEX:31995 L0046:EN:HTML

Gutwirth, S. 2012. "Short Statement about the Role of Consent in the European Data Protection Directive." In: *The Selected Works of Serge Gutwirth.* Accessed April 14. http://works.bepress.com/serge_gutwirth/80

Győző, S. E. 2011. "New Principles – in the Light of the Discussions within the Council Conclusions on the Commission's Communication." Presentation to the International Data Protection Conference, Budapest, June 16 and 17.

Hijmans, H. 2011. "Principles of Data Protection: Renovation Needed?" Presentation to the International Data Protection Conference, Budapest, June 16 and 17.

Knyrim, R., and G. Trieb. 2011. "Smart Metering under EU Data Protection Law." *International Data Privacy Law* 1 (2): 121–128.

Moerel, L. 2011. "The Long Arm of EU Data Protection Law: Does the Data Protection Directive Apply to Processing of Personal Data of EU Citizens by Websites Worldwide?" *International Data Privacy Law* 1 (1): 28–46.

Papakonstantinou, V., and P. De Hert. 2009. "The PNR Agreement and Transatlantic anti-Terrorism co-Operation: No Firm Human Rights Framework on Either Side of the Atlantic." *Common Market Law Review* 46: 885–919.

Limits and challenges of the expanding use of covert CCTV in the workplace in Spain – beyond jurisprudential analysis

José R. Agustina[a] and Fanny Coudert[b]

[a]Department of Criminal Law and Criminology, Faculty of Law and Political Sciences, Universitat Internacional de Catalunya, 08017, Barcelona, Spain; [b]Interdisciplinary Centre for Law & ICT, Faculty of Law, Katholieke Universiteit Leuven, 3000 Leuven, Belgium

This paper analyzes the expanding use of legitimate covert CCTV in the workplace in Spain. By examining the recent evolution of the jurisprudence in that field, we focus on the legal reasons that support court decisions from 2000 to the present and add some criminological and ethical perspectives to better comprehend not only the legal rationale, but also some other collateral effects that employers should take into account in implementing covert surveillance. We conclude that verification of a previous objective pattern of risk involving criminal behavior is crucial for ceding the general principles on respecting privacy. The central argument involves the exceptional case an employer may find when there is a continuous situation and the only way to stop it is by discovering the wrongdoers in action. The paper shows the method for further research and a more detailed rationale for improving legal and decision-making analyses in this field.

Introduction

The present article explores some privacy issues within the broad context of surveillance in the workplace. Concretely, it focuses on the use of covert CCTV in the workplace for crime control purposes. In doing so, it is addressing an interdisciplinary and under-researched topic area. Although there is a wealth of published material on CCTV, there are few studies that specifically consider CCTV in the workplace (McCahill and Norris 1999), even more so where it is used covertly for crime prevention purposes.

From a general perspective, the topic of surveillance in the workplace has been debated since the early 1980s. Since then, academics in organizational behavior disciplines, organizational sociologists and occupational psychologists have investigated the effects of monitoring and surveillance but tend to write about the phenomena in different ways in their respective publication venues (Ball 2010). However, the approach taken in this article is essentially based on criminological and legalistic perspectives, although some managerial and ethical considerations are also made. Certainly, the complexity of the real issue calls for an interdisciplinary and integrated approach, but, in getting closer to the issue, one or another focus should be taken as predominant. Therefore, the intended approach seeks to find a balanced and practical analysis by merging overall legal (normative) and criminological (empirical) considerations. As Gary Marx (2005, 395) has put it, "[w]e need, if not marriages, at least more cohabitation involving the empirical analyses of the social sciences with the normative analyses of the law and ethics".

Looking back at the recent changes in the field, the diffusion of CCTV in society and particularly in the workplace has increased dramatically (McCahill and Norris 1999; Norris 2009). CCTV has become a major weapon and common prevention strategy in the fight against crime and its use appears to be expanding (Gill 2006, 438). However, from a critical perspective, it could be argued that the use of CCTV in the workplace is not so much about deterring crime as it is about enhancing control over workers and increasing organizational efficiency and productivity. In fact, although the growth of CCTV surveillance in the private sector can largely be accounted for by the increased recognition of the impact of business victimization (e.g. internal and external threats), CCTV use unexpectedly proved to be more valuable in checking whether staff were meeting company requirements (e.g. compliance with till procedures; McCahill and Norris 1999, 219).

In the workplace context, CCTV provides useful tools for a series of legitimate purposes, such as the monitoring of employees' productivity, the maximization of the productive use of apparatus, the investigation of complaints of employees' misconduct or the preparation of the employer's defense in lawsuits or administrative complaints – such as those brought by employees related to discrimination, harassment, discipline or termination of employment (Lasprogata, King, and Pillay 2004). However, this paper only addresses a special case among a vast range of monitoring goals, that is, the use of covert CCTV based on a crime occurrence, and it is based on the crucial distinction between ordinary and exceptional monitoring cases.

In terms of privacy concerns, as Kristie Ball has synthesized, in recent years a combination of available technologies and a management culture that emphasizes individual measurement and management has resulted in an extension and intensification of individual monitoring. The implication is that surveillance at work is, first, a necessity, and second, a normal, taken-for-granted element of working life. Among the various monitoring practices, which may focus on measuring employees' performance, their behavior or their personal characteristics, surveillance in the workplace is developing in three directions – the increased use of personal data, biometrics and of covert surveillance (Ball 2010, 88–91).

Within that context, this paper aims to analyze the recent evolution of court decisions' rationale in Spain regarding one of the three fields just mentioned where workplace surveillance is expanding – covert CCTV systems. Nouwt, de Vries, and Prins (2005) have analyzed from a comparative perspective privacy case law and surveillance practices and perceptions relating to CCTV in the workplace in 11 countries, but they did not focus specifically on covert surveillance, despite the fact that it is not an infrequent practice as the number of cases analyzed in the present paper reveals.

Regarding the interest of the research topic addressed in this paper, it is worth noting that much of the recent literature on surveillance in the workplace focuses on improving worker performance and electronic monitoring, rather than on crime prevention or reaction and CCTV systems. Looking to fill this gap, it is important to remark that we exclude from our focus what is probably the primary aim in using CCTV, namely, that businesses are keen to maintain productivity. In doing so, we assume that covert CCTV follows a rationale completely different from what we refer to as "ordinary monitoring". As we will examine, only in "exceptional monitoring" cases, within which covert surveillance fits, can companies *not* inform workers of the extent to which they are being watched. Because of that exceptional nature, covert CCTV systems are rarely justified. On the contrary, ordinary monitoring focused on labor performance has to be transparent and, based on its transparency, allows a much greater extent of pervasiveness.

In our analysis we will go beyond the legal reasons that support the court decision sample analyzed in order to add some criminological and ethical perspectives that help us better comprehend not only its own legal rationale but also some other collateral effects that employers should take into account in implementing covert surveillance. Moreover, as one important practical insight, in recognizing important changes in surveillance practices, law and crime prevention, it is analyzed how the use of CCTV surveillance systems in the workplace means that issues relating to trust, transparency and proportionality need to be revisited.

Three preliminary clarifications

For the purposes of the present paper three previous clarifications are needed in relation to three main concepts, i.e. "CCTV", "crime prevention and crime reaction", and the "workplace".

Concept of CCTV

In line with the UK doctrine (Norris 2009; von Silva-Tarouca 2011), we have opted to use the term "CCTV" as generic term to cover any video-surveillance system irrespective of the technology used, that is, whether it is a closed television system relying on analogue technology or a network IP video system that runs on a local area network. Nevertheless, it is important to stress the fact that CCTV systems may differ considerably in their technological components and capabilities, and such differences have important implications, especially on legal and ethical grounds (von Hirsch 2000; von Silva-Tarouca 2011).

CCTV as crime prevention and crime reaction tool

In controlling crime, CCTV may help to prevent potential offenses and may also help in the reaction to actual crimes once they have occurred, in order to provide evidence. From *situational crime prevention* strategies, CCTV allegedly demotivates potential offenders, who seek to target a place without any kind of surveillance. Within such logic, "opportunity makes the thief" (Felson and Clarke 1998). However, a given situation only creates an opportunity for crime *if* there is a lack of capable guardians or managers around. Thus, lacking other human resources, cameras may foster rational choice considerations by increasing perceptions of the probabilities of being caught (e.g. Clarke 1995). Nevertheless, implementing CCTV systems is only *one* measure within a vast range of alternatives in preventing crime, and their effectiveness is not clear among scholars. CCTV works best in small, well-defined sites, and in combating property crimes rather than violence or disorder (Ratcliffe 2006). All in all, for some scholars the small number of evaluations can be a limiting factor in arriving at conclusions about an intervention's effectiveness, as well as being able to generalize results (Welsh, Farrington, and O'Dell 2010, 33).

On the other hand, CCTV may be an effective tool in reacting to crime that has occurred within a company in order to detect the wrongdoers and eradicate the problem if it persists. In fact, prevention and reaction may be seen as a continuum and, hence, by having the power to react, a preventative function becomes more effective. However, crime reaction operates upon a given fact, while prevention operates only upon suspicion. As we will see, such a difference becomes relevant in terms of legitimating privacy limitations.

Based on prevention and reaction differences, the present paper is *not* going to analyze CCTV as a crime prevention tool in the workplace. Neither is it going to deal with a general approach to employee crime prevention strategies or the CCTV's alleged effectiveness. Certainly, in the framework of employee or corporate crime and in organizational settings, there are some duties of surveillance and control by the employer that may trigger different kinds and degrees of liability for those crimes committed by others within the organization (e.g. Agustina 2010). Such duties and responsibilities are much more related to general preventative surveillance measures. In contrast, we will analyze the use of hidden cameras upon the understanding that it is an exceptional form of monitoring and it is only legitimate when addressed under certain and restrictive circumstances (i) to protect corporate interests from employees' wrongdoings and (ii) to protect the company from legal liabilities.

Extended concept of workplace

An important point related to CCTV in operation at a workplace is the concept of "workplace" itself. In this regard, as our concern focuses on crime reaction in the workplace, both internal and external threats should be included within the "workplace", as they both may lead to damage to company assets. Such kinds of crime may occur at different places depending on the type of services a company is providing. Moreover, given the technological revolution and its implications for labor relationships, the traditional physical boundaries are no longer the limits of many workplaces. The head-cams worn by police officers or CCTV systems in operation on buses may be examples of CCTV uses that should not be excluded from our concerns. However, some places within the physical boundaries of the workplace, inasmuch as they can affect intimacy expectations, will exceed boundaries for covert cameras' purposes (e.g. changing rooms or toilets).

Methodology

To analyze the recent evolution of the jurisprudence on covert CCTV at workplace in Spain in order to comprehend the rationale behind such evolution we have begun from the first constitutional court decision in which that issue was addressed – the above-mentioned Spanish Constitutional Court decision STC 186/2000. Searching at CENDOJ, which is the official Spanish jurisprudence database, using the words "cámara oculta" and "trabajador", we found 35 matches. After reviewing them, the sample finally was limited to 22 relevant cases for the purposes of the research (=22).

We analyzed quantitatively the following parameters in order to obtain some patterns: (i) jurisdictional organ; (ii) way of providing evidence to the Court – videographic or photographic recordings and forensic expert exposition; (iii) quotation of

STC 186/2000; (iv) previous notification to the Workers' Committee of Representatives; (v) previous criminal pattern of risk; (vi) privacy violation claim; (vii) type of company by sector; and (viii) type of worker and extent of dependency in the employment relationship. As for the qualitative analysis, we examined throughout the 22 cases the relevant facts of each case and the rationale of the Court regarding the evidence obtained by covert CCTV.

Such analysis had not been carried out previously in Spain. Through it we have discovered not only the expansion of the legitimate role of covert surveillance for crime prevention at workplace, but also the common patterns in the 22 cases where this issue was addressed. Once patterns have been described, data are appropriately framed in a legal, ethical and criminological context in order to propose some boundaries and restrictions to maintain this expansion within reasonable and legitimate purposes.

Table 1. Quantitative analysis of court decisions on covert CCTV at workplace ($N = 22$).

	Number	Percentage
1. Jurisdictional organ		
Civil courts	1	4.5
Criminal courts	2	9.1
Labor courts	19	86.4
Administrative courts	0	0.0
2. Method of providing evidence to courts		
Video-graphic recordings	15	68.2
Photographic recordings	5	22.7
Forensic expert exposition	1	4.5
N/A	1	4.5
3. Quotation of the STC 186/2000		
Yes	5	22.7
No	17	77.3
4. Previous notification to the Workers' Committee of Representatives		
Yes	0	0.0
No	22	100.0
5. Previous criminal pattern of risk		
Yes	14	63.6
No	8	36.4
6. Privacy violation claim		
Yes	6	27.3
No	16	72.7
7. Type of company by sector		
Food sector	5	22.7
Transportation sector	3	13.6
Industry sector	3	13.6
Store sector	3	13.6
Service sector	3	13.6
Others	5	22.7
8. Type of worker and extent of dependency in the employment relationship		
Dependent	17	77.3
Supervisor	5	22.7

The precedent – the Spanish Constitutional Court decision STC 186/2000

As mentioned above, the evolution of covert CCTV in Spain cannot be understood without the analysis of the Spanish Constitutional Court decision STC 186/2000. That case, which could be called the ENSIDESA case (the name of the company) was the first of its kind at a constitutional level on covert video-surveillance monitoring. By that decision an important precedent was established and, as we will see, it has helped the expansion of such covert surveillance practices. Briefly, the facts underlying the decision were the following.

As a result of repeated unbalanced accounting records in the textile and shoe section of a company and some advance warning about the irregular conduct of the cashiers, the directors of the company contracted with a private security company to install closed circuit television cameras. The covert surveillance camera system, installed on the roof, only focused on three cash registers and the counter, with the estimated radius reaching the hands of the cashier. As a result of the surveillance, the employer verified and corroborated the suspicion that had prompted the adoption of a hidden control system, and determined the disciplinary action against the three workers, providing video-graphic recordings as evidence.

In accordance with the established doctrine of the European Court of Human Rights, the Spanish Constitutional Court started off by stating that the measure at stake has to go through a three-part test: (1) the "suitability" test, which defines whether the measure is reasonably likely to achieve its objectives; (2) the "necessity" test, which evaluates whether there are other less restrictive means capable of producing the same result; and (3) the "strict proportionality" test, which consists of a weighing of interests in which the consequences on fundamental rights are assessed against the importance of the objective pursued (Tridimas 2006, 139). This three-part test, called by the Spanish Constitutional Court the "proportionality principle" test, has to be applied case by case. The more severe the infringement, the more important the legitimate objective in each case will need to be (Liberty 2007).

In this sense, the Constitutional Court argued that the measure adopted by the employer was (1) *justified*, as there was a reasonable suspicion over the employees of having committed some deviances in their scope of employment, and *suitable* for the purpose, to verify that the employees were stealing money from the cashier machine and, if so, to discipline them; (2) necessary – as the recording was going to provide evidence of such deviant acts; and (3) proportional – inasmuch as the recording was limited to the area of the cash machine and to the time needed to check that it was not only an isolated act or a confusion but a repetitive misconduct.

Therefore the Justices argued in their rationale that the use of hidden cameras was justified upon the previous verification of an "objective pattern of risk" for the company. The previous victimization was the basis upon which the employer could justify the covert way for implementing CCTV regardless of the transparency rules that are mandatory in a normal scenario. Note that such a precedent could be extended to other means of covert surveillance – at least to the extent permitted by general rules on the legal analogy. In this sense, the rationale of the constitutional adequacy of covert video-surveillance systems can be set as a paradigm in business crime prevention strategies. Note too that the Court also found it justified that the installation of CCTV was not previously communicated to the Workers' Committee of Representatives.

Analysis of data – the 22 cases

As we can see in Figure 1, the great majority of cases were brought before Labor Courts (86.4%), while only 9.1% were criminal cases and the remaining 4.5% civil cases. In all cases there was no previous notification to the Workers' Committee of Representatives.

Many cases are related to fraudulent paid sick days; some to employee theft losses; others to "theft of time", that is, different sorts of absenteeism. For instance, an employee and his immediate boss manipulated the parking lot ticketing machine and extracted money from it just when visible CCTV systems were not in operation. The employer set a covert camera and sees who had been manipulating the machine (STSJ Madrid 11649/2010). In another case, the employer installed a covert CCTV camera focusing on a refrigerator that had been intentionally unplugged repeatedly, spoiling food (STSJ Madrid 3598/2006). An employee was caught and fired after being identified by covert CCTV at a grocery store repeatedly taking dried fruit and chocolate (STSJ Cantabria 720/2004). An employer detected deficient cleaning, installed a covert camera and obtained evidence to prove that the employee was working only 7 hours per week and not 12 hours as agreed by contract (STSJ Comunidad Valenciana 2170/2004). In an armed robbery at the premises of the company an employee helped the robbers by opening the door for them, switching off the lights and giving testimony in court in a contradictory way. The evidence provided by covert CCTV was admitted, although the Court did not accept the company's version of the facts (STSJ Madrid 21797/2007).

As for the specific pattern of risk, in 63.6% of cases it was found that there were reasonable grounds for suspicion of a criminal or deviant act committed by an employee that was causing damage to the company.

Surprisingly, in all cases analyzed, the evidence provided from covert CCTV was admitted in Court. However, the evidence was determinant for the purpose in only 61% of cases. As for the way of providing evidence, this was done in the majority of cases as video-graphic evidence (68.2%), while in 22.7% of the cases it was by photographic evidence; only in 4.5% of the cases was a forensic expert exposition; and in the remaining 4.5% there was no reference at all. The STC 186/2000 precedent was formally invoked in 22.7% of cases.

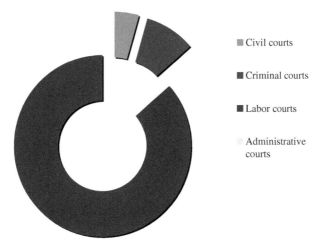

Figure 1. Jurisdictional organ.

Figure 2. Type of worker and extent of dependency in the employment relationship.

Regarding the types of workers, in 77.3% of cases the employee caught by covert CCTV was a dependent employee and in 22.7% was a supervisor (Figure 2). As for the sectors or types of companies, as we can see in Figure 3, the majority were food-sector companies (22.7%), while transportation, industry, storage and service sectors comprised most of the remainder (13–14% each).

Framing data and discussion

The Data have shown that the STC 186/2000 precedent has meant a legitimization of covert practices under certain circumstances in Spain. However, it is also worth noting that employee monitoring, and in particular video surveillance, has become an important means of detection of employee wrongdoing. In that sense, unlawful interference with the right to privacy of employees suspected of wrongdoing may make the evidence produced by the employer null and void in civil and criminal proceedings. The question of hidden employee monitoring will trigger a delicate balance to be struck by judicial authorities. Whereas the case-law in countries such as Belgium or France was first favorable to employees and systematically dismissed evidence obtained in breach of the obligation of transparency, more recent case-law

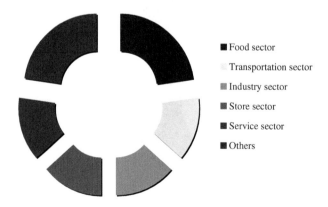

Figure 3. Type of company by sector.

in these countries, in line with the European Court of Human Rights case-law, seems to point towards a change in the balance in favor of employers. Compliance with the right to due process and the possibility given to the employee to contest the accuracy of the evidence produced will in those cases act as a counterweight.[1]

Looking at the evolution of Spanish jurisprudence on covert CCTV in the workplace and all the patterns mentioned above, we can highlight some trends, challenges and limits from legal, ethical and criminological perspectives. What causes and/or correlations may be behind the new trend legitimizing covert CCTV?

Employee theft losses are a good reason

As Read Hayes has put it, asset protection studies indicate the same thing year in and year out: employees account for much, if not most, of a company's losses. Research has shown that as many as 75% of all employees have stolen or otherwise harmed their employer (Hollinger and Clark 1983; Harper 1990). Coffin (2003) reports that employee dishonesty is the fastest growing organizational problem for many companies (Hayes 2008).

However, although the significant amount of money in company losses may trigger business crime prevention and detection strategies, employee theft losses should not justify *in general* certain covert practices. As we will discuss, transparency is required except when the employer has verified a certain pattern of risk that legitimizes covert and exceptional means.

Technology increases the ability to set a watch

Recently, the US Supreme Court ruled in a very timely case[2] that the police violated the Constitution when they placed a Global Positioning System (GPS) tracking device on a suspect's car and monitored its movements for 28 days. A set of overlapping opinions in the case collectively suggests that a majority of the Justices are prepared to apply broad privacy principles to bring the Fourth Amendment's ban on unreasonable searches into the digital age, when law enforcement officials can gather extensive information without ever entering an individual's home or vehicle.

In debating the rationale for the decision Justices were divided, with the majority saying the problem was the placement (or setting) of the device on private property. Moreover five justices also discussed their discomfort with the government's use of or access to various modern technologies, including video surveillance in public places, automatic toll collection systems on highways, devices that allow motorists to signal for roadside assistance, location data from cell phone towers and records kept by online merchants.

As in the case of GPS, technology makes the setting of new covert CCTV systems even more easy and privacy-challenging, especially because surveillance devices may go with the employee wherever he goes. The issue will be more and more pervasive (see von Silva-Tarouca 2011).

Be careful of collateral effects on productivity – a decrease of trust, morale and motivation

From an anthropological approach to the culture of work and the organizational aspects necessary to run an enterprise, a company certainly requires a minimum of trust and a modicum of control (Brisebois 1997; Weckert 2002). The sum of individual efforts needs at the same time certain patterns of coordination, direction and control to provide unity and meaning to individual work within the more general corporate purpose. In this context, confidence and control are two elements equally necessary and interdependent, and "there is no functional alternative to trust" (Brisebois 1997, 16–19). Whereas human dignity will call for relationships based on trust and mutual respect, some complementary monitoring activity might appear necessary to maintain such a relationship. Such monitoring activity takes place because, in practice, a personal relationship based on an expectation of trust has previously been generated. Such attitudes are therefore not contradictory but complementary, being a faithful reflection of the anthropological roots that underpin both the dynamics of trust and the logics of control in the field of business.

Here there is a fundamental contradiction: monitoring comes from a fear, that of being betrayed – thus of mistrust. In this sense, monitoring intervenes and is necessary because the relationship is based on a relative trust. Trust is something that does not come as a given but is built. Only time can ground relationships on trust. Work relationships are too sporadic to rely 100% on trust. They are moreover power relationships and thus the same level of trust cannot exist as, for example, in the case of friendship. Monitoring activities therefore intervene here to compensate for this inherent part of mistrust, so the employer can rest assured that her fundamental assets are protected. This could explain what we say about covert CCTV.

When analyzing CCTV in the workplace, account should be taken of the important shift that has occurred. The contagion of the "society of risks" has led to an increasing "culture of control" with a direct impact on trust as a key factor of work relationships. However, following Weckert (2002), we have to take into account the following:

- While there is a need to create and maintain a climate for trust, there is also a need to minimize opportunities for workplace crime. However, while trust is difficult to build, it is rather fragile and easy to demolish.
- While it might be assumed that electronic monitoring improves productivity and quality, a former study by Stanton and Julian (2002) casts some doubt on this. Based on this study, the greater the use of employers' monitoring and surveillance techniques, the greater the climate of mistrust within the organization.
- There is a high price to pay for a lack of trust. However, it does not follow from this that employee monitoring and surveillance are never justified.
- If trust is robust in a generally trusting workplace environment, it can withstand some monitoring and surveillance and some untoward behavior, but not too much. Once some threshold is reached, trust is lost, and then it is difficult to regain. For a workplace to reach its full potential, trust is important. It is important that further research be conducted to help our understanding of how much monitoring and surveillance workplace trust can withstand.

Is transparency an untouchable barrier?

The reality of employee crime has some fuzzy edges (see Agustina 2010).[3] Those crimes committed against the company suffer, in many cases, from a diffuse character that makes them "invisible crime" without an apparent victim and have a continued performance over time. This imperceptible character thus impedes the drawing of a clear line between *crime* and *irregularities*, at least in terms of the economic effects and impact on the company. This does not prevent continuous addition of small irregularities from actually generating a devastating effect, and sometimes irreparable outcomes. Laureen Snider has aptly described the development of this phenomenon as "theft of time", as it is a continuum that arises from workers' misuse of employer's time (Snider 2001, 105–120).

However, the law should reflect a quest for a harmonious balance between trust and control, as we have just mentioned. The concept of trust is reflected through the general law principle of "good faith" in the execution of contractual obligations. Both the employer and the employee should act in good faith when complying with their rights and obligations. A breach of "good faith" will be acknowledged as an abuse of rights that entitles the counterpart to be restored in their rights.

In this context, workers' participation in the process of designing and implementing security systems strengthens the legitimacy and transparency of actions that could be considered *prima facie* an invasion of privacy. The participation of workers may be active (based on free consent), or merely passive (through information notices). From an ethical standpoint, notice would be enough to prevent an alleged surreptitious surveillance. However, there are two different types of surveillance that could justify an extraordinary non-transparent surveillance: (1) hidden surveillance measures taken for the benefit of employees; and (2) cases that do not directly benefit workers, but are justified to defend the assets of the business or comply with a duty to guarantee no damages that requires the employer to seriously react in a hidden way (e.g. Agustina 2010).

What happens with hidden or transparent monitoring in terms of transparency? Obviously any control measure implemented without the knowledge of workers (although it is for their own benefit) demands *prima facie* some requirements from the company to be justified. Consider, for example, the installation of hidden cameras to curb the escalation of petty theft in units of the company. The fight against petty thefts whose victims are the employees may justify hidden measures of surveillance to detect the offenders. However, if one accepts the legitimacy of a hidden control in this case, it is difficult to bring serious objections when it is the employer's property threatened by a number of thefts and employees are *not* directly threatened. Of course, in either case, the legitimacy of the non-transparent nature of the surveillance is necessarily restricted in time: once the worker had been identified, the employer would have to make a formal communication to workers if cameras were to in operation. In this case, the purpose would clearly be preventive and *not* reactive in the sense that the employer was not attempting to solve an on-going case.

In this regard, the communication strategies for designing and implementing monitoring systems should be able to resolve the ethical dilemma raised and provide solutions that harmonize positions (see Alder 1998). In fact, the adequacy of the system in delimitating privacy at work is closely related to proper communication. Thus, the ethical-communicative element within control policies becomes a crucial factor in the rating of a particular ethical business practice. Only a policy manifestly unreasonable, even if properly communicated, would be unethical. In this sense, the abusive nature of such problems and the circumstances of each company lead us to different methods and solutions, tailored to the specific case (made-to-measure).

The translation of the need for proper communication policies into the legal framework should be found in the principles of fairness and the introduction of consultation procedures. Concretely, in terms of employee monitoring, this will imply an obligation to inform and consult employees before the introduction, modification or evaluation of any system likely to be used for monitoring/surveillance of workers. Employee monitoring is usually subject to prior notice to employees through the employment regulations, internal memoranda or *ad hoc* notices form attached to the work contract. This requirement echoes that of fairness (and thus of good faith) in the relationship. The data protection framework explicitly introduces such principle. In words of Bygrave (2002), "the notion of fairness further implies that the processing of personal data be transparent for the data subject". In that sense, the Data Protection Directive (95/46/EC Directive) stipulates that "if the processing of data is fair, the data subject must be in a position to learn of the existence of a processing operation and; where data are collected from him, must be given accurate and full information, bearing in mind the circumstances of the collection" (Recital 38). Fairness is closely linked to the reasonable expectations of the data subject (here the employee) that are generated by the data processing activity (see Kuczerawy and Coudert 2011). Employees, when informed about the purpose and means of the video surveillance processing, can thus adjust their conduct accordingly.

However, owing to the inherently imbalanced nature of the relationship, such notice should usually be completed by prior information and/or consultation of employees' representatives. The role of employees' representatives will be to counterbalance any potential abuse of monitoring powers by the employer, and thus a failure of self-restraint, suggesting and negotiating solutions that are more balanced and less intrusive to employees' fundamental rights. Employees are generally not considered to be in a position where they can give a free consent or to freely negotiate the conditions of such monitoring. As stressed by the European Commission,[4] the effectiveness of employees' protection relies to a great extent on collective rights regarding involvement of workers' representatives. These rights supplement the worker's individual rights to information and participation. In that sense, the European Commission, building on the International Labour Organization Code of Conduct on the protection of workers' data (1996) referred to the need to include within the European framework information and consultation of workers' representatives with a view to reaching an agreement before the introduction or modification of (1) automated systems permitting the processing of workers' personal data, (2) any technical devices that can be used for monitoring/surveillance of workers at workplace and (3) questionnaires as well as tests of any form including medical, genetic and personality tests used at the stage of recruitment or during employment. The involvement of workers' representatives is finally advocated as regards evaluation concerning the aforementioned issues.

Transparency appears to be a pivotal element in the fairness of video surveillance implementation. However, as we have seen, covert surveillance cases lead us to modulate that formal principle based on a strict analysis of the context and the exceptional need to protect other rights/interests apart from privacy. The issue will then lie in the proportionality rationale, which probably needs a clearer construction. Our understanding is that some proportionate reasons will diminish the general standards of transparency. However, what does proportionality mean in practice?

In this context, one of the tangible concepts, which may help us in clarifying the rationale behind covert surveillance cases, is the so-called "(un)observable observer".

When being subjected to CCTV in an operation zone, workers should at least know that they are being watched and therefore legitimately bring their conduct out of the scope of the third person's observation. As noted by von Hirsch (2000), the "observable observer" allows people (to the extent that what others might think affects them) to adjust their behavior when they know they are being watched: a worker who, while doing manual work, has the habit of talking out loud about intimate things to his dead wife, does not do so when others are passing near him.

According to von Hirsch, hidden observation presents problems of legitimacy for two reasons. First, the behavior of the person is being recorded without any warning and they may reasonably think that they are free from observation by others, when in reality they are not. In addition, it can produce an intimidating effect on people (*a chilling effect*); once people are aware that checks are carried out covertly, there can be generated a general feeling of control when circulating in public spaces. Allowing general covert surveillance can seriously compromise not only the privacy of individuals, but also the whole system of freedoms and civil rights. In the more specific context of work relationships, it also increases the impact on trust.

However, employees do *not* have the right of being protected from an unobservable observer when there is an expectation of wrongdoing. Legitimate expectations of privacy (which entail a right to transparency) should hence be given up before a legitimate reason such as a serious suspicion of crime. The employee, when committing a crime, breaches trust and loses their legitimate expectation of privacy.

Proportionality and a given pattern of risk – ex ante and ex post facto perspectives

From a general viewpoint, ethical principles that limit surveillance within a company should take into account the *object* of the action, the *aim* pursued and the given *circumstances* (Alder 1998). The intrinsic moral/ethical goodness or badness (object) could be mitigated or aggravated based on the aim and the circumstances – the object being something unchangeable. However, consequentialist conceptions of ethics would only seek to qualify the action according to the consequences that come with the action. That is, some sacrifices could be justified by higher individual and social benefits that the action entails. According to this theory, in the overall balance, taking into account all the consequences of a specific company policy, the negative effects of a particular action could be minimized or justified.

Among all of the instruments of management, monitoring the activity of workers should be assessed in a "neutral" manner – at least as far as possible. The object of such action is not conditional on the effects or the intrinsically positive or negative ethical analysis. As argued by Alder (1998), the complexity of the debate over electronic monitoring of employees should not be simplistically resolved (*win–lose approach*), as if the object of action was, in absolute terms, not inherently good or bad.

In that regard, the balance of arguments and considerations should be provided jointly: (1) teleological arguments in terms that highlight the positive effects of surveillance on the grounds that monitoring benefits organizations, customers and society in general; and (2) arguments in terms of ethics by which limits are imposed, understanding that monitoring dehumanizes workers, invades privacy of individuals, increases levels of stress, damages health and reduces the quality of life at work. As it seems logical, most arguments in favor of electronic monitoring of employees have a background based on the utilitarian argument.

According to the consequentialist perspective, organizational practices (among which is electronic surveillance) are evaluated in terms of maximizing profits (*the greatest balance of good over evil*) – understanding profits in a broad sense. Thus, any negative consequence has to be balanced with all the outcomes derived from the action or policy. In this sense, the ability to assess the effectiveness and competitiveness through the data provided by electronic monitoring becomes essential to compete in a global market. It has been shown repeatedly in this regard that effective monitoring leads to increased productivity, improving service quality and lowering costs. Companies that have installed a control system for phone calls can expect at least a 10% reduction in telephone bills and simultaneously a productivity increase. Listening to phone calls is also an effective tool in the training of operators and ensures the quality of service. For all the reasons before mentioned, Alder finally concludes that, although it is difficult, if not impossible, to empirically assess the overall results that electronic monitoring has on the whole society, practices that benefit businesses should also benefit indirectly the whole society.

The law should determine, by setting up a series of principles and objective standards, the boundary line that cannot be crossed by the employer. At the same time, some room has to be left for the autonomy of the employer's control and privacy policies in order to make feasible what best suits the needs of the company and the particularities of workers. Ultimately it is the employer who should be self-limited, as the way she solves the tension between privacy and control will directly affect the productivity of the company.

In this sense, proportionality is crucial: the existence of an end (if legitimate) justifies the adoption of some (legitimate) means. That is, the means–end relationship means that (1) without a lawful final cause no means is justified, and (2) only certain means are legitimate, those that are proportionate to the end appointed. The scope and intensity of monitoring should be adapted to the purpose, searching from the various techniques available for those that minimize the erosion of privacy.

However, such analysis of adequacy should be performed on a case-by-case basis. That is, depending on the examination of the factual situation and level of threats and dangers of specific business environment, the intensity and extent of the covert surveillance measures to be taken could be justifiable. Only the specific purpose here and now that drives the installation of cameras and the circumstances of the case should define the proper criteria for the analysis of proportionality of the measures to be taken.

Conclusions

The results of covert employee monitoring can only provide evidence in legal actions and become a risk-management tool under exceptional circumstances. Case law in Spain goes towards the legitimization of covert monitoring whenever the employer can justify a legitimate interest, but one wonders whether this trend may be abused, encouraged by new technological developments. Whereas it is not possible to compel the employer to give prior notice to the employee in the cases we have analyzed for obvious reasons, alternative measures could be looked for. In this sense, the rationale used in cases of access to lockers of employees suspected of wrongdoing could be somehow applied.

Questions therefore arise in terms of accountability of the employer in a context of hidden employee monitoring. The verification of a previous objective pattern of risk involving criminal behavior should be crucial for ceding the general principles of respecting privacy. The central argument would be the exceptional case an employer may find when there is a continuous situation and the only way to stop it is by discovering the wrongdoers in action. This has to do with the criminological characteristics of employee crime (Agustina 2010, 336).

However, an accountability check of the employer assessment of the above-mentioned "objective pattern of risk" cannot only be left to Courts, but should also be integrated to internal processes of companies in order to ensure good faith in working relationships (as the employer can check the compliance with employees' obligations, employees should be given some means to do the same through consultative procedures). Whereas information to the Workers' Council may not be the best way to install such control, owing to inherent risks of "leaks", we can envision that independent parties such as data protection officers, where they exist, could play such a moderating role. In that sense, the proposal from the European Commission to make the appointment of data protection officers mandatory for public authorities, controllers who employ more than 250 people and whose core activity consists of individual monitoring, can only be applauded.[5] If approved, this proposal would foster stronger accountability mechanisms, which take into account the specificities of each data processing environment.

Looking at the court decisions sample analyzed, a more detailed rationale is needed for legal and decision-making analyses in this field. This paper has shown some ways to put into tangible terms the abstract concepts developed within the framework of the well-known proportionality principle.

Notes

1. European Commission, Second stage consultation of social partners on the protection of workers' personal data, 2002.
2. See *New York Times*, 24 January 2012, at http://www.nytimes.com/2012/01/24/us/police-use-of-gps-is-ruled-unconstitutional.html?_r=1&scp=1&sq=police%20gps&st=cse
3. Employee crime can be difficult to detect, but detection is crucial for companies. Employees can cause devastating effect with just a click of a mouse (Porter and Griffaton 2003).
4. European Commission, Second stage consultation of social partners on the protection of workers' personal data, 2002.
5. European Commission, Article 32 of the Proposal for a regulation of the European Parliament and of the Council on the protection of individuals with regard to the processing of personal data and on the free movement of such data (General Data Protection regulation), COM (2012) 11 final, Brussels, 25 January 2012.

References

Agustina, J. R. 2010. "Risks in Preventing Crime by Limiting Employees' Privacy: Analysing Employers' Duties and Faculties Versus Privacy Interests in Controlling E-mails at the Workplace." *International Journal of Private Law* 3 (4): 333–357.
Alder, G. S. 1998. "Ethical Issues in Electronic Performance Monitoring: A Consideration of Deontological and Consequentialist Perspectives." *Journal of Business Ethics* 17: 729–743.
Ball, K. 2010. "Workplace Surveillance: An overview." *Labor History* 51 (1): 87–106.
Brisebois, R. 1997. "Sobre la confianza." *Cuadernos Empresa y Humanismo* 65: 3–65.
Bygrave, L. 2002. *Data Protection Law: Approaching its Rationale, Logic and Limits.* Hague, London, New York: Kluwer Law International.

Clarke, R. V. 1995. "Situational Crime Prevention." *Crime and Justice* 9: 91–150.

Coffin, B. 2003, August. "Breaking the Silence on White Collar Crime." *Risk Management* 60 (9): 40.

Felson, M., and R. Clarke. 1998. *Opportunity Makes the Thief. Practical Theory for Crime Prevention.* Police Research Series, Paper 98, edited by Barry Webb, 1–36. London: Home Office, Policing and Reducing Crime Unit Research, Development and Statistics Directorate.

Gill, M. 2006. "CCTV: Is it Effective?" In *The Handbook of Security*, edited by M. Gill, 438–461. London: Palgrave Macmillan.

Harper, D. 1990. "Spotlight Abuse – Save Profits." *Industrial Distribution* 79: 47–51.

Hayes, R. 2008. *Strategies to Detect and Prevent Workplace Dishonesty.* Connecting Research in Security to Practice (CRISP). Alexandria, VA: ASIS International Foundation, Inc.

Hollinger, R. C., and J. P. Clark. 1983. *Theft by Employees.* Lexington, MA: Lexington Books.

Kuczerawy, A., and F. Coudert. 2011. "Privacy Settings in Social Networking Sites: Is It Fair?" In *Privacy and Identity Management for Life 6th IFIP AICT 352*, edited by S. Fischer-Hübner, P. Duquenoy, M. Hansen, R. Leenes and G. Zhang, 231–243. Berlin: Springer.

Lasprogata, G., N. King, and S. Pillay. 2004. "Regulation of Electronic Employee Monitoring: Identifying Fundamental Principles of Employee Privacy through a Comparative Study of Data Privacy Legislation in the European Union, United States and Canada." *Stanford Technology Law Review* 4: 1–46.

Liberty, 2007. *Overlooked: Surveillance and Personal Privacy in Modern Britain.* Accessed September 15, 2011. http://www.liberty-human-rights.org.uk/issues/3-privacy/pdfs/liberty-privacy-report.pdf

Marx, G. 2005. "Seeing Hazily (but not Darkly) Through the Lens: Some Recent Empirical Studies of Surveillance Technologies." *Law and Social Inquiry*, Spring 30 (2): 339–399.

McCahill, M., and C. Norris. 1999. "Watching the Workers: Crime, CCTV and the Workplace." In *Invisible Crimes. Their Victims and their Regulation*, edited by P. Davis, P. Francis and V. R. Jupp, 208–231. London: Palgrave Macmillan.

Norris, C. 2009. *A Review of the Increased Use of CCTV and Video Surveillance for Crime Prevention Purposes in Europe.* Study P.E. 419.588.

Nouwt, S., B. de Vries, and C. Prins. 2005. *Reasonable Expectations of Privacy? Eleven Country Reports on Camera Surveillance and Workplace Privacy.* The Netherlands: Universiteit van Tilburg.

Porter, W. G., II, and M. C. Griffaton. 2003. "Between the Devil and the Deep Blue Sea: Monitoring the Electronic Workplace." *Defense Counsel Journal*, January, 70: 65.

Ratcliffe, J. 2006. *Video Surveillance of Public Places.* Problem-Oriented Guides for Police Response Guides, Series Guide No. 4. US Department of Justice, Office of Community Oriented Policing Services.

Snider, L. 2001. "Crimes against Capital: Discovering Theft of Time." *Social Justice* 28 (3): 105–120.

Stanton, J. M., and A. L. Julian. 2002. "The Impact of Electronic Monitoring on Quality and Quantity of Performance." *Computers in Human Behavior* 18: 85–101.

Tridimas, T. 2006. *The General Principles of EU Law.* 2nd ed., 139. Oxford: Oxford EC Law Library.

von Hirsch, A. 2000. "The Ethics of Public Television Surveillance and CCTV." In *Ethical and Social Perspectives on Situational Crime Prevention*, edited by A. von Hirsch, D. Garland and A. Wakefield, 59–76. London: Hart.

von Silva-Tarouca, L. B. 2011. *Setting the Watch. Privacy and the Ethics of CCTV Surveillance.* Oxford: Hart.

Weckert, J. 2002. "Trust, Corruption, and Surveillance in the Electronic Workplace." In *Human Choice and Computers: Issues of Choice and Quality of Life in the Information Society, 17th IFIP World Computer Congress,* Montreal, edited by K. Brunnstein and J. Berleur, 109–120. Boston, MA: Kluwer.

Welsh, B. C., D. P. Farrington, and S. J. O'Dell. 2010. *Effectiveness of Public Area Surveillance for Crime Prevention: Security Guards, Place Managers and Defensible Space.* Stockholm, Sweden: Swedish National Council for Crime Prevention, Information and Publications.

Evaluating privacy impact assessments

Kush Wadhwa and Rowena Rodrigues

Trilateral Research & Consulting, London, UK

> Privacy impact assessments (PIAs) are emerging as an important privacy management tool for public and private sector organizations. However, a key concern of PIA policy and practice is the lack of follow-up and means to evaluate its conduct at different levels, particularly so that different stakeholders can make sense of PIA practice as evidenced in PIA reports. This article first outlines the evaluation criteria established under the EU Privacy Impact Assessment Framework project and attempts to find the best means of extending their application to help assess PIAs, based on good practice.

Introduction

Privacy impact assessment (PIA) is emerging as a critical privacy management tool for public and private sector organizations alike. Several countries mandate their use for public sector projects to deploy new systems, and the proposed data protection regulation from the European Commission mandates PIAs where sensitive data are processed. The European Parliament Resolution on a comprehensive approach on personal data protection in the European Union (European Parliament 2011) "Considers it essential to make Privacy Impact Assessments mandatory in order to identify privacy risks, foresee problems, and bring forward proactive solutions". The Privacy and Data Protection Impact Assessment Framework for Radio Frequency Identification (RFID) applications (European Commission 2011) also illustrates the importance of PIAs in privacy and data protection.

According to Wright and De Hert (2012a), a PIA is a "methodology for assessing the impacts on privacy of a project, policy, program, service, product or other initiative and, in consultation with stakeholders, for taking remedial actions as necessary in order to avoid or minimise negative impacts". PIAs, which are contemporary privacy protection mechanisms, surfaced initially and developed from the mid-1990s in Australia, Canada, Hong Kong, New Zealand and the United States. They have their roots in environmental impact assessments and social impact assessments (SIAs).[1]

The UK Information Commissioner's PIA Handbook (2009) outlines why PIAs are required:

- to identify and manage privacy risks (signifying good governance and good business practice);
- to avoid unnecessary costs (of problems discovered at later stages);
- to avoid inadequate solutions implemented at later stages;
- to avoid loss of trust and reputation by addressing concerns;
- to inform the organization's communications strategy (through understanding perspectives); and
- to meet and exceed legal requirements.

Currently, in locations where PIAs are required, or required under particular circumstances – Australia (Office of the Privacy Commissioner 2010), Canada (Treasury Board of Canada Secretariat 2002), Ireland (Health Information and Quality Authority 2010), New Zealand (Office of the Privacy Commissioner 2007), UK (ICO 2009), United States (Office of Management and Budget 2003) – they are intended to be performed early in the project life cycle so that there is an opportunity to have an impact on the implementation of the project, enhancing privacy and reducing the myriad privacy and data protection related risks. However, although standards for the PIA process have taken root at the government level in some countries, their uptake is not uniform, nor is the actual implementation of the process.

One of the key concerns of PIA policy and practice is the lack of follow-up and means to evaluate its conduct at different levels, particularly for different stakeholders to make sense of PIA practice, as evidenced in PIA reports. This article first outlines the evaluation criteria established under the EU Privacy Impact Assessment Framework (PIAF) project[2] and tries to find the best means of extending their application to help assess PIAs, based on good practice.

The PIAF criteria

Background

The PIAF report (Wright et al. 2011), reviewing the PIA methodologies of seven countries, presented the most complete compendium and analysis of PIA policies and practices yet compiled and published. It reviewed and compared PIA methodologies (policies and practice) in Australia, Canada, Hong Kong, Ireland, New Zealand, the UK and the United States. The study uniquely presented and applied a list of criteria for evaluating the effectiveness of PIAs based on PIA reports.

Statement of the criteria

The PIAF report used the following criteria to measure the effectiveness of PIA reports and, through them, to assess the overall PIA process:

(1) early initiation of PIA;
(2) identification of who conducted the PIA;
(3) description of the project to be assessed, its purpose and any relevant contextual information;

PRIVACY AND SECURITY IN THE DIGITAL AGE

  (4) mapping of information flows (i.e. how information is to be collected, used, stored, secured and distributed and to whom and how long the data is to be retained);

  (5) checking of the project's compliance against relevant legislation;

  (6) identification of the risks to or impacts on privacy;

  (7) identification of solutions or options for avoiding or mitigating the risks;

  (8) recommendations;

  (9) publication;

(10) stakeholder consultation.

These criteria guided the evaluation of 10 PIA reports (two reports per country) from Australia, Canada, New Zealand, UK and the United States. The analysis revealed that the PIA reports commonly contained, in some form and to varying degree, the following: a project description, a statement of purpose, relevant contextual information, identification of privacy risks and impacts, and identification of solutions or options for risk avoidance and mitigation. In relation to the other evaluation criteria, there were significant differences in practice. PIA reports vary as much between jurisdictions as within.

Employing the criteria for PIA enhancement

This paper intends to take the criteria and lessons learnt from the first PIAF report and seeks to apply them to help enhance the effectiveness of PIAs.

The need to enhance PIAs

PIAs, as currently conducted, although a positive development, have a lot of room for improvement. Wright (2011) states

> Making privacy impact assessments mandatory is not the end of the story. Audits and metrics are needed to make sure that PIAs are actually carried out and properly so and to determine if improvements to the process can be made.

One of the more severe criticisms is that PIAs often resemble no more than window dressing or represent "another ritualised hurdle to jump over" (Marx 2012). In this respect, one of the significant challenges is the lack of post-PIA evaluation. The effectiveness of PIAs needs enhancement. This can happen only if the PIA process is dynamic and PIAs have some sort of follow-up. One means of achieving this is by evaluating PIA reports. However, currently, there is no easy, standardized means of conducting this evaluation. To achieve this end, we propose a PIA Evaluation and Grading System (PEGS).

Related work

There are a number of PIA risk assessment tools, which help organizations assess privacy risks and facilitate the PIA process (note, as compared with PEGS, which evaluates the actual PIA process post facto, although it may be also employed to guide the PIA process). Among privacy risk assessment tools are: the AIPCA/CICA privacy risk assessment tool; the Security and Privacy Impact Assessment (SPIA)

Tool of the University of Pennsylvania; the GS1 RFID Privacy Impact Assessment (PIA) tool; the Vienna University intelligentPIA tool for RFID applications; and the Privacy Impact Assessment Tool for Cloud Computing proposed by Tancock, Pearson, and Charlesworth (2010). We briefly summarize (for full and up to date information, the reader should refer to the respective websites) and then assess each of these tools against the following yardsticks:

Operational usability	Is the tool itself simple and intuitive to use with a minimum need for training?
Contextual usability	Are the questions asked/examined when using the tool easy to understand with a minimum need for training?
Applicability	Is the tool equally applicable to a broad range of applications and technologies?
Thoroughness	Are the questions examined in using the tool broad/sufficiently detailed in scope?
Accessibility	Is the tool easy to find on the Internet? Is it costly to gain access to the tool?
Privacy focus	Is the tool focused only on privacy-related issues, or is it a subset of a larger evaluation process?

We next analyze the different PIA tools, outline their advantages and disadvantages and comparatively illustrate how they fare against the above listed yardsticks.

The AICPA/CICA privacy risk assessment tool

The Privacy Risk Assessment Tool developed by the American Institute of Certified Public Accountants (AICPA) and the Canadian Institute of Chartered Accountants (CICA) aims to help organizations perform privacy risk assessments. The tool, designed in spreadsheet form, is based on the 10 principles and 73 criteria contained in the AICPA/CICA Generally Accepted Privacy Principles (GAPP).[3] The tool comprises a Scoring Input Template (10 separate files with unique names to accommodate 10 assessors) and a Scoring Summary. This model uses a three-point scoring system (i.e. 2 = low risk, 5 = medium risk or 8 = high risk) to evaluate the GAPP criteria against the following: likelihood of control failure, business impact and mitigation/prevention costs. After the scoring is complete in the individual assessment templates, the tool summarizes the scoring for all GAPP criteria under the relevant GAPP principle and graphically illustrates the results.

The AICPA/CICA Privacy risk assessment tool is comprehensive and has the ability to accommodate multiple assessors. The accompanying guidance is good. It is a good initial assessment measure. However, although intended to be user-friendly and intuitive, it is slightly complex. It is designed for use by "privacy professionals who have a good understanding of privacy laws and regulations, privacy best practices, business operations, risk assessments, and current privacy practices and controls within the organization" (AICPA/CICA 2010).

The SPIA risk assessment tool of the University of Pennsylvania

The University of Pennsylvania has a SPIA risk assessment tool (also in spreadsheet format) for its schools/centers that "offers suggestions for what safeguards may be appropriate in order to mitigate the most common threats and provides a reporting template to help synthesize the learning and proposed changes that result from the SPIA process" (University of Pennsylvania 2007). The tool is designed as a "roadmap to help organizations identify areas of risk and select appropriate strategies and timeframes to mitigate those risks" (University of Pennsylvania 2007). The tool enables organizations to take probability rankings and threat consequences and automatically score risk into categories of "High", "Significant", "Moderate" or "Low". Threats (security and privacy) are broadly identified. In its scoring of threats, the tool employs a six-point scale:

0 = Threat does not apply to this application/database.
1 = Rare – the event would only occur under exceptional circumstances.
2 = Unlikely – the event could occur at some time, but probably will not.
3 = Moderate – the event should occur at some time.
4 = Likely – the event will probably occur at some time.
5 = Almost certain – the event is expected to occur in most circumstances.

After the current probability of each threat is scored against each application/database, the current potential consequences of the threat being realized are evaluated on a scale of 0–5 (0 = threat is not applicable, 1 = insignificant, 2 = minor, 3 = moderate, 4 = major, 5 = disastrous). The results then help in the re-evaluation of each threat, this time taking into account planned risk mitigation safeguards to obtain a revised risk value.

The SPIA risk assessment tool is versatile and adaptable enough to include additional threats. It is designed to be objective. On the downside, the tool is rather overwhelming at first glance, consisting of several disconnected spreadsheets to drive the assessment process. Moreover, the SPIA tool looks at security risks as well as privacy impacts, requiring much broader analysis and risking the possibility of losing sight of privacy issues amongst the myriad security issues that may need to be addressed.

GS1 EPC/RFID PIA tool

GS1, an international association dedicated to the design and implementation of supply chain standards, has implemented a PIA tool for use in the design phase of RFID applications. The tool aims to help large and small-scale enterprises evaluate whether an application meets "consumer privacy expectations" (GS1 2012). Similar to the SPIA tool, it uses spreadsheets with detailed screens. The tool, according to GS1, is designed to

- rapidly perform *a comprehensive assessment of privacy risks* of any new EPC/RFID implementation within your company;
- identify *privacy controls* to be built in at the early stages of the specification or development process;
- comply with the *European Commission's RFID Recommendation* and best practices on privacy and data protection, including the EPC Privacy Guidelines.

The GS1 EPC/RFID PIA tool has three parts: the Assessment Setup; the Initial Assessment; and the Detailed Assessment. In the Assessment Setup, the RFID

Application Operator provides general information about the organization, the RFID application and its operations. The Initial Assessment determines the need for a detailed PIA and to complete this, the RFID Application Operator answers four questions that determine whether the assessment is complete or whether level 1, 2 or 3 detailed assessments are required. The detailed assessment addresses predefined specific risks, the likelihood of their occurrence, the impacts of the risk and risk mitigation controls. A series of questions helps judge the levels of privacy risks (likelihood and impact) and controls. The effectiveness of controls is evaluated on a scale of 1–5 (least to most). A control rated less than 3 calls for detailed explanation of the control.

The Impact is multiplied by the Likelihood and subtracted from the Controls to attain the scoring. If a risk has no controls, a penalty is assigned. The scores of all controls are tallied and totalled against each risk, and scores from all risks are totalled and tallied for the overall assessment score.

The GS1 EPC/RFID PIA Tool has its advantages. It is available in two Excel versions (2007/2010 and 2003). GS1 recommends that generated reports are made available to data protection authorities and thus advocates the principle of oversight. The tool is simpler than the AICPA/CICA and the SPIA tools. One of its disadvantages is that it is incompatible with older computers. The tool is tailored to RFID implementations rather than a broader range of systems and applications that could be privacy intrusive.

The intelligentPIA tool for RFID applications

The intelligentPIA (iPIA) tool is a PIA for RFID applications.[4] The tool, designed by the Institute for Management Information Systems, Vienna University, is an open source application written in PHP and JavaScript using jQuery UI.

There are eight steps in the assessment process: characterization of the application; initial analysis; definition of privacy targets; evaluation of degree of protection demand for each privacy target; identification of threats; identification and recommendation of controls; consolidated view of controls; assessment and documentation of residual risks.

First, the RFID application must be characterized. This involves describing "scenarios and use cases, systems and system components, interfaces, data flows and involved parties", and identifies "the scope, boundaries and assets (resources and information) that need to be protected" (Institute for Management Information Systems 2012). Next, an initial analysis (based on a decision tree taken from the official RFID PIA framework) follows to determine the type of PIA required; that is, full-scale, small-scale or none. The tool outlines privacy targets next. The tool lists 16 privacy targets derived from the European Data Protection Directive 95/46/EC (European Parliament and the Council 1995.). Additional targets may be added, as required. The tool then evaluates the degree of protection for each target based on three demand categories: low, scored at 1; medium scored at 2; and high, scored 3.

The next step is identifying threats for each privacy target. The tool lists 60 such likely threats and enables the inclusion of additional threats. Controls, either of technical (access control mechanisms, authentication mechanisms and encryption methods) or non-technical nature (management and operational controls as well as accountability measures, policies or operational procedures and information measures taken with regard to data subjects), are to be identified next. The intelligentPIA tool offers 27 controls, with provision to add additional controls. The tool presents the identified controls in a consolidated, tabular form, allowing one to judge if the control has been implemented, planned or unplanned. The last step is an assessment and documentation of residual risks. The tool generates the report as a PDF file.

The intelligentPIA tool is a simple and systematic tool. However, its scope is limited to RFID applications.

The privacy impact assessment tool for cloud computing proposed by Tancock, Pearson and Charlesworth

Tancock, Pearson, and Charlesworth (2010) present a design for a PIA tool for cloud computing. The tool (not implemented at time of this assessment) addresses "the complexity of privacy compliance requirements for organizations (both public and private sector), by highlighting privacy risks and compliance issues for individuals within the organization who are not experts in privacy and security, so they can identify solutions in a given situation" (Tancock, Pearson, and Charlesworth 2010). The tool is expected to work as a "service accessible from a web browser, using a Software as a Service (SaaS) model, in which external organizations can ask to use that service (probably on a pay-per-use basis), in order to generate PIA reports based on their input, as required. In this model, security mechanisms are used in order to protect any confidential information that is transferred or stored by the service" (Tancock, Pearson, and Charlesworth 2010).

This PIA tool is envisaged as a decision support system (DSS) with a knowledge base (KB) maintained on an ongoing basis by privacy experts. The tool comprises templated questions and answers based on different contexts. After use, a detailed output report is generated including the risk levels of privacy domains.

The advantages are that the tool is designed for use in both full-scale and small-scale PIA. It is thus efficiently tailored. Its web-based nature eliminates the cumbersomeness of using spreadsheet-based solutions. It can be run at different stages of a project's development process lifetime, each time producing output and advice appropriate to that stage.

The disadvantages are that this tool might prove expensive to implement and maintain. It is tailored to the cloud computing environment and is not adapted for broader application.

Table 1 lists the advantages and disadvantages of how the tools fare comparatively against the yardsticks outlined previously. The analysis shows that most of the reviewed existing PIA tools are spreadsheet-based applications, which are quick, easy to access, easily available and affordable. Web-based applications, on the other hand, require more resources, and are more expensive to deploy and maintain.

The PIA tools examined in Table 1 all facilitate the PIA process. They help organizations comply with privacy requirements. The output of these PIA tools are PIA reports that embody an organization's approach to privacy for a specific application. None of the tools, however, provides a means of evaluating this output. This evaluation, we suggest, is an important element of accountability.

Table 1. Comparative analysis of selected PIA tools.

		The AICPA/CICA privacy risk assessment tool	The SPIA tool	GS1 EPC/RFID PIA Tool	iPIA tool	Cloud computing PIA tool
Operational usability	Is the tool itself simple and intuitive to use with a minimum need for training?	No	No	Yes	Yes	Intention expressed
Contextual usability	Are the questions asked/ criteria examined when using the tool easy to understand with a minimum need for training?	No	No	Yes	Yes	Unclear (tool not deployed)
Applicability	Is the tool equally applicable to a broad range of applications and technologies?	Yes	Yes	No	No	No
Thoroughness	Are the questions examined in using the tool broad/ sufficiently detailed in scope?	Yes	Yes	Yes	Yes	Unclear (tool not deployed)
Accessibility	Is the tool easy to find on the Internet? Is it costly to gain access to the tool?	Easy to find/free	Easy to find/free	Easy to find/free	Easy to find/free	Not implemented yet (intended to be a pay for access tool)
Privacy focus	Is the tool focused only on privacy-related issues, or is it a subset of a larger evaluation process?	Privacy focussed	Security and privacy focussed	Privacy focussed	Privacy focussed	Privacy focussed

PEGS

How might we add value to the work of these PIA tools? We examine this next and propose one specific means of doing so. The PIA Evaluation and Grading System, or PEGS, is primarily a PIA enhancement tool designed to make the PIA process more effective through the provision of a useful and efficient means of evaluating and grading PIA reports. This evaluation and grading has both a broad and specific purpose. The broad and overarching purpose is to enhance the effectiveness of PIAs with the help of the rich experience of PIA policy and practice as evidenced in the PIAF project. The specific, underlying purpose is to provide a practical means of determining how a PIA fares in relation to other PIAs.

PIA guidance has been criticized for being too burdensome, cumbersome and contrary to the "KISS principle, that is, keep it simple stupid" (Flaherty 2000). Therefore, we need a simple, convenient means of embodying the PIA evaluation criteria identified before. At the same time, we need to expand the criteria to include the whole gamut of the PIA process. Moreover, the evaluation means need to be adaptable, given that PIA requirements are not universal or might change with the passage of time (i.e. to maintain the dynamism of PIAs).

Checklists are a widely used methodology in environmental (Morgan 1999), health (Kemm, Parry, and Palmer 2004) and regulatory impact assessment (Radaelli and de Francesco 2010). Checklists are popular in privacy assessment too, as evident in the cases of Australia (Office of the Privacy Commissioner 2006), Canada (OCIPO 2010; Treasury Board of Canada Secretariat 2002) and the UK (ICO 2009). Scriven (2007) describes the usefulness of checklists in detail, and stresses how they are "easier for the lay stakeholder to understand and validate", reduce the "influence of the halo effect, i.e. the tendency to allow the presence of some highly valued feature to over influence one's judgment of merit" and economically incorporate "huge amounts of specific knowledge".

The PIA evaluation criteria are, therefore, first presented as a checklist (see Table 2), which is based upon several key sources, including the work of the PIAF project (Wright et al. 2011), as well as published research on the state of the art (Wright 2012) and on best practices (Wright and Paul 2012b) in privacy impact assessments.

The checklist avoids the problem of "dumbing down" the PIA process by providing a column on "scope for improvement" – it is more than a "mere box-ticking" exercise (Wright 2011).

Once our criteria are recognized, we apply weighting in line with the relative importance of each criterion. The weighting in Table 3 illustrates the high-level criteria (not the full detailed criteria in Table 2), and is based on the lessons learnt from the PIAF Report.

The criteria have been awarded weights in three categories – 1, 2 and 3, with 1 representing the least important and 3 representing the most important. The weighting is a subjective indication based on lessons learnt from the PIAF project.

We next determine the least important and the most important criteria. The basic criteria carry a weight of 1 (i.e. clarification of early initiation, identification of who conducted the PIA and publication). These criteria are in the nature of contextual details of the PIA process. While it is good practice to provide these elements, their absence is not such as to make the PIA a failure or useless. While these details are important, their absence can typically be addressed by contacting the PIA

PRIVACY AND SECURITY IN THE DIGITAL AGE

Table 2.   PIA evaluation checklist

PIA evaluation criteria	Yes	No	Scope for improvement
Early initiation	Tick where		
Was the PIA initiated early enough to influence project design?	applicable		
Does the PIA report state whether the PIA was initiated early?			
Does the PIA report outline how the PIA influenced project design?			
Conduct of PIA			
Does the PIA report identify who conducted the PIA and their expertise/experience in PIA conduct?			
Does the PIA report identify when the PIA was conducted?			
Does the PIA report identify its target audience (i.e. for whom it was prepared)?			
Does the PIA report provide contact details for further information in relation to the PIA?			
Does the PIA outline/document the PIA process?			
Does the PIA report outline what guidance it followed?			
Does the PIA report state who approves it?			
Does the PIA outline a post-implementation review/audit process?			
Project description, purpose and relevant contextual information			
Does the report sufficiently describe the project being assessed and provide relevant contextual information (such as business rationale, project scope, or relevant social, economic or technological considerations)?			
Does the report describe the purpose and objectives of the project?			
Information flow mapping			
Does the PIA map the information flows? (i.e. how information is to be collected, used, stored, secured and distributed and to whom and how long the data is to be retained)			
Legislative compliance checks			
Has all law relevant to the project been surveyed and the project checked for compliance?			
Identification of privacy risks and impacts[a]			
Does the PIA assess risks to data privacy?			
Does the PIA assess and indicate the level of risks to privacy of the person?			
Does the PIA assess and indicate the level of risks to personal behavior?			
Does the PIA assess and indicate the level of risks to personal communications?			

PRIVACY AND SECURITY IN THE DIGITAL AGE

Table 2 (*Continued*)

PIA evaluation criteria	Yes	No	Scope for improvement
Does the PIA caution project managers and assessors that the risks listed in the PIA guide are not exhaustive?			
Does the PIA report make provisions to address issues arising out of future changes to the project?			
Does the PIA analyze the public acceptability of the scheme and its applications?			
Identification of solutions/options for risk avoidance, mitigation			
Does the PIA identify means/solutions for risk avoidance?			
Does the PIA identify means/solutions for risk mitigation?			
Recommendations			
Does the PIA make recommendations?			
Are the recommendations accompanied by timeframes for implementation?			
Have the recommendations been implemented/ incorporated in project design?			
Publication			
Has the PIA report/executive summary/edited version been published?			
If the PIA report is not published, has an explanation to that effect been made public?			
Identification of stakeholder consultation			
Have stakeholders been consulted as part of the PIA procss? Was the consultation adequate (representative of relevant interests)?			
Did stakeholders have the chance to provide information and comment?			
Does the PIA report document the stakeholder involvement and engagement process?			
Does the PIA incorporate stakeholder engagement throughout the project life cycle?			

Note: the term project may refer to a project, product, service, program or other initiative, including legislation and policy.
[a] The present article deliberately does not define and limit here what comes within the scope of the terms data privacy, privacy of the person, personal behavior or personal communications. We suggest the organizations refer to appropriate national PIA guidance for this information.

sponsoring organization; however, in some cases, their absence is an early warning in identifying other flaws in the process or the outcomes.

As one can see in Table 3, criteria that are important, carrying a weight of 2 (i.e. project description, information flow mapping, legislative compliance checks and identification of stakeholder consultation), are process-focussed. The elements these criteria look at must be included in the PIA report; their absence would make the PIA report ineffective and deficient, as they are a reflection of the thoroughness of the PIA process. These elements reflect how deeply the PIA process investigated the system, how

Table 3. Evaluation criteria and weights.

Evaluation criteria	Criteria weight
Clarification of early initiation	1
Identification of who conducted PIA	1
Project description, purpose and relevant contextual information	2
Information flow mapping	2
Legislative compliance checks	2
Identification of privacy risks and impacts	3
Identification of solutions/options for risk avoidance, mitigation	3
Recommendations	3
Publication	1
Identification of stakeholder consultation	2
Score	20

thoroughly it applied evaluation criteria, and how well it engaged stakeholders in the process.

Finally, the essential criteria carry a weight of 3 (i.e. identification of privacy risks and impacts, identification of solutions for avoidance, mitigation of privacy risks and recommendations). A PIA report that fails to incorporate these elements would be a failure, as these are the intended core outcomes of the PIA process itself.

To help determine whether the criteria are met or not and make an initial evaluation, we outline a detailed, descriptive checklist[5] with questions to help gage whether the criterion is fulfilled. The checklist was based on the best elements of PIA policy and practice identified in the PIAF Report and as outlined by Wright in his paper on the state of the art in PIA (Wright 2012).

The next task was to assign values – here too, we use a three-point scale with 2 indicating non-compliance, 5 part compliance and 8 indicating an effective level of compliance. In this respect, PEGS follows the AICPA/CICA scoring model.

Grades were assigned based on the following scores. Scores in the range of 141–160 are indicative of an excellent or effective PIA and graded as A+. Scores in the range of 121–140 are indicative of a very good PIA and graded as A−. Scores in the range of 101–120 are good and graded as B+. Scores between 81–100 are acceptable and graded as B−. Scores in the range of 61–80 are indicative of inadequate PIAs and are graded as C. Scores between 40 and 60 are indicative of poor PIAs and graded as D.

An excellent PIA is one that fulfills all the criteria to an exceptionally high degree. One must note, however, that there is no such thing as a perfect PIA, and yet efforts must be made to achieve that ideal. A very good PIA is one that is of high quality and yet not effective enough to meet the A+ standard. A good PIA is one that fulfills the necessary criteria and can be seen to be effective in most parts. It might be lacking in minor details. An acceptable PIA is one that fulfills the major requirements, yet leaves much to be desired. An inadequate PIA is one in need of major revision, and a failure refers to a PIA that fails to meet all or a substantial number of criteria.

The PEGS system and process

How does PEGS work in practice? Like some privacy risk assessment tools, PEGS could be embedded in a spreadsheet. PEGS could also be implemented as a web-based application.

There are two basic steps in the PEGS process. The first involves completing the checklist and the second involves the scoring and grade allocation.

Test driving PEGS

We now examine how PEGS could work in practice with the help of two case studies.

Case study 1 – the New Zealand Google street view PIA

As a first step, we analyze the New Zealand Google Street View PIA against the established evaluation criteria. Google Street View is a Google Maps application used to explore places through 360°, street-level imagery from public spaces and privately owned properties (that have permitted such access; Google Inc 2012). Google collects this imagery from its vehicles driving past locations, processes it and subsequently puts it online. Google Street View launched in New Zealand in 2008.

During the course of filming in New Zealand, Google's Street View vehicles collected open Wi-Fi information[6] (easily accessible Wi-Fi information such as network names) and payload information (the actual contents of communications) from unsecured Wi-Fi networks. When the revelation surfaced (New Zealand Privacy Commissioner 2010a), investigations followed. The Privacy Commissioner conducted an inquiry (New Zealand Privacy Commissioner 2010b), and eventually imposed several requirements on Google. One of the key requirements was to conduct a PIA on "new Street View data collection activities in New Zealand", and provide a copy of the PIA to the Privacy Commissioner.[7]

Google Inc. published an 11-page PIA report on its website (Google Inc 2011). We now examine it against the PEGS evaluation criteria.

The Google Street View PIA report does not satisfy the first criterion. The PIA was not initiated early enough to influence project design. The PIA is an example of a retrofit and was initiated as the result of obligation imposed upon Google by the New Zealand Privacy Commissioner after an inquiry into Street View's unauthorized collection of Wi-Fi information.

In relation to the second criterion (identification of who conducted the PIA), the Google Street View PIA report does not identify who conducted the PIA or name the author(s) of the PIA report.

Next, we checked compliance of the Street View PIA report to the third criterion – project description, purpose and relevant contextual information. The PIA report sets out a project description (overall aims, scope, extent and links of Street View to other projects). However, this is rather too brief (the project description minus the section on links to other projects is only a page long). Therefore, we find in favor of a part compliance score.

The Google Street View PIA partly fulfilled the fourth criterion, information flow mapping. Although information flows were mapped, their description left much to be desired (the New Zealand PIA Handbook recommends that flow charts clearly depict the manner of data collection, internal circulation and dissemination beyond the organization; Office of the Privacy Commissioner 2007).

Next, we analyzed compliance with the fifth criterion, legislative compliance checking. The PIA report mentions a "comprehensive legal assessment" (Google Inc 2011). However, the report does not explain how Google Street View complies specifically with relevant legislation, particularly the Information Privacy Principles of the Privacy Act 1993. The Report states that Google transfers Street View data outside New Zealand, yet does not (as the NZ PIA Handbook recommends) recognize any special sensitivities in this respect.

The Google Street View PIA Report highlights the privacy risks and impacts as necessitated by the sixth criterion (identification of privacy risks and impacts) and thus received a positive grading. The report covers the following privacy risks: generation of images incidentally featuring passers-by and information such as vehicle license plates; images triggering privacy-related sensitivities based on person–place association and images featuring sensitive locales (e.g. women's refuges; Google Inc 2011). However, when evaluated against the detailed checklist, it failed to demonstrate effective risk assessment; that is, there was no indication of risk levels, just an overall broad picture. The PIA report does not caution that the risks listed in the PIA are not exhaustive, or analyze the public acceptability of the scheme and its applications (this was particularly relevant given that Street View practices were found to be violating data protection law). Therefore, the report receives a part compliance score for this criterion.

The Google Street View PIA report fares well in relation to the seventh criterion – identification of solutions/options for risk avoidance, mitigation. The report outlines the measures taken to address privacy concerns prior to publication of images on Google Maps and Google Earth, for example, training of Street View vehicle operators prior to and during collection of imagery as well as guidance on appropriate route planning; disclosure to the public of collection activities (transparency about Street View's collection activities); outreach and education to sensitive groups regarding the launch and flagging process (which refers to the process whereby Street View users flag inappropriate content or sensitive imagery for Google to review and remove), delayed publication of images and automatic blurring of faces and license plates prior to the posting of imagery; and making available the "Report a Problem" tool (which enables members of the public to report a problem such as privacy concerns that they might have with the images Google captures). The tool is available as a link at the bottom left of a Street View image.

The Google Street View PIA report fulfills the eighth criterion in part – it includes recommendations in the PIA report (Google Inc 2011), but it does not provide any timeframes for implementation/incorporation in project design.

The Google Street View PIA report also fulfills the publication criterion. It is one of the few private company-based PIA reports in the public domain. It thus sets a good example for other companies in this respect.

In relation to the tenth criterion, stakeholder consultation, the Google Street View PIA report makes no mention of consultation whatsoever, especially of those stakeholders most affected by the implementation of Street View's collection and use of their personal information.

Case study 2 – the Australian EVI PIA

Our second case study concerns the Australian PIA on the proposal to amend the Anti-Money Laundering and Counter-Terrorism Financing Act 2006 (AML/CTF Act) to authorize the use and disclosure of credit reporting information for electronic identity verification (EV; hereinafter the Australian EVI PIA; IIS 2009).

The Australian EVI PIA states that the PIA was initiated early enough to enable it to influence the proposal (ALRC 2008). Thus, it fulfills the first criterion. The

Australian EVI PIA report also identifies who conducted the PIA; that is, it was conducted by Information Integrity Solutions Pty Ltd for the Attorney-General's Department.

The Australian EVI PIA report adequately describes the proposal and its purpose, and provides relevant contextual information as required by the third criterion. It also complies with the information flow-mapping criterion. It contains a tabular analysis of the potential information flows (collection, use, disclosure, retention) if the use of credit information (CRI) for EV is authorized.

In relation to legislative compliance checks, the next criterion, the Australian EVI PIA report provides an overview of credit reporting and applicable regulations and how it would comply with those. Thus, it can be said to fulfill this criterion.

The next criterion is identification of privacy risks and impacts. This is the most detailed part of the Australian EVI PIA Report. The report identifies various privacy risks if identity information held by credit reporting databases were made available for electronic identity verification under the Anti-Money Laundering and Counter-Terrorism Financing Act 2006. It also considers the consequences of rejection/failure including black lists or other EV harms and the impact on individual control over their personal information.

An effective PIA should identify solutions and options for risk avoidance and/ or mitigation. The Australian EVI PIA Report contains recommendations (based on a "layered defence approach") categorized into two parts – recommendations relating to the law and recommendations relating to governance (including transparency and accountability). Thus, it scores well on both these criteria. A full score is awarded on the publication criterion, as the Australian EVI PIA report is publicly available.

It is only in relation to stakeholder consultation that the report falls short, according to our criteria. Although key stakeholders including privacy and consumer advocates, reporting entities and their representatives, CRAs and other EV service providers were consulted, the consultation seems to have been rather limited, given the scope of the proposal. Only 10 stakeholders were consulted, and only 10 submitted comments on the draft PIA report. Therefore, a part fulfillment of the last criterion is adduced.

Comparative analysis of the case studies. Based on the above analysis, we derive the results in Table 4, shown as a scorecard.

The New Zealand Google Street View PIA receives a score of 94, which makes it an acceptable PIA. The Australian EVI PIA on the other hand, scores very well and receives an A+ grade.

Role, functions and utility. PEGS is useful for a number of reasons.

First, evaluating a PIA will help increase transparency in PIAs. Second, it will help improve the quality of the PIAs. The PIAF Report recommended that PIA reports be quality assured by senior management (Wright et al. 2011). The PIA grading tool could facilitate this task. Third, it will increase accountability, particularly in the implementation of PIA recommendations. PEGS thus presents a viable, accessible and simple means of evaluating the rigor of an organization's PIA process.

Like the Privacy and Data Protection Impact Assessment Framework for RFID Applications, PEGS is sufficiently general in its approach – this means that it is dynamic enough for application across technologies and sectors.

PEGS could be used at different levels: by organizations to self-evaluate PIAs and meet and exceed legal requirements; by national data protection authorities to review

Table 4. Comparative chart with results of PIA report evaluation under PEGS.

Evaluation criteria for PIA reports	Criteria weight	Google streetview [NZ] compliance	Google streetview [NZ] Score	EVI [AU] compliance	EVI [AU] score
Clarification of early initiation	1	2	2	8	8
Identification of who conducted PIA	1	2	2	8	8
Project description, purpose and relevant contextual information	2	5	10	8	16
Information flow mapping	2	5	10	8	16
Legislative compliance checks	2	2	4	8	16
Identification of privacy risks and impacts	3	5	15	8	24
Identification of solutions/options for risk avoidance, mitigation	3	8	24	8	24
Recommendations	3	5	15	8	24
Publication	1	8	8	8	8
Identification of stakeholder consultation	2	2	4	5	10
Score	20	44	94	77	154
Grade			B −		A +

Grade chart			Score assignment	
Excellent	A +	141–160	Complies fully	8
Very good	A −	121–140	Complies in part	5
Good	B +	101–120	Does not comply	2
Acceptable	B −	81–100		
Inadequate/requires improvement	C	61–80		
Failure	D	40–60		

PIAs conducted by organizations; and by third-party certification bodies and other stakeholders who need a user friendly means of determining in an objective manner whether a PIA is effective. Companies can use the PIA checklist/grading system as a self-evaluation mechanism to determine if their PIAs have been effective, or need to be improved and revised. It may even serve as a check on whether an organization is meeting its PIA commitments and as a reminder to the organization of its privacy commitments.

National data protection authorities or privacy commissioners can use the checklist/grading system to review and monitor PIA conduct and implementation. They can then provide feedback to the organizations in relation to the elements of the criteria found lacking. When data protection breaches occur, PEGS could be used to evaluate whether an organization had satisfied the requirements of PIA best practice, as outlined in the evaluation criteria. As such, the results of PEGS could become evidence of an organization's having exercised due diligence in relation to its PIA process.

PEGS is also useful to third party certification bodies. PEGS is based on international PIA best practice and presents a good model for third-party certification bodies to assess PIAs and determine privacy and data protection adequacy. Other stakeholders such as academics and the public could use either the checklist or the grading system to assess the quality of an organization's PIA. There is little to no guidance on how a layperson might assess a PIA. PEGS could fill that lacuna.

At this stage, we must also note the limitations of PEGS. Despite its intent to be as objective as possible, it is likely that some subjectivity owing to evaluator perceptions might creep into a PEGS analysis. Using two or more independent persons/parties to conduct the PEGS evaluation could address this.

Conclusion

This paper presents a model for PIA evaluation and grading that will enhance the effectiveness of PIAs. In this, it advances the state of the art in PIAs. However, to work effectively and to enhance the social value of PIAs, PEGS must be visible to stakeholders. This could be actualized by a central PIA registry[8] (or an online PIA portal like www.AllRovi.com) that uses PEGS to score and grade PIAs. This can be a "window of access" to PIAs and essential to build a PIA culture where organizations at different levels can learn from each other's experience and improve PIAs (Wright et al. 2011). This is all the more relevant given the policy thrust towards making PIAs more publicly accessible.

If the PEGS model is adopted, it will deliver further structure and standardization to the PIA process. The PEGS will be a means of informing and communicating with stakeholders about PIAs and their relative effectiveness. It will facilitate a judgment on a PIA's efficiency potential (i.e. how good a PIA is and to what it should aspire, and how future PIAs could be enhanced). One of the main reasons that companies conduct PIAs is to build trust – the PEGS results may be used to promote and advertise the achievement of that goal.

Acknowledgments

The authors prepared this paper on behalf of Trilateral Research & Consulting LLP based on research undertaken in the Privacy Impact Assessment Framework for Data Protection and

Privacy Rights (PIAF) project, funded by the European Commission's Directorate-General Justice under grant agreement number JUST/2010/FRAC/AG/1137-30-CE-0377117/00-70.

Notes

1. SIAs aim at ensuring that developments or planned interventions maximize the benefits and minimize the costs of those developments, including, especially, costs borne by the community.
2. The project began in January 2011 and its final deliverable was published in December 2012. Its objective was "encourage the EC and Member States to adopt a progressive privacy impact assessment policy as a means of addressing needs and challenges related to the processing of personal data"; PIAF. http://piafproject.eu/
3. Generally Accepted Privacy Principles is a comprehensive privacy framework, developed under a joint effort of the CICA and the AICPA, designed to assist organizations create effective privacy programs addressing privacy risks and business opportunities. Available from: http://www.cica.ca/service-and-products/privacy/gen-accepted-privacy-principles/index. aspx
4. The tool's scope extends to RFID tags and readers as well as all connected backend systems and the communication infrastructure.
5. The checklist is not only useful post-PIA. It can serve as an effective aide memoir in preparing for a PIA, during the conduct of a PIA, preparing a PIA report or reviewing a draft version. The checklist is to be read in conjunction with PIA Guidance. This will help eliminate the "tunnel vision" problem associated with checklists. See Bisset (2001).
6. According to the New Zealand Privacy Commissioner, open Wi-Fi information includes the device's unique identity number, a user's network name, information on whether the network is secured or unsecured and signal strength.
7. Other requirements include making a statement about its Street View Wi-Fi collection activities on its official New Zealand blog (including an apology and acknowledgment of better transparency), improving privacy and information security training for all of its employees, improving review processes for its products and services and deleting payload data. These undertakings are in force for three years from 14 December 2010.
8. An example is the OIPC (2013).

References

AICPA/CICA. 2010. *AICPA/CICA Privacy Risk Assessment Tool User Guide.* 4. http://www. aicpa.org/interestareas/informationtechnology/resources/privacy/privacyservices/downloadable documents/10684-378_privacy%20risk%20assessment%20tool.pdf

ALRC (Australian Law Reform Commission) 2008. *For Your Information: Australian Privacy Law and Practice. ALRC Report 108. Recommendation 57–4.* Accessed on November 21, 2012. http://www.alrc.gov.au/publications/57.%20Use%20and%20Disclosure%20of%20Credit% 20Reporting%20Information/use-and-disclosure

Bisset, R. 2001. "Developments in EIA Methods." In *Environmental Impact Assessment: Theory and Practice*, edited by P Wathern, 47–61. London: Routledge.

European Commission. 2011. *Privacy and Data Protection Impact Assessment Framework for Radio Frequency Identification (RFID) Applications of 12 January 2011.* http://ec.europa.eu/ information_society/policy/rfid/pia/index_en.htm

European Parliament. 2011. *Resolution on a Comprehensive Approach on Personal Data Protection in the European Union, 2011/2025(INI).* Strasbourg: European Parliament.

European Parliament and the Council. 1995. "Directive 95/46/EC of 24 October 1995 on the Protection of Individuals with Regard to the Processing of Personal Data on the Free Movement of Such Data." *Official Journal* L281: 31–50.

Flaherty, David H. 2000. *Privacy Impact Assessments: An Essential Tool for Data Protection. A Presentation to a Plenary Session on New Technologies, Security and Freedom. 22nd Annual Meeting of Privacy and Data Protection Officials.* Venice. 27–30. http://aspe.hhs.gov/ datacncl/flaherty.htm

Google Inc. 2011. *Google Street View New Zealand Privacy Impact Assessment*. Accessed November 21, 2012. http://google-au.blogspot.in/2011/05/privacy-impact-assessment-for-street.html

Google Inc. 2012. *Using Street View*. Accessed November 21, 2012. http://maps.google.co.nz/intl/en/help/maps/streetview/learn/using-street-view.html

GS1 (2012). GS1 EPC/RFID. *Privacy Impact Assessment Tool*, http://www.gs1.org/epcglobal/pia

Health Information and Quality Authority. 2010. *Guidance on Privacy Impact Assessment in Health and Social Care*. Dublin. http://www.hiqa.ie/resource-centre/professionals

ICO (Information Commissioner's Office) 2009. *Privacy Impact Assessment Handbook. Version 2.0*. Cheshire. http://www.ico.gov.uk/for_organisations/topic_specific_guides/pia_handbook.aspx

IIS (Information Integrity Solutions Pty Ltd) 2009. *Privacy Impact Assessment Report, Electronically Verifying Identity Under the Anti-Money Laundering and Counter-Terrorism Financing Act 2006 Using Credit Reporting Information. For the Attorney General's Department*. http://www.ag.gov.au/www/agd/rwpattach.nsf/VAP/(8AB0BDE05570AAD0EF9C283AA8F533E3)~Privacy+Impact+Assessment+Report+-+Electronically+verifying+identity+under+the+AML+CTF+Act+using+credit+reporting+information.pdf

Institute for Management Information Systems. 2012. *Intelligent PIA User Manual*. Vienna University. Accessed November 21, 2012. http://www.wu.ac.at/ec/research/user_manual.pdf

Kemm, John, Jayne Parry, and Stephen Palmer, eds. 2004. *Health impact assessment: Concepts, Theory, Techniques and Applications*. Oxford: OUP.

Marx, Gary T. 2012. "Foreword: Privacy is Not Quite Like the Weather." In *Privacy Impact Assessment*, edited by David Wright and Paul de Hert, v–xiv. Springer: Dordrecht.

Morgan, Richard K. 1999. *Environmental Impact Assessment: A Methodological Approach*. United Kingdom: Chapman and Hall.

New Zealand Privacy Commissioner. 2010a. *Google and Wi-Fi Information Collection*. http://privacy.org.nz/media-release-google-and-wi-fi-information-collection/

New Zealand Privacy Commissioner. 2010b. *Google's Collection of WiFi Information During Street View Filming. Executive Summary*. http://privacy.org.nz/google-s-collection-of-wifi-information-during-street-view-filming/

OCIPO (Office of the Chief Information and Privacy Officer). 2010. *Privacy Impact Assessment Guide for the Ontario Public Service*. Canada: Queen's Printer for Ontario.

Office of Management and Budget. 2003. *OMB Guidance for Implementing the Privacy Provisions of the E-Government Act of 2002*. Washington, DC. http://www.whitehouse.gov/omb/memoranda/m03-22.html

Office of the Privacy Commissioner. 2006. *Privacy Impact Assessment Guide*. Sydney, NSW. http://www.privacy.gov.au.

Office of the Privacy Commissioner. 2007. *Privacy Impact Assessment Handbook*. Auckland: Office of the Privacy Commissioner.

Office of the Privacy Commissioner. 2010. *Privacy Impact Assessment Guide*. Sydney, NSW. http://www.oaic.gov.au/publications/guidelines.html#privacy_guidelines

OIPC (Office of the Information and Privacy Commissioner of Alberta). 2013. *PIA Registry*. http://www.oipc.ab.ca/pages/PIAs/Registry.aspx

Radaelli, Claudio, and Fabrizio de Francesco. 2010. "Regulatory Impact Assessment." In *The Oxford Handbook of Regulation*, edited by R. Baldwin, M. Cave and M. Lodge, 279–301. Oxford: OUP.

Scriven, Michael. 2007. *The Logic and Methodology of Checklists*. http://www.wmich.edu/evalctr/archive_checklists/papers/logic&methodology_dec07.pdf.

Tancock, David, Siani Pearson, and, Andrew Charlesworth. 2010. "A Privacy Impact Assessment Tool for Cloud Computing." *Second IEEE International Conference on Cloud Computing*. Indiana University: USA, 667–676.

Treasury Board of Canada Secretariat. 2002. *Privacy Impact Assessment Guidelines: A Framework to Manage Privacy Risks*. Ottawa. http://www.tbs-sct.gc.ca/pubs_pol/ciopubs/pia-pefr/paipg-pefrld1-eng.asp.

University of Pennsylvania. 2007. *Introduction to the SPIA Program*. http://www.upenn.edu/computing/security/spia/spia_step_by_step.pdf

Wright, David. 2011. "Should Privacy Impact Assessments be Mandatory?" *Communications of the ACM* 54 (8). http://cacm.acm.org/magazines/2011/8. doi:10.1145/1978542.1978568

Wright, David. 2012. "The State of the Art in Privacy Impact Assessment." *Computer Law & Security Review* 28 (1): 54–61. doi:10.1016/j.clsr.2011.11.007.

Wright, David, and Paul De Hert. 2012a. "Introduction to Privacy Impact Assessment." In *Privacy Impact Assessment*, edited by David Wright and Paul De Hert, 3–32. Springer: Dordrecht.

Wright, David, and Paul De Hert. 2012b. "Findings and Recommendations." In *Privacy Impact Assessment*, edited by David Wright and Paul De Hert, 445–481. Dordrecht: Springer.

Wright, David, Kush Wadhwa, Paul De Hert, and Dariusz Kloza, eds, 21 September 2011. *PIAF: A Privacy Impact Assessment Framework for data protection and privacy rights*, Deliverable D1, Prepared for the European Commission Directorate General Justice, JLS/ 2009-2010/DAP/AG. First deliverable (D1) prepared for the European Commission's Directorate-General Justice under Grant Agreement Number JUST/2010/FRAC/AG/ 1137- 30-CE-0377117/00-70.

Regulating privacy enhancing technologies: seizing the opportunity of the future European Data Protection Framework

Gerrit Hornung

Chair of Public Law, IT Law and Legal Informatics, University of Passau, Innstr. 39, D-94032 Passau, Germany

> Privacy enhancing technologies (PETs) have long been discussed as a valuable tool to protect personal data. Apart from some examples at the Member State level (such as Germany), however, there is still a lack of legal instruments and requirements concerning these technical instruments. Without mandatory requirements and legal incentives, there is the risk that developers and controllers will not provide PETs to their respective customers. As European data protection law will undergo substantial changes in the coming years, there is now an opportunity to implement at least basic legal instruments to supplement and foster the development and implementation of PETs. This opportunity must not be missed: given the long reform cycles of European data protection law, any regulation that does not end up being part of the current reform may have to wait for another 15–20 years for the next opportunity.

Introduction

After years of stagnation, reforming the European Union law of data protection has gained new momentum. The 2012 proposals of the Commission are likely to supersede the respective discussions at Member State level. In the case of Germany, several alterations to the Federal Data Protection Act were made in response to the so-called data protection scandals of 2008.[1] After more than 10 years of debate on substantial reforms of the national data protection law,[2] another impetus has been provided by a position paper published by the national conference of the German Data Protection Supervisory Authorities (Konferenz der Datenschutzbeauftragten des Bundes und der Länder 2010).

The paper contains essential ideas and proposals for revising the current legal framework in Germany, for example, concerning the possibility of technology-based data protection. However, it remains silent as to the requirements and limitations established by European law with regard to a national modernization of data protection law – which appears somewhat remarkable, taking into account the detailed regulations established by the EU Data Protection Directive of 24 October 1995.[3]

In November 2010 the European Commission took action and published a communication on "A comprehensive approach on personal data protection in the

European Union" (European Commission 2010). It formed the basis of the three documents, released by the Commission in January 2012, namely the comprehensive Communication on the overall reform proposal (European Commission 2012a) and the drafts of a General Data Protection Regulation (GDPR, European Commission 2012b), as well as a Directive for data protection in the fields of criminal offences and criminal penalties (European Commission 2012c).[4]

The GDPR is supposed to replace the current Data Protection Directive and would form the sole legal basis for data protection in most data processing areas. Hence, it is of utmost importance that the current reform takes into consideration important findings of practical and scientific work on data protection law which were not available 15 years ago. One of the key areas is the concept of data protection through technology, which provides considerable opportunities for data protection. The concept is included in the GDPR, but unfortunately falls short of its potential.

The concept of data protection through technology or "privacy by design"

The basic idea of technology-based data protection has been discussed for years: if threats to and violations of data protection are factually impossible, then there is no need to impose legal restrictions. Such traditional restrictions encompass obligations and prohibitions, but because of their very nature require a case of breach. Ideally, they become obsolete in the case of – effectively organized – data protection through technology. By executing normative requirements as to the use of personal data, law and technology complement each other and form an "alliance" (Roßnagel 2001) to protect personal rights.

This alliance becomes increasingly important as traditional regulatory instruments are often unable to cope with the challenges of modern data processing. Being tied to the conventional enforcement authorities of national states, such regulatory instruments lose their effectiveness in the disembodied social sphere of the internet (Roßnagel 1997a). Under these circumstances, effective data protection cannot be guaranteed by legal instruments alone, but requires the availability of privacy enhancing technologies (PETs).[5] As data processing becomes pervasive, such technologies are increasingly important. In ubiquitous computing (see e.g., Fleisch and Mattern 2005; Mattern 2007; Roßnagel, Sommerlatte, and Winand 2008), it appears to be a misperception to believe that it is possible to secure personal privacy and informational self-determination without technologies that provide anonymity, pseudonymity and transparency in a user-controlled way without hampering the user in his or her everyday business (Kühling 2007; Roßnagel 2007; Hildebrandt 2008; Hornung 2010a). Concepts for such technologies are already available. They could provide privacy-friendly default settings, implement the opt-in principle, allow for personalized user-settings for routine data processing, carry out automatic deleting routines, support personalized identity management or transmit, organize and document declarations of consent that the data subject has issued for a group of data processes.

Furthermore, enforcing technology-based data processing rules allows for the precautionary principle to gain further importance for data protection (Roßnagel 2011). In the future, it will become increasingly relevant since the growing amount of data processed increases the risk that data subjects become identifiable where initially identification was not possible (Roßnagel and Scholz 2000, 728 et seq.; Roßnagel 2007, 185 et seq.). This leads to problems under the current data protection regime, which does not cover the data in the beginning (see Art. 3 of the Data Protection Directive, which restricts the scope to personal data in the meaning of Art. 2 lit. a) and lays down neither requirements nor legal consequences for data becoming personal at a later date. Assuming that further storage or other processing of data becomes unlawful the moment it becomes identifiable (Roßnagel and Scholz 2000, 730), controllers still face the severe problem of identifying that precise moment. Technological instruments can help to entirely avoid data that is "not yet" attributable to a specific person or to subject it to a regime of processing regulations.

Target groups of the concept

Data protection through technology can only be successful if PETs are both available and implemented in practice. These requirements are complementary: the conception, research and development of PETs will have no bearing on the protection of personal rights if these technologies are not being used in practice – whether this is due to a lack of publicity, usability or affordability or alternatively because powerful market actors prevent them from being widely distributed. Vice versa, even the greatest willingness among market actors and private persons to use these technologies will be futile in the absence of fundamental research and practical implementation.

This conclusion suggests that any concept for data protection through technology needs to have two sets of target groups: producers of the respective technologies (for the actual availability of technology) and users, that is, controllers and processors (for the practical application). Both target groups depend on criteria for the development and application of privacy-friendly technology. At this point, the law comes into play and receives particular importance since future-oriented criteria for the design of technology can be derived from it (Roßnagel 1993, 2011, 54 et seq.). At the same time, the law provides opportunities to create incentives and conditions for the use of such technology.

As experience shows, market forces are not a sufficient impetus for the development and spreading of PETs. There are various reasons for this. Technology is often designed according to functional requirements. However, enhancing privacy is, from a technical point of view, a non-functional requirement *per se*. The intrinsic (and legitimate) aim of producers and users is the maximization of profit. In this field, data protection could become relevant as long as there is demand on the market. On the other hand, in the absence of such demand it may quickly become a mere cost driver or end up being irrelevant in the design process because it neither causes nor reduces costs.

On that account, it is crucial to emphasize the idea of product responsibility when targeting producers. Laws can assist in doing so and have an impact in several respects:

- The first is by providing extrinsic incentives, such as binding requirements and restrictions or liability regulations.
- The second is by exerting influence on intrinsic goals, that is, stimulation of the market for PETs using data protection audits or quality seals (see Roßnagel 1997b, 2000, 2003a, 2010; Bäumler 2001, 2002, 2004).
- The third is by establishing guidelines for the participation of scholars and practitioners in interdisciplinary research developing methods for privacy enhancing design of new technologies.[6] Apart from legal experts, such research

should also bring together other experts from a wide range of areas relevant to the topic, for example, computer science, organization and management science, economics and political science. In this area, funding institutions can use their influence when awarding research grants by taking into account or even requiring that issues of data protection are dealt with in the course of researching new information technology (European Data Protection Supervisor 2008). In recent years there has been a desirable tendency among funding institutions towards incorporating such criteria into their processes.

The practical application constitutes an even more significant problem. In fact, PETs are available in many cases, partly because of the intrinsic motivation of technical research scientists developing, for example, concepts and solutions for particular components: encryption and signature routines, systems for anonymization and pseudonymization, methods for a user-centric identity management, the possibility of privacy enhancing default-settings or anonymous payment procedures. In addition to that, there are concepts for entire applications, such as location-based services (e.g. Ranke 2004; Jandt 2008; Schnabel 2009). However, users face considerable inhibitions to actually make use of the available technology. In that context, the law can serve as a catalyst through the incentive mechanisms mentioned above. Apart from that, there are additional instruments that can be used especially for controllers and processors. One example is legislation creating transparency duties in cases of so-called "personal data breaches" (e.g. Art. 4 (3) of the amended Directive 2002/58/EC on privacy and electronic communications) that are intended to urge users to take effective measures ensuring data protection (Gabel 2009; Eckhardt and Schmitz 2010; Hanloser 2010; Hornung 2010b). The Commission has proposed such an instrument in Articles 31 and 32 GDPR.

Presumably, those measures can only have an impact if they are implemented on a European, or even on a global level. Considering the course of technological development, especially regarding the internet, one could get the impression that companies such as Apple, Google or Facebook are the key protagonists when it comes to determining standards for processing personal data. This holds true for new applications such as cloud computing as well: the standards providers such as Amazon and Google set in this field raise data protection issues that have so far only partly been covered by research but at any rate will hardly cause infrastructural decisions to be revised once these decisions have been made. That bears the danger of globally operating corporations establishing factual rules, as was historically the case with the medieval *lex mercatoria*, the customary law of merchants. Prospectively, such a customary law of the digital sphere, a *lex mercatoria digitalis* of some sort (Hornung 2010c), could prove to be more relevant than national regulatory efforts – simply because large (and typically US) corporations with hundreds of millions of users create their own rules.

To counterbalance this development, it is necessary to understand the use of PETs as a socio-technological system and to take on an actor-centred perspective: instead of focusing on the outcome of the development process, that is, the specific technology (where it regularly turns out to be impossible to predict what it will or should be like), emphasis should be placed on guidelines and incentives for the behaviour of protagonists and the organization of development processes. Influencing these processes and raising awareness for the impacts of technological decisions could then be more effective than specific requirements for single technologies.

Regulatory instruments: the status quo

When examining the regulatory instruments for data protection through technology *de lege lata*, it appears appropriate to distinguish between substantial requirements for technology itself and procedural requirements for the process of developing and applying technology. Both can be established on a European as well as on a Member State level, albeit to a different extent. For the latter, Germany serves as a useful example.

Since 1997, the German data protection law has contained provisions that provide for the selection and design of data processing systems in accordance with the principles of data avoidance and data minimization. After a first introduction specifically for the area of telecommunication and media services by the identical § 3 (4) Teledienstedatenschutzgesetz 1997 and § 12 (5) Mediendienstestaatsvertrag 1997,[7] a general provision was created as part of the Federal Data Protection Act in the course of the 2001 amendment,[8] which was later extended in 2009 to include requirements for the collection, processing and use of personal data. In its current wording,[9] the amended § 3a of the Federal Data Protection Act covers two groups of protagonists and three steps: the provision is directed at producers (first step: design of systems) and users (i.e. controllers and processors in the second and third steps: choice of systems and application) and demands that they adhere to the principles of data minimization, particularly anonymization and pseudonymization.

When discussing issues of data protection, § 3a of the Federal Data Protection Act is often used as a supporting argument for establishing rules of conduct for responsible bodies. It is used in both data authorities applying it in practice and in scientific publications (dealing with it theoretically). In these publications, it has been argued whether the provision establishes a real statutory duty.[10] In so far as the provision proscribes mandatory minimum requirements for the design, selection and application of technology, such duty can be identified. However, legally the provision is somewhat ineffective, as a violation neither leads to the unlawfulness of the resulting data processing nor results in any other legal consequences such as claims by the data subjects, possibilities for supervisory measures or administrative offences. Thus it remains a case of "soft law". It also appears that so far there is no empirical research on the practical impact of § 3a of the Federal Data Protection Act (on the economic opportunities of PETs see London Economics 2010).

On the procedural side – which could promote the implementation of the norm – legal provisions are still missing on the federal German level. The adoption of an act of parliament on a data protection audit, as announced in 1997 by § 17 Mediendienstestaatsvertrag and in 2001 by § 9a of the Federal Data Protection Act, failed finally in the course of the 2009 reform after the drafts had evoked unanimous criticism among experts (Roßnagel 2010, 274 et seq.). On the contrary, there are also success stories in Germany: in Schleswig-Holstein, the responsible data protection authority (Unabhängiges Landeszentrum für Datenschutz, ULD) awards a quality seal based on the Land's data protection audit regulation to IT products that are in conformity with data protection requirements according to accredited experts (Bäumler 2002, 2004; Schläger 2004). The opportunity has been seized by a number of producers of a wide range of products.[11] It has certainly been promoted by the fact that, according to § (2) of Schleswig-Holstein's Data Protection Act, the state administration shall preferably use products that comply with the regulations on data protection and data security as established by the procedure prescribed by the data protection audit regulation. A similar provision exists in Nordrhein-Westfalen, however, without an audit regulated by state law. Another less successful example can be found in Bremen (Holst 2004). In 2007 and 2008 the Schleswig-Holstein auditing formed the nucleus of the "European Privacy Seal (EuroPriSe)", which also includes several partners from other EU Member States (Meissner 2008).

Beyond this project, funded by the European Commission, there are currently neither procedural nor substantial regulations on a European level as to data protection through technology. It is possible to establish a relation between § 3a of the German Federal Data Protection Act and the provisions of the Data Protection Directive, for instance in regards to the principle of necessity (Art. 6 (1) lit. c of the Directive; see Brühann 2003, para. 30; Bizer 2006, para. 32; Scholz 2011, para. 17). However, the German provision aims further as it constitutes a rule of preference for the design and selection of data processing systems and even requires the data controller to reconsider the purpose of processing in accordance with the data minimization principle (Roßnagel, Garstka, and Pfitzmann 2001, 101 et seq.; Bizer 2006, para. 2; Scholz 2011, para. 34; Roßnagel 2011, 44 et seq.). Thus the substantial requirements in § 3a of the Federal Data Protection Act as well as the procedural rules in Schleswig-Holstein and Bremen were developed on a Member State level, which will be of relevance when dealing with the question of the future level of harmonization in the European Union.

The amendment of the Directive

The current process of revising the Data Protection Directive provides an opportunity to establish rules for data protection through technology on a European level. Respective statements by the Commission can be found in the Commission's proposal (5.1), although they should be tightened substantially (5.2). Finally, conclusions for the future regulatory strategy of the Union can be drawn from national experiences with the concept of data protection through technology (5.3).

The Commission's proposal

The Commission's 2010 communication emphasizes the importance of data protection through technology on several occasions. It states, for instance, that PETs, the promotion of which the Commission had already suggested in a 2007 communication (European Commission 2007), as well as the application of the "privacy by design" concept could play a major role in data security and the possible introduction of the principle of accountability (European Commission 2010, 11 et seq.).

However, the Commission's proposals remain vague, even in its latest 2012 proposal. Article 23 (1) GDPR states that the controller shall, both at the time of the determination of the means of processing and at the time of the processing itself, implement appropriate technical and organizational measures and procedures in such a way that the processing will meet the requirements of the GDPR and ensure the protection of the rights of the data subject. Also, the controller must strictly adhere to the principle of necessity (Art. 23 (2) GDPR). However, the draft lacks any binding statement concerning the design of the technology and does not mention general principles of data protection through technology at all (Hornung 2012, 75 et seq.). Most notably, anonymization and pseudonymization are not mentioned at all.[12] From a German point of view, it appears that the normative substance even falls short of § 3a of the Federal Data Protection Act. Under the current draft, the practical effect of data protection by design will depend entirely on delegated acts and technical standards of the Commission pursuant to Articles 23 (3) and (4) as well as Article 30 (3) GDPR. Unfortunately, the Commission has so far shown little interest in establishing legally binding obligations to that effect.

Article 39 GDPR contains provisions concerning certification as well as data protection seals and marks. However, these rules are phrased even more vaguely (Hornung 2012, 76), as they merely ask Member States and the Commission to "encourage" the establishment of respective tools. The draft lacks any statement as to the competent authority, the procedure, the applicable criteria and the legal consequences of certification.[13] Consequently, it is entirely unclear by which standards the Commission is expected to make use of its power to adopt delegated acts and lay down technical standards pursuant to Articles 39 (2) and (3) GDPR.

At any rate, it is striking that the Commission, in its 2010 Communication, did not classify both points mentioning data protection through technology under the chapter on "Strengthening individuals' rights" but rather under the chapter on "Enhancing the internal market dimension".[14] It remains to be seen what the implications for the further amending process will be. In any case, it is desirable that the concept of data protection through technology will not be discussed predominantly with regard to harmonizing economical parameters. As essential as this is in certain areas – purely national quality seals do not make sense in a single European market – it would fall short of the basic idea of the concept of supporting data subjects in their self-determined handling of personal data with technological means.

Desirable changes for the future

To make technological mechanisms for a self-determined data protection a success, it is possible to (a) require mandatory use of specific technologies, (b) to trust in market forces alone, and (c) to follow a mixed approach. The first approach is promising when dealing with the introduction to the market of a specific technology design or application which by its nature can be subject to mandatory government regulations. The privacy-friendly design of the electronic proof of identity of the new German ID card is an example (see Roßnagel, Hornung, and Schnabel 2008; Hornung and Roßnagel 2010; Hornung and Möller 2011). However, directly regulating specific technologies should not constitute the general regulatory concept of data protection law as continuous technological change would either lead to the inadequacy of these regulations or to a never-ending process of amending the existent data protection laws.

The second approach makes sense in areas where it appears that the desired mechanisms of supply and demand actually do exist. Obviously, this is still not the case in the area of PETs. If it were correct that "all those involved in processing of personal data would benefit from a wider use of PETs" – as the Commission put it in its 2007 communication (European Commission 2007, 6) to which it refers in the 2010 paper – then they would prevail on the market all by themselves. Under that precondition, all that remained to be done would be to raise awareness of the benefits of PETs among market participants. Such efforts to spread information constitute reasonable and vital measures. However, in light of the intense discussion on data protection through technology in the last years, one should not assume that the lack of distribution is solely due to the incapability or reluctance of producers and users to acknowledge the benefits they could achieve for themselves by using PETs. On the contrary, it appears that PETs are still not part of business cases, and it is very doubtful whether the current market incentives will suffice to change that in the future (London Economics 2010).

Thus, the third approach is the most promising for a general concept of data protection through technology. It provides legally governed market incentives, pursues concepts of regulated self-regulation and establishes requirements for the procedures of developing and implementing technology.[15] It also includes – unlike the Commission's proposals – mandatory requirements. These are not structured in a traditional regulatory manner, but do set standards for producers and designers of technology, contain requirements for processing data, and undertake a legally induced process of influencing the market.

With regard to the organization of technological development, the latter approach could be promoted by a number of measures: Fixed targets for specific sectors or technologies could determine privacy friendly results and leave it to the creativity and innovative ability of the developers to achieve them. Duties to inspect and report would allow for supervision of the results and moreover stimulate self-reflection by developers on the privacy-related implications of their work. The mandatory involvement of internal and external data protection authorities could make use of their expertise and create more transparency throughout the design process. Strengthening the Article 29 Data Protection Working Party (or the future European Data Protection Board pursuant Article 64 GDPR) could contribute to an enhanced structuring of the development process of PETs, for example, by empowering it to guide the respective processes. The outcomes of these processes would be enhanced through the market should audits and quality seals provide market incentives by certifying a high level of data protection that has been verified in a legally governed procedure. In that context, the debate will have to focus on whether to prefer the awarding of such audits and quality seals on a European or rather on a Member State level. Apart from that, giving data subjects legal claims wherever distinguishably defined duties can readily be observed by the respective responsible institutions could foster data subjects' rights – an example would be the establishment of a right to privacy enhancing default settings.

It is essential to involve the European Data Protection Supervisor in any further amending process. He first published a statement dealing with the Commission's communication on 18 January 2011. In the paper, the concept of privacy by design is linked to the principle of "accountability" in the same manner as by the Commission. Unlike the Commission though, he derives consequences from that linkage for mandatory statutory duties: under certain circumstances data controllers shall be obliged to prove that they make use of PETs (European Data Protection Supervisor 2011, 23). The European Data Protection Supervisor (2011, 23) suggests a "binding provision setting forth a "privacy by design" obligation". In his 2012 statement on the Commission's proposal, the Supervisor notes the lack of such a binding provision (European Data Protection Supervisor 2012, 29 et seq.).

Such form of an obligation is supported by the present perception of the principle of accountability. So far, the principle has been largely unknown to the law of data protection, although it can be found in no. 14 of the 1980 OECD Guidelines on the Protection of Data and Transborder Flows of Personal Data[16] and was incorporated in the Privacy Framework of the Asia-Pacific Economic Cooperation. The principle of accountability was introduced into the European reform debate through a working document of the Article 29 Data Protection Working Party (2010). As a result, it is currently subject to an intense debate among experts.[17]

The concept originates in the common law tradition. Despite all uncertainty regarding terminology and content (see e.g. Arnull and Wincott 2002; Harlow 2002; Bovens 2007), the obvious aim is to accept verifiable responsibility (Fisher 2004, 496 et seq.). Taking up this notion, the Article 29 Data Protection Working Party (2010, 21) construes accountability as the establishment of provisions requiring data controllers to take adequate and effective measures to implement the basic principles and obligations of the directive and to prove their implementation efforts. If connected with applying concepts of data protection through technology, this approach could actually mean a step forward.

According to the considerations of the European Data Protection Supervisor (2011, 23 et seq.), obligations imposed on controllers should additionally be complemented by a provision for developers and producers of technology; mandatory regulations to that effect have been suggested as well. Furthermore, it is stipulated that data protection authorities should be provided with enforcing measures, at least for cases where obvious breaches of these obligations occur. These suggestions should be adopted as they lead the further reform process into the right direction. Beyond that, the statement also supports the plans regarding certification systems (European Data Protection Supervisor 2011, 24). For unknown reasons, the Supervisor remains silent on this point in his 2012 paper.

Directive or regulation? The margin of the Member States

Considering the results that have been achieved concerning data protection through technology, it is possible to draw a number of conclusions for possible regulatory strategies of the EU, particularly the issue of the adequate regulatory margin of Member States.

The Commission, supported strongly by the European Data Protection Supervisor (2011, 15, 2012, 9 et seq.), proposes to adopt a Regulation instead of the current Data Protection Directive. This approach is expected to create both an effective protection of fundamental rights and a single European market for personal data. So far, the Directive has merely led to a formal unification of data protection laws in Europe, while the actual level of protection varies considerably.

The discussion on the regulatory instrument also refers to the controversial question of whether or not the current Data Protection Directive constitutes a full harmonization of data protection law in Europe. According to the European Court of Justice, the Directive "amounts to harmonization which is generally complete" (European Court of Justice 2003, para. 96, 2008, para. 51). At the same time, however, it "allows the Member States a margin for manoeuvre in certain areas and authorizes them to maintain or introduce particular rules for specific situations" (European Court of Justice 2003, para. 97), as long as such possibilities are made use of in the manner provided for by the Directive and in accordance with its objective of maintaining a balance between the free movement of personal data and the protection of private life. Ultimately, it is difficult to give a generalized answer regarding the question of the regulatory margin available to Member States regarding the Directive as such.[18] In contrast, it must be established in every single case exactly what the respective provision mandates and how much discretion it leaves for Member States to depart from that general provision.

A prospective regulatory strategy should also take into account the aforementioned considerations. Directives sometimes contain extensive and detailed requirements, while Regulations may also define margins for manoeuvre for Member States. Hence, considerations should not focus on what instrument to use, but rather on the exact extent of the margin each instrument should grant to Member States.

It cannot be generalized to what extent such margins are desirable in all areas of data protection law. One should instead distinguish according to the principle of subsidiarity (Art. 5 (3) TEU) and ask whether the specific regulatory objectives can rather, by reason of the scale or effects of the proposed action, be better achieved at Union level. This will, for example, be the case for terminology issues, where national variations are impractical.[19] In some areas, though, it is desirable to create room for Member States to become innovative. In particular, the concept of data protection through technology is a prime example for this: the substantial requirements of § 3a of the German Federal Data Protection Act as well as the audit and quality seal procedures have been developed within the margin of the current Directive's regime and are now returned to the European sphere as part of the current European reform discussion. This would not have been possible under different, stricter European parameters.

This experience is not necessarily an argument against a further harmonization process nor against a change to the instrument of a Regulation. However, it clearly suggests leaving room for innovation to Member States in areas where long-term determinations are not (yet) possible owing to the rapid development and therefore the competition of ideas between Member States should not be obstructed but rather be supported. This does especially apply to the development of new protection concepts in the area of data protection through technology, to concretizations of general principles of data protection to suit new technology, and to the development of guidelines for innovative PETs. It thus appears that the Commission's proposal should be both tightened and untightened: while there is good reason to include binding obligations as regards the use of PETs by controllers and processors, Member States should be given margins for innovative regulatory tools.

In the specific case of certification and seals, it must be ensured that these are recognized in all Member States in order to maintain an incentive for companies to voluntarily undergo such certification procedures. In principle, there are two approaches: first, all auditing and certification processes could be conducted on a European level – depending on the number of processes this may prove to be an impossible undertaking; second, national supervisory authorities or other bodies could assume these tasks. In that case, the awaited data protection regulatory regime would have to contain an effective instrument to ensure the mutual recognition of such certifications and seals.

Conclusion

The concept of data protection through technology is a key component of modern data protection law and has been specified by preliminary work and experience to the point where the renewed regulatory regime in the European Union should contain mandatory requirements. To abstain from this step would mean to obstruct a worthwhile concept for a long period of time since the reform cycles of the Union are of extraordinary length. The first draft of the Commission concerning the current Data Protection Directive dates back to 5 November 1990[20] – a point in time when there was no World Wide Web. Although this had changed by the date of adoption on 24 October 1995, data processing has changed fundamentally in the meantime and today has little in common with the conditions of that time.

As it may well be that the next reform will not take place before another 20 year interval has elapsed, the current modernization process needs to provide instruments that keep pace with technological progress. Since the outcome of this progress is still unknown, "learning" mechanisms are necessary. One possible European instrument to ensure this is the adoption of delegated acts by the European Commission in accordance with Article 290 of the Treaty on the functioning of the European Union (TFEU). Thereby, the Commission may adopt non-legislative acts of general application to supplement or amend certain non-essential elements of the legislative act. Whilst this instrument could be a useful tool in data protection law, the current proposal of the Commission clearly does not meet the requirements set forth in Article 290 (1) TFEU as regards the restriction to "non-essential elements". The Commission proposes to grant itself implementing powers as regards virtually all provisions of the GDPR (see the extensive lists in Articles 86 and 87 GDPR). In the case of PETs, certification and seals in particular, the Commission would reserve the right to decide on all major regulatory issues. In the light of the aforementioned considerations, such powers and rights appear unreasonable (Hornung 2012, 80 et seq.).

In light of the scarce experience with the instruments of Article 290 TFEU, any potential concept should be complemented by margins for a competition of ideas among the Member States. It will become even more crucial the more technological innovations confront the entire law of data protection with conceptual problems.[21] The European system of data protection law can only adequately react to such a challenge when it features "self-learning" processes. Therefore, the recommended course of action must be twofold. On the one hand, mandatory requirements for designing and applying PETs and a legally governed system to provide market incentives for PETs through certification and seals must be introduced. On the other hand it is necessary to abstain from regulating technologies that are still largely unknown. Instead, a framework for technological but also legal innovations must be established that includes learning mechanisms on both the European and the Member State level.

Acknowledgements

The text is a revised version of a paper that was published in German in the *Zeitschrift für Datenschutz* 2011, 51–57 – the journal has given its permission to publish the revised English version – and based on a talk given by the author at the conference of the Alcatel–Lucent Stiftung für Kommunikationsforschung: Datenschutz in Europa. Recht und Technik in der Novellierung der europäischen Datenschutzrichtlinie, 6 May 2011, Stuttgart. The author is grateful to the two anonymous reviewers for their valuable comments and to Mr Markus Lieberknecht and Mr Ray Migge for their support on the revised version.

Notes

1. See e.g. Eckhardt (2009), Gola and Klug (2009), Roßnagel (2009), Scheuring (2010) and Kühling and Bohnen (2010).
2. On this debate, see Roßnagel, Garstka, and Pfitzmann (2001), Ahrend et al. (2003), Bizer (2001, 2004) and Roßnagel (2005).

PRIVACY AND SECURITY IN THE DIGITAL AGE

3. Directive 95/46/EC of the European Parliament and of the Council of 24 October 1995 on the protection of individuals with regard to the processing of personal data and on the free movement of such data, *Official Journal*, 23 November 1995 no. L. 281, 31.
4. For first views on the proposals, see De Hert and Papakonstantinou (2012), Hornung (2012) and Bäcker and Hornung (2012).
5. On this concept, see Borking (1998, 2001), Hansen (2003) and Scholz (2003, 357 et seq. with further references), as well as the papers in Roßnagel (2001); on the economic opportunities, see London Economics (2010).
6. For a current example on this, see the project "Gestaltung technisch-sozialer Vernetzung in situativen ubiquitären Systemen (VENUS)" at the University of Kassel, http://www.uni-kassel.de/einrichtungen/iteg/venus
7. The basis of these provisions was formed by an expert opinion of the Projektgruppe verfassungsverträgliche Technikgestaltung (1996).
8. On the development, see e.g. Roßnagel (2011, 42 et seq., 49 et seq.), Scholz (2011, para. 1 et seq.), critically Albers (2005, 554), Bull (2006). Most of the Data Protection Acts of the German Länder contain similar provisions.
9. "Personal data shall be collected, processed and used, and data processing systems shall be chosen and designed in accordance with the aim of collecting, processing and using as little personal data as possible. In particular, personal data shall be rendered anonymous or pseudonymous as allowed by the purpose for which they are collected and/or further processed, and as far as the effort required is not disproportionate to the desired purpose of protection."
10. While there are several voices in favor of this (Bäumler 1999, 260; Dix 2003, para 23; Bizer 2006, para. 41; Scholz 2011, para. 27), others are more skeptical (Wuermeling 1997, 8; Gola and Schomerus 2011, para. 2; Schaffland and Wiltfang 2011, para. 2).
11. For further information and the list of products, see https://www.datenschutzzentrum.de/guetesiegel/index.htm
12. The Article 29 Data Protection Working Party (2012, 11) has called for such a definition.
13. The question of which criteria products must meet to receive data protection seals was one of the most controversial issues in the parliamentary proceedings in Germany and contributed to the failure to pass a federal Act of Parliament on the issue (Roßnagel 2010, 276 et seq.).
14. Both dimensions are part of the current Directive and amount to one of its key problems: the European requirements are meant to both serve the common market and protect the privacy of the persons concerned (Ehmann and Helfrich 1999, para. 4; Kuner 2007, 20).
15. On this concept, see from a German perspective Hoffmann-Riem (1998a, 535 et seq., 1998b, 687 et seq.), Nedden (2001), Roßnagel (2003b, 2007), 175 et seq., 2011, 62 et seq.); see also the earlier works of Podlech (1972/1973) and Podlech et al. (1982).
16. OECD document C (80) 58.
17. See particularly the conference on "Privacy and Accountability 2011" originating in the PATS project (http://pats-project.eu/).
18. There are different views on the issue: while some argue in favor of the general margins of the Member States (Jacob 1993; Simitis 1997, 282, 1998, 2476, 2000, 714; Dammann and Simitis 1997, para. 10; Roßnagel, Garstka, and Pfitzmann 2001, 55 et seq.), others emphasize the harmonizing effects of the Directive (Brühann 2009; Hoeren 2009). There are also differentiating views (Lütkemeier 1995, 598).
19. By way of example, there are no benefits to the varying terminology of Article 2 of the Data Protection Directive and § 3 of the German Federal Data Protection Act respectively.
20. *Official Journal*, 5 November 1990, no. C 277, 3.
21. This is particularly the case as regards the technological innovations in the area of ubiquitous computing, see Roßnagel (2007), 155.

References

Ahrend, V., B.-C. Bijok, U. Dieckmann, B. Eitschberger, M. Guthmann, H. Eul, M. Schmidt, and P.-D. Schwarzhaupt. 2003. Modernisierung des Datenschutzes? *Datenschutz und Datensicherheit* 27 (7): 433–438.

Albers, M. 2005. *Informationelle Selbstbestimmung*. Baden-Baden: Nomos.

Arnull, A., and D. Wincott, eds. 2002. *Accountability and legitimacy in the European Union*. Oxford: Oxford University Press.

Article 29 Data Protection Working Party. 2010. Opinion 3/2010 on the Principle of Accountability – Adopted on 13 July 2010 [online]. Accessed September 10, 2012. http://ec.europa.eu/justice/policies/privacy/docs/wpdocs/2010/wp173_en.pdf

Article 29 Data Protection Working Party. 2012. Opinion 01/2012 on the Data Protection Reform Proposals, 23 March 2012 [online]. Accessed September 10, 2012. http://ec.europa.eu/justice/data-protection/article-29/documentation/opinion-recommendation/files/2012/wp191_en.pdf

Bäcker, M., and G. Hornung. 2012. EU-Richtlinie für die Datenverarbeitung bei Polizei und Justiz in Europa. Einfluss des Kommissionsentwurfs auf das nationale Strafprozess- und Polizeirecht. *Zeitschrift für Datenschutz* 2 (4): 147–152.

Bäumler, H. 1999. Das TDDSG aus Sicht eines Datenschutzbeauftragten. *Datenschutz und Datensicherheit* 23 (5): 258–262.

Bäumler, H. 2001. Audits und Gütesiegel im Datenschutz. *Computer und Recht* 17 (11): 795–800.

Bäumler, H. 2002. Marktwirtschaftlicher Datenschutz. *Datenschutz und Datensicherheit* 26 (6): 325–329.

Bäumler, H. 2004. Ein Gütesiegel für den Datenschutz: Made in Schleswig-Holstein. *Datenschutz und Datensicherheit* 28 (2): 80–84.

Bizer, J. 2001. Ziele und Elemente der Modernisierung des Datenschutzrechtes. *Datenschutz und Datensicherheit* 25 (5): 274–277.

Bizer, J. 2004. Strukturplan modernes Datenschutzrecht. *Datenschutz und Datensicherheit* 28 (1): 6–14.

Bizer, J. 2006. Kommentierung zu § 3a BDSG. In *Bundesdatenschutzgesetz*, edited by S. Simitis, 295–315. 6th ed. Baden-Baden: Nomos.

Borking, J. 1998. Einsatz datenschutzfreundlicher Technologien in der Praxis. *Datenschutz und Datensicherheit* 22 (11): 636–640.

Borking, J. 2001. Privacy-enhancing Technologies (PET). *Datenschutz und Datensicherheit* 25 (10): 607–615.

Bovens, M. 2007. Analysing and Assessing Accountability: A Conceptual Framework. *European Law Journal* 13 (4): 447–468.

Brühann, U. 2003. Europarechtliche Grundlagen. In *Handbuch Datenschutzrecht: Die neuen Grundlagen für Wirtschaft und Verwaltung*, edited by A. Roßnagel, 131–155. Munich: C.H. Beck, chapter 2.4.

Brühann, U. 2009. Mindeststandards oder Vollharmonisierung des Datenschutzes in der EG. Zugleich ein Beitrag zur Systematik von Richtlinien zur Rechtsangleichung im Binnenmarkt in der Rechtsprechung des Europäischen Gerichtshofs. *Europäische Zeitschrift für Wirtschaftsrecht* 20 (18): 639–644.

Bull, H. P. 2006. Zweifelsfragen um die informationelle Selbstbestimmung – Datenschutz als Datenaskese? *Neue Juristische Wochenschrift* 59 (23): 1617–1624.

Dammann, U., and S. Simitis. 1997. *EG-Datenschutzrichtlinie*. Baden-Baden: Nomos.

De Hert, P., and V. Papakonstantinou. 2012. The Proposed Data Protection Regulation Replacing Directive 95/46/EC: A Sound System for the Protection of Individuals. *Computer Law & Security Review* 28 (2): 130–142.

Dix, A. 2003. Konzepte des Systemdatenschutzes. In *Handbuch Datenschutzrecht: Die neuen Grundlagen für Wirtschaft und Verwaltung*, edited by A. Roßnagel, 363–386. Munich: C.H. Beck, chapter 3.5.

Eckhardt, J. 2009. BDSG: Neuregelungen seit 01.09.2009. *Datenschutz und Datensicherheit* 33 (10): 587–595.

Eckhardt, J., and P. Schmitz. 2010. Informationspflicht bei Datenschutzpannen. *Datenschutz und Datensicherheit* 34 (6): 390–397.

Ehmann, E., and M. Helfrich. 1999. *EG-Datenschutzrichtlinie*. Köln: Schmidt.

European Commission. 2007. *Promoting Data Protection by Privacy Enhancing Technologies (PETs)*. COM (2007) 228 final, Brussels.

European Commission. 2010. *A Comprehensive Approach on Personal Data Protection in the European Union*. COM(2010) 609 final, Brussels.

European Commission. 2012a. *Safeguarding Privacy in a Connected World – A European Data Protection Framework for the 21st Century.* COM(2012) 9 final, Brussels.

European Commission. 2012b. *Regulation on the Protection of Individuals with Regard to the Processing of Personal Data and on the Free Movement of such Data (General Data Protection Regulation).* COM(2012) 11 final, Brussels.

European Commission. 2012c. *Directive on the Protection of Individuals with Regard to the Processing of Personal Data by Competent Authorities for the Purposes of Prevention, Investigation, Detection or Prosecution of Criminal Offences or the Execution of Criminal Penalties, and the Free Movement of Such Data.* COM(2012) 10 final, Brussels.

European Court of Justice. 2003. Judgment of 6 November 2003 – C-101/01 – Lindqvist.

European Court of Justice. 2008. Judgment of 16 December 2008 – C-524/06 – Huber.

European Data Protection Supervisor. 2008. The EDPS and EU Research and Technological Development [online]. Accessed September 10, 2012. http://www.edps.europa.eu/EDPSWEB/ webdav/shared/Documents/EDPS/Publications/Papers/PolicyP/08-04-28_PP_RTD_EN.pdf

European Data Protection Supervisor. 2011. Opinion on the Communication from the Commission to the European Parliament, the Council, the Economic and Social Committee and the Committee of the Regions – "A comprehensive approach on personal data protection in the European Union" [online]. Accessed September 10, 2012. http://www.edps. europa.eu/EDPSWEB/webdav/site/mySite/shared/Documents/Consultation/Opinions/2011/ 11-01-14_Personal_Data_Protection_EN.pdf

European Data Protection Supervisor. 2012. Opinion of the European Data Protection Supervisor on the Data Protection Reform Package [online]. Accessed September 10, 2012. http://www.edps.europa.eu/EDPSWEB/webdav/site/mySite/shared/Documents/Consultation/ Opinions/2012/12-03-07_EDPS_Reform_package_EN.pdf

Fisher, E. 2004. The European Union in the age of accountability. *Oxford Journal of Legal Studies* 24 (3): 495–515.

Fleisch, E., and F. Mattern. 2005. *Das Internet der Dinge: Ubiquitous Computing und RFID in der Praxis: Visionen, Technologien, Anwendungen, Handlungsanleitungen.* Berlin: Springer.

Gabel, D. 2009. Informationspflicht bei unrechtmäßiger Kenntniserlangung von Daten. *Betriebsberater* 64 (39): 2045–2049.

Gola, P., and C. Klug. 2009. Die BDSG-Novellen 2009 – Ein Kurzüberblick. *Recht der Datenverarbeitung,* Beilage, 25 (4): 1–5.

Gola, P., and R. Schomerus. 2011. Kommentierung zu § 3a BDSG. In *Bundesdatenschutzgesetz,* edited by P. Gola and R. Schomerus, 103–107. 10th ed. München: C.H. Beck.

Hanloser, J. 2010. Europäische Security Breach Notification. *Multimedia und Recht* 13 (5): 300–303.

Hansen, M. 2003. Privacy Enhancing Technologies. In *Handbuch Datenschutzrecht: Die neuen Grundlagen für Wirtschaft und Verwaltung,* edited by A. Roßnagel, 291–324. Munich: C.H. Beck, chapter 3.3.

Harlow, C. 2002. *Accountability in the European Union.* Oxford: Oxford University Press.

Hildebrandt, M. 2008. A Vision of Ambient Law. In *Regulating Technologies,* edited by R. Brownsword and K. Yeung, 175–191. Oxford: Hart.

Hoeren, T. 2009. Die Vereinbarkeit der jüngsten BDSG-Novellierungspläne mit der Europäischen Datenschutzrichtlinie. *Recht der Datenverarbeitung* 25 (3): 89–95.

Hoffmann-Riem, W. 1998a. Informationelle Selbstbestimmung in der Informationsgesellschaft. *Archiv des öffentlichen Rechts* 123 (4): 513–540.

Hoffmann-Riem, W. 1998b. Weiter so im Datenschutzrecht? *Datenschutz und Datensicherheit* 22 (11): 684–689.

Holst, S. 2004. Bremische Datenschutzauditverordnung in Kraft. *Datenschutz und Datensicherheit* 28 (12): 710–711.

Hornung, G. 2010a. Kontrollierte Vernetzung – vernetzte Kontrolle? Das Recht in Zeiten des ubiquitous computing. In *Sichtbarkeitsregime. Überwachung, Sicherheit und Privatheit im 21. Jahrhundert,* edited by L. Hempel, S. Krasmann and U. Bröckling, 245–262. Berlin: VS-Verlag.

Hornung, G. 2010b. Informationen über "Datenpannen" – Neue Pflichten für datenverarbeitende Unternehmen. *Neue Juristische Wochenschrift* 63 (26): 1841–1845.

Hornung, G. 2010c. Regelungsinstrumente im virtuellen Raum [online]. Unabhängiges Landeszentrum für Datenschutz Schleswig-Holstein. Accessed September 10, 2012. https://www.datenschutzzentrum.de/sommerakademie/2010/

Hornung, G. 2012. A General Data Protection Regulation for Europe? Light and Shade in the Commission's draft of 25 January 2012. *SCRIPTed* 9 (1): 64–81. Accessed September 10, 2012. http://script-ed.org/?p=406.

Hornung, G., and J. Möller. 2011. *Passgesetz und Personalausweisgesetz*. München: C.H. Beck.

Hornung, G., and A. Roßnagel. 2010. An ID card for the Internet. The new German ID card with "electronic proof of identity". *Computer Law and Security Review* 26 (2): 151–157.

Jacob, J. 1993. Die EG-Datenschutzrichtlinie aus Sicht des BfD. *Recht der Datenverarbeitung* 9 (1): 11–14.

Jandt, S. 2008. *Vertrauen im Mobile Commerce. Vorschläge für die rechtsverträgliche Gestaltung von Location Based Services*. Baden-Baden: Nomos.

Konferenz der Datenschutzbeauftragten des Bundes und der Länder. 2010. Resolution of the 79th Conference of the Data Protection Commissioners of the Federation and of the Länder. *Ein modernes Datenschutzrecht für das 21. Jahrhundert*, Stuttgart, March 17–18.

Kühling, J. 2007. Datenschutz in einer künftigen Welt allgegenwärtiger Datenverarbeitung – Aufgabe des Rechts? *Die Verwaltung* 40 (2): 153–172.

Kühling, J., and S. Bohnen. 2010. Zur Zukunft des Datenschutzrechts – Nach der Reform ist vor der Reform. *Juristenzeitung* 65 (12): 600–610.

Kuner, C. 2007. *European Data Protection Law*. 2nd ed. Oxford: Oxford University Press.

London Economics. 2010. Study on the Economic Benefits of Privacy Enhancing Technologies [online]. The European Commission DG Justice, Freedom and Security. Accessed September 10, 2012. http://ec.europa.eu/justice/policies/privacy/docs/studies/final_report_pets_16_07_10_en.pdf

Lütkemeier, S. 1995. EU-Datenschutzrichtlinie – Umsetzung in nationales Recht. *Datenschutz und Datensicherheit* 19 (10): 597–603.

Mattern, F. 2007. *Die Informatisierung des Alltags. Leben in smarten Umgebungen*. Berlin: Springer.

Meissner, S. 2008. Zertifizierungskriterien für das Datenschutzsiegel EuroPriSe. *Datenschutz und Datensicherheit* 32 (8): 525–531.

Nedden, B. 2001. Datenschutz und "Privacy Enhancing Technologies". In *Allianz von Medienrecht und Informationstechnik?* edited by A. Roßnagel, 67–75. Baden-Baden: Nomos.

Podlech, A. 1972/1973. Verfassungsrechtliche Probleme öffentlicher Informationssysteme. *Datenverarbeitung im Recht* 1 (2): 149–169.

Podlech, A. 1982. Individualdatenschutz-Systemdatenschutz. In *Beiträge zum Sozialrecht. Festgabe für Hans Gründer*, edited by K. Brückner and G. Dalichau, 451. Percha: Schulz.

Projektgruppe verfassungsverträgliche Technikgestaltung. 1996. Entwurf gesetzlicher Regelungen zum Datenschutz und zur Rechtssicherheit in Online-Multimedia-Anwendungen Gutachten für das Bundesministerium für Bildung, Wissenschaft, Forschung und Technologie [online]. Accessed September 10, 2012. http://www.provet.org/bib/mmge/

Ranke, J. 2004. *M-Commerce und seine rechtsadäquate Gestaltung*. Baden-Baden: Nomos.

Roßnagel, A. 1993. *Rechtswissenschaftliche Technikfolgenforschung. Umrisse einer Forschungsdisziplin*. Baden-Baden: Nomos.

Roßnagel, A. 1997a. Globale Datennetze – Ohnmacht des Staates – Selbstschutz des Bürgers. *Zeitschrift für Rechtspolitik* 30 (1): 26–30.

Roßnagel, A. 1997b. Datenschutz-Audit. *Datenschutz und Datensicherheit* 21 (9): 505–515.

Roßnagel, A. 2000. *Datenschutzaudit. Konzeption, Durchführung, gesetzliche Regelung*. Wiesbaden: Vieweg-Verlag.

Roßnagel, A. 2001. *Allianz von Medienrecht und Informationstechnik?* Baden-Baden: Nomos.

Roßnagel, A. 2003a. Datenschutzaudit. In *Handbuch Datenschutzrecht: Die neuen Grundlagen für Wirtschaft und Verwaltung*, edited by A. Roßnagel, 437–484. Munich: C.H. Beck, chapter 3.7.

Roßnagel, A. 2003b. Konzepte der Selbstregulierung. In *Handbuch Datenschutzrecht: Die neuen Grundlagen für Wirtschaft und Verwaltung*, edited by A. Roßnagel, 387–436. Munich: C.H. Beck, chapter 3.6.

Roßnagel, A. 2005. Modernisierung des Datenschutzrechts für eine Welt allgegenwärtiger Datenverarbeitung. *Multimedia und Recht* 8 (2): 71–75.

Roßnagel, A. 2007. *Datenschutz in einem informatisierten Alltag.* Berlin: Friedrich-Ebert-Stiftung.

Roßnagel, A. 2009. Die Novellen zum Datenschutzrecht – Scoring und Adresshandel. *Neue Juristische Wochenschrift* 62 (37): 2716–2722.

Roßnagel, A. 2010. Datenschutzaudit – ein modernes Steuerungsinstrument. In *Sichtbarkeitsregime. Überwachung, Sicherheit und Privatheit im 21. Jahrhundert,* edited by L. Hempel, S. Krasmann and U. Bröckling, 263–280. Berlin: VS-Verlag.

Roßnagel, A. 2011. Das Gebot der Datenvermeidung und -sparsamkeit als Ansatz wirksamen technikbasierten Persönlichkeitsschutzes? In *Innovation, Recht und öffentliche Kommunikation,* edited by M. Eifert and W. Hoffmann-Riem, 41–66. Berlin: Dunker& Humboldt.

Roßnagel, A., and M. Scholz. 2000. Datenschutz durch Anonymität und Pseudonymität. *Multimedia und Recht* 3 (12): 721–731.

Roßnagel, A., H. Garstka, and A. Pfitzmann. 2001. *Modernisierung des Datenschutzrechts.* Expert Opinion for the Federal Ministry of the Interior. Berlin: Bundesministerium des Innern.

Roßnagel, A., G. Hornung, and C. Schnabel. 2008. Die Authentisierungsfunktion des elektronischen Personalausweises aus datenschutzrechtlicher Sicht. *Datenschutz und Datensicherheit* 32 (3): 168–172.

Roßnagel, A., T. Sommerlatte, and U. Winand, 2008. *Digitale Visionen. Zur Gestaltung allgegenwärtiger Informationstechnologien.* München: C.H. Beck.

Schaffland, H.-J., and N. Wiltfang. 2011. *Bundesdatenschutzgesetz.* Berlin: Erich-Schmidt Verlag.

Scheuring, M. 2010. Das Gesetz zur Änderung datenschutzrechtlicher Vorschriften – die richtige Antwort auf die Datenskandale? *Neue Zeitschrift für Verwaltungsrecht* 29 (13): 809–811.

Schläger, U. 2004. Gütesiegel nach Datenschutzverordnung Schleswig Holstein. *Datenschutz und Datensicherheit* 28 (8): 459–461.

Schnabel, C. 2009. *Datenschutz bei profilbasierten Location Based Services.* Kassel: Kassel University Press.

Scholz, P. 2003. *Datenschutz beim Internet-Einkauf.* Baden-Baden: Nomos.

Scholz, P. 2011. Kommentierung zu § 3a BDSG. In *Bundesdatenschutzgesetz,* edited by S. Simitis, 393–411. 7th ed. Baden-Baden: Nomos.

Simitis, S. 1997. Die EU-Datenschutzrichtlinie – Stillstand oder Anreiz? *Neue Juristische Wochenschrift* 50 (5): 281–288.

Simitis, S. 1998. Datenschutz – Rückschritt oder Neubeginn? *Neue Juristische Wochenschrift* 51 (34): 2473–2479.

Simitis, S. 2000. Auf dem Weg zu einem neuen Datenschutzkonzept. *Datenschutz und Datensicherheit* 24 (12): 714–726.

Wuermeling, U. 1997. Neues Multimediarecht ab 1. *Datenschutzberater* 21 (7–8): 6–10.

Index

absenteeism 151
abuse, children at risk of 124
access to justice 134, 137–8, 142
accountability: biometric systems 47–8; cloud computing 4, 8–9, 13–31, 167; data protection 2, 47, 134, 138, 139–42, 186; privacy enhancing technologies (PETs) 186, 188–9; PIA Evaluation and Grading System (PEGS), proposal for 175; privacy impact assessments (PIAs) 167; private and public accountability, combination of 28–31; prospective accountability 27–8; Spain, use of covert CCTV in workplace in 159
accuracy of data 46, 51
ACLU polls 85
acquis communautaire 102
ADHD, children with 74
affective computing 4, 74–5
age *see* generational and age-cohort views of information privacy
AIPCA/CICA privacy risk assessment tool 163, 164, 166, 168
aircraft, piloting 75
Alder, GS 157–8
algorithmic surveillance 59
Allanson, Jennifer 73
already connected generations 82–3, 106
Amazon 10, 184
ambient assisted living 75
American Civil Liberties Union (ACLU) polls 126
American Life Project 83
anonymity 39, 49, 182, 184, 186–7
Anti-Money Laundering and Counter-Terrorism Act 2006 (Australia) 174–5
Antón, AI 26
APEC *see* Asia-Pacific Economic Cooperation (APEC)
Apple 184
arbitration 38
Armstrong, G 59
Article 29 Working Party 16–17, 121, 133, 188–9

artifacts 61, 72–3, 76
Asia-Pacific Economic Cooperation (APEC) 12, 15, 22, 188
assistance systems for safety-critical applications 75
assumption of innocence 38, 51
audits 11, 13, 18, 24, 28–30, 183, 185–6, 190
Australia: Anti-Money Laundering and Counter-Terrorism Act 2006 174–5; cloud computing 15; credit reporting information for electronic identity verification 174–5; EVI PIA 174–6; privacy impact assessments (PIAs) 161–3, 174–6; surveys 101
automated decision-making 46, 51
autonomic technologies 10–12
autonomy 12, 76, 120, 158

Baby Boomers (born from 1946–1964), attitudes of 84, 89, 90–8
Ball, Kristie 146
Beck, Ulrich 122
behavioural data 74, 76, 78
Belgium, employee monitoring in 152–3
benefit fraud 123
Bennett, CJ 57
Benyon, D 76
Berger, PL 61
Binding Corporate Rules (BCR) 12, 20–1
biocybernetic adaptation 4, 71–8; adaptivity of ICT systems 72–3; affective computing 4, 74–5; ambient assisted living 75; assistance systems for safety-critical applications 75; behavioural data 74, 76, 78; biosignals 77; brain-computer interfaces 74; codes of conduct 78; companions and interaction partners, computers as 74; crime 77; culture 78; data protection 4, 74–8; definitions and guiding visions 72–4; emotional/affective behaviour of artifacts 76; ethics 76, 78; European Union 71, 77–8; generational changes 78; health care 74, 77–8; intimate data 75; 'mind-reading' 77;

INDEX

neuro-physiological computing 73, 78; physiological computing 73, 78; privacy-by-design 77–8; regulation 4, 74, 77–8; relationships with artifacts, development of 76; sensitive personal data 72–3, 74–6, 78; validation 77

biofeedback games for children with ADHD 74

biology, pursuit of standardization in synthetic 72

biometrics 125 *see also* future biometric systems for crime prevention and human rights

biosignals 77

blogs and online magazines 62–3, 65

bodily integrity 57

brain-computer interfaces 74

brain, engineering the 72

Brandeis, Louis 103, 121

Breaux, TD 26

Brokaw, Tom 84

burden of proof, reversal of 141

Bush, George W 124

Bygrave, L 156

Cambridge Reports National Omnibus Survey 85

Canada 22, 101, 128, 161–3

Cantril, Albert H 88

Cantril, Susan Davis 88

capture of data 36, 39, 41, 48–50

cars, tracking devices on 153

CCTV: covert monitoring 148; crime prevention 145, 147–8; crime reaction tool, as 147–8; criminological perspective 145–6; Croatia 103, 106, 109–10, 112–14; legalistic perspective 145; managerial perspective 145; public attitudes 103, 106, 109–10, 112–14; workplace monitoring 145, 148 *see also* Spain, use of covert CCTV in workplace in

Centre for Information Policy Leadership 17

certification 177, 187, 189–90

Charlesworth, Andrew 164, 167

Charter of Fundamental Rights of the EU 38, 42–3, 45–6, 48, 120, 127

cheap and portable computer technology, widespread use of 76

Chen, S 25

children 74, 106, 124

choice of law 12

Churchill, GA 109

civil liberties 3, 85–6 *see also* human rights

Civil Rights Movements 84

class 88, 106, 114

close circuit TV *see* CCTV

cloud computing 164, 167–8 *see also* cloud computing and accountability; cloud computing and data protection

cloud computing and accountability 4, 8–9, 13–31: audits 18, 24; cloud service providers (CSPs) 20–1, 23–4; contract 14, 20–1, 23–4, 26–9, 31; data protection 15, 17–21; decryption keys 24–5, 27; definition 8–9, 14–16, 18, 30–1; design of solutions 22–30; encryption 24–7, 30; EU law 15–20; interoperability 20; legislation 14, 21–2, 30–1; machine readable policies 24–6; OECD Guidelines 14; potential hazards 18–20; personally identifiable information (PII) 14–15, 18–19, 21, 25, 28; policy 21, 24–7, 30; privacy impact assessments (PIAs) 23, 27–30; procedural measures 23–4, 26–30; regulation 14–22, 28, 30–1; responsibility, allocation of 21–2; risk and trust assessment 27–8; security techniques 25; self-regulation 18–19; service level agreements (SLAs) 23–4, 27, 30; technological measures 14, 21–3; transparency 15–21, 25, 28; Trust Authorities 24–7; user trust 21

cloud computing and data protection 7–31: administrative policies 14; audits 11, 13; autonomic technologies 10–12; cloud service providers (CSPs) 8–12; commercial customers 8, 9; command and control regulation 7–8, 13; contract 9; cross-border services 7–8; data protection 8, 11, 138; definition of cloud computing 8, 9; deployment models 9; enforcement 12; EU law 7–8, 11, 14, 30; fair information principles (FIPs) 14; jurisdiction 11, 12; mapping legal and regulatory approaches 12–13, 26–7; multi-tenancy 10; offshoring 10–12, 23; outsourcing 10–13, 20, 23; personally identifiable information (PII) 8–9, 11–14; public law 9; regulation 4, 7–9, 12–13, 30; risk assessment 11–14; security risks 4, 11, 21, 23–4; self-regulation 8, 9, 14, 30; server farms 10; service level agreements (SLAs) 11; site inspections 11; software licensing 10–11; standards 8, 11–12, 21, 27–9; technical measures 9, 10–14; transparency 13; virtual machines (VMs) 9–10, 12; virtualization 9–12 *see also* cloud computing and accountability

Cloud Security Alliance (CSA) 11, 25

command and control regulation 7–8, 13

companions and interaction partners, computers as 74

COMPANIONS project 76

confidentiality 2, 8, 10–11, 24, 30, 102–4, 135, 167

INDEX

consequentialism 157
constitutional law 36, 38–48, 54
cookies 47
covert monitoring 88 *see also* Spain, use of covert CCTV in workplace in
Cowper, M 15
Creative Commons copyright licence model 26
credit reporting information for electronic identity verification 174–5
crime prevention/detection: benefit fraud 123; biocybernetic adaptation 77; biometrics 36–54; CCTV 64–6, 145, 147–9, 150–5, 157, 159; criminal offences and penalties, proposal for directive on field of 182; criminological perspective 5, 145–6, 147, 159; Croatia 101, 111, 113–14; European Union 36, 38–9, 41–3, 45–7, 50, 54; managerial-regulative definition of crime 64; organized crime 36, 40, 126; privacy enhancing technologies (PETs) 182; public attitudes 101, 111, 113–14; Spain, use of covert CCTV in workplace in 149, 150–5, 157, 159
Croatia, public attitudes to privacy and surveillance in 100–14; age 107–8, 111–13; CCTV 103, 106, 109–10, 112–14; crime prevention 101, 111, 113–14; data protection 101–14; demographic differences 5, 105–14; educational level 107–8, 111–13; effectiveness, perceptions of 109–10, 112; employment status 108, 111–12; enforcement 101, 103, 109, 111–13; European Union 101, 104; gender 107–8, 111–14; government use of data 106, 114; income levels 107–8, 111–13; manipulation of data 109–13; 'nothing to hide' argument 105, 114; opinion polls and survey 101, 106–8, 113–14; policies, design of 105; privacy and data protection, citizens concerned about 5, 106, 111–13; pro-surveillance citizens 5, 106, 109–13; security 101, 105–6; socio-economic status 114; surveillance, definition of 105; surveilled, citizens who are concerned about being 5, 101, 106, 109–13; terrorism 111, 113; transparency 102; trust 105, 109, 111–12, 114
Crompton, M 15
Cronbach coefficients 109–10
cross-border services 7–8
CSIRO 25–6
culture: biocybernetic adaptation 78; generational attitudes 82–4, 88; privacy 1, 57–8, 101; relativism 57–8; smart CCTV 58, 61–2, 67–8; surveillance 58, 153–4
customary law 184

cybernetics *see* biocybernetic adaptation

Daimler 75
data abuse pyramids 105
data protection: accountability 2, 15, 17–21; adequacy 177; biocybernetic adaptation 4, 74–8; biometric systems 36, 38–9, 41–4, 45–51; cloud computing 7–31; Croatia 101–14; data abuse pyramid 105; data controllers 2, 135, 137–41, 188–90; data protection commissioners 60, 65, 67; data protection through technology 182–3, 185–7, 189–90; European Union 39, 43, 45–6, 104; Germany 39, 46, 66; harmonization 121, 134–5, 138, 186–7, 189; PIA Evaluation and Grading System (PEGS), proposal for 175, 17; privacy enhancing technologies (PETs) 181–91; privacy impact assessments (PIAs) 47–8, 121, 161–2, 166; public attitudes 101–14; right to privacy 120–2; security 105, 123–4, 126–7, 129; smart CCTV 60, 65–7; surveillance 60, 65–7, 100; transparency 2, 41–2, 134, 138–9, 142, 156 *see also* Data Protective Directive; Data Protection Regulation, proposal for; sensitive personal data
Data Protective Directive: accountability 15, 47; biometric systems 39, 43, 45–7; cloud computing 8, 11, 15; Data Protection Regulation, proposal for 133–40, 182, 186, 189–91; privacy enhancing technologies (PETs) 182, 186, 189–91; right to privacy 121; sensitive personal data 46; Spain, use of covert CCTV in workplace in 156; transparency 156; Vienna University intelligentPIA tool for RFID applications 166
Data Protection Regulation, proposal for 133–42: access to justice 134, 137–8, 142; accountability 134, 138, 139–42, 186; adequacy criterion 135; biocybernetic adaptation 78; 'closest to the home' individual redress right, creation of 137–8; cloud computing 138; data minimization principle 135; Data Protection Directive 133–40, 182, 186, 189–91; data protection principles 5, 134–7; data quality 136–7; directive or regulation, using 189–90; Fair Information Principles 139; harmonization 134–5, 138; impact assessments 135, 140; lawfulness, principle of 136–7; notifications 135, 140–1; personal data processing 134–42; privacy-by-design 135, 140–1; privacy enhancing technologies (PETs) 5, 181–2, 186–91; privacy impact assessments (PIAs) 5, 161; proportionality 134, 140; rectification 135; right to privacy 121–2;

INDEX

sensitive personal data 78; terrorism 136; transparency 134, 138–9, 142
Data Retention Directive 1–2, 124
De Hert, Paul 161
de Vries, B 146
decryption 24–5, 27
definition of privacy *see* privacy, definition of
demographics 101, 105–14 *see also* gender; generational and age-cohort views of information privacy
design: biometric systems 38–54; cloud computing 22–30; policies 105; privacy-by-design 14, 39, 47–8, 77–8, 135, 140–1, 182–3, 186, 188; privacy enhancing technologies (PETs) 5, 182–3, 185–8, 191; public attitudes 105
Desoi, M 51–3
digital natives 82–3, 106
disabilities, persons with 74
discrimination 45, 57, 66–7
drowsiness when driving 75
due process 153
Dutton, WH 87–8

education, level of 88, 98, 107–8, 111–13
effectiveness 109–10, 112, 134, 162–9, 177
e-learning 74–5
electronic identity verification, credit reporting information for 174–5
emotional/affective behaviour of artifacts 76
employee monitoring 88, 145, 148 *see also* Spain, use of covert CCTV in workplace in
employee representatives 156
encryption 24–7, 30
energy grids 4
enforcement: biometric systems 38; cloud computing 12; data protection 139; privacy enhancing technologies (PETs) 182–3, 189; public attitudes 101, 103, 111–13
ENISA (European Network and Information Security Agency) 11
EnCoRe 27
environment 161, 169
EPAL 25
ePrivacy Directive 47
Equifax 86, 105
Ericson, RV 58
ethics 3, 5, 76, 78, 147, 157–8
ethnicity 44, 46, 88
ETICA project 77–8
European Convention on Human Rights (ECHR): biometrics 38, 42–6; Court of Justice, overlap of ECtHR with 45; ECtHR, case law of 43–5; margin of appreciation 45; positive obligations 44, 45; Spain, use of covert CCTV in workplace in 150, 153

European Data Protection Board (EDPB) 121, 188
European Data Protection Supervisor (EDPS) 78, 177–9
European Privacy Seal 186
European Technology Assessment Group (ETAG) 71
European Union: accountability 15–20; *acquis communautaire*, definition of 102; biocybernetic adaptation 71, 77–8; biometric systems 36, 38–9, 41–3, 45–7, 50, 54, 125; Charter of Fundamental Rights of the EU 38, 42–3, 45–6, 48, 120, 127; cloud computing 7–8, 11, 14, 15–20; criminal offences and penalties, proposal for directive on field of 182; crime prevention 36, 38–9, 41–3, 45–7, 50, 54, 126, 182; data protection 1–2, 39, 43, 45–6, 104, 124, 126; ECtHR, case law of 43–5; ePrivacy Directive 47; European Convention on Human Rights, accession to 45, 101–2; freedom, security and justice, rea of 127; fundamental rights 36, 38–9, 41–3, 45–7, 50, 54, 120; Group of Personalities (GoP) 125, 127; GS1 RFID Privacy Impact Assessment (PIA) tool 165; illegal immigration 126; Lisbon Treaty 43; nationality discrimination 45; non-legislative acts of general application 191; police and criminal justice area 43, 45–6; PRISMS project 119, 127–9; privacy-by-design 39, 47, 188; privacy impact assessments (PIAs) 47–8; public attitudes 101, 104; regulation 182, 186, 189–90; Safe Harbor Agreement with US 18, 20; Science and Technology Options Assessment panel (STOA) 71–2; security and privacy trade-off paradigm 119–22, 125–6; Spain, use of covert CCTV in workplace in 159; supremacy of EU law 43, 46; terrorism 126; treaties 39, 42–4, 191 *see also* Data Protective Directive; Data Protection Regulation, proposal for
evaluation systems *see* PIA Evaluation and Grading System (PEGS), proposal for
evergreening process 28

Facebook 82
facial recognition systems 59, 60
fair information principles (FIPs) 14, 139
false hits 37, 40, 42, 46, 48, 51
Federal Data Protection Act (Germany), amendment of 185–7, 190
Filipczak, B 84
fingerprints 36–7, 40, 48–9, 51–2
France, employee monitoring in 152–3
freedom of association 1

INDEX

freedom of expression 1, 2

freedom of movement 38, 51

freedom, security and justice, area of 127, 136

fundamental rights *see* human rights

future biometric systems for crime prevention and human rights 36–54: accountability 47–8; adapting behaviour 41; aid, data collection as mere 41; anonymization 39, 49; automated decision-making 46, 51; Biometric Template Protection 52; capture of data 39, 41, 48, 49–50; Charter of Fundamental Rights of the EU 38, 42–3, 45–6, 48; coarse scans 48–9; constitutional law 36, 38–48, 54; data protection 36, 38–9, 41–3, 45–51, 54; design 38–54; enforcement 38; error rates, defining and testing 51; EU law 36, 38–9, 41–3, 45–7, 50, 54, 125; European Convention on Human Rights 38, 42–6; false hits 37, 40, 42, 46, 48, 51; foreseeability 43–4; German constitutional law 36, 38–46, 54; high scatter 41–2, 44, 49, 52, 54; identifiability, reducing 52; legality 38–48; limitations on use 42, 50, 52, 54; necessity 40, 44; police 36–54; privacy-by-design 39, 47–8; privacy impact assessments 38, 47–8; privacy in public 41; proportionality 39, 40, 44–5; proposals for design 48–54; regulation 38–9; science and technology by legal technology design, governing 38–9, 47; security of data 42, 50, 54; self-determination 38–9; sensitive personal data 37–8, 44, 46, 54; suitability 40; surveillance 38–9, 41–2, 44–6, 52; terrorism 36, 40; 'three-step' model 51–3; transparency 41–2, 44, 46, 48–9, 51–2, 54; travel, right to 38, 51; uniform personal identifiers 42, 50, 54; use of information 39, 42, 50, 52, 54; wanted lists 37–40, 49; watched, feelings of being 41

Gallup 85

Galway Project 16

games and interactive media 74

Gazso, A105

gender 83, 85, 88–90, 92–3, 95–8, 106–8, 111–14

General Data Protection Regulation (GDPR), proposal for *see* Data Protection Regulation, proposal for

General Social Survey 85, 90, 93

Generally Accepted Privacy Principles (GAPP) 164

Generation X (born between 1965–1980), attitudes of 84, 89–90, 93–7

generational and age-cohort attitudes to information privacy 5, 81–98: Baby Boomers (born from 1946–1964) 84, 89, 90–8; biocybernetic adaptation 78; civil liberties 85–6; Croatia 107–8, 111–13; culture 82–4, 88; digital natives/always connected generation 82–3; educational level 88, 98; ethnicity 88; federal government use of data 89, 93–7; gender 83, 85, 88–90, 92–3, 95–8; generation, definition of 83–4; Generation X (born between 1965–1980) 84, 89–90, 93–7; government use of data 89, 93–7; Greatest Generation (born before 1928) 84, 89, 90–7; income level 88, 98; lifecycles 84–5; middle-aged persons 82, 84, 88–98; Millennials (born after 1980) 82–3, 84, 89, 93, 95, 97; older generation 84, 88–97; opinion polls and surveys 84–90, 98; Pew delineation of generations 84; political parties 88, 98; rural culture 88; seminal events 84; Silent Generation (born from 1928–1945) 84, 89, 90–7; social networking 82–3; socio-economic status 88; time, attitudes over 85–8; urban culture 88; wiretapping 89, 90–3, 96–8; younger people 82–3, 84, 88–9, 93–7

Germany: anonymity 186–7; audits 185–6; biometrics 36, 38–46, 54; Bremen 186; certification 187; constitutional law 36, 38–46, 54; data protection 39, 46, 66, 181, 185–8; Federal Data Protection Act, amendment of 181, 185–7, 190; identity cards 187; minimization of data 185–6; Nordrhein-Westfalen 186; privacy enhancing technologies (PETs) 181, 185–8; Schleswig-Holstein 185–6; seals and marks 187; security of data 185–6; smart CCTV 4, 58, 60, 62, 65–8; soft law 185; standards 187; telecommunications 185

Giddens, A 122

Global Positioning System (GPS) tracking device 153

globalization 16, 20, 122

good faith 155–6, 159

Google: cloud computing 10; data protection 184; New Zealand Google Street View PIA 173–4, 175–6; Street View 134, 173–4, 175–6

Goold, BJ 104–5, 114

government: civil rights and government 3; Croatia 106, 114; parliamentary documents 62–3; public attitudes 89, 93–7, 106, 114; surveillance 101; Trusted Cloud Initiative 25

Generation X (born between 1965–1980), attitudes of 84, 89–90, 93–7

grading systems *see* PIA Evaluation and Grading System (PEGS), proposal for

INDEX

Greatest Generation (born before 1928), attitudes of 84, 89, 90–7
Group of Personalities (GoP) 125, 127
GS1 RFID Privacy Impact Assessment (PIA) tool 164, 165–6, 168

Haggerty, KD 58, 68, 105
Hague program 125
harmonization 121, 134–5, 138, 186–7, 189
Harris-Equifax Consumer Privacy Survey 88
Hartigan index 110
Hayes, Read 153
health 44, 46, 74, 76–8
historically relative, privacy as 58
Hong Kong 161–2
Hoofnagle, C 83
Howe, N 84
human dignity 38
human rights: biometric systems 36–54; Charter of Fundamental Rights of the EU 38, 42–3, 45–6, 48, 120, 127; data protection 189; privacy enhancing technologies (PETs) 189; security and privacy trade-off paradigm 120, 125; Spain, use of covert CCTV in workplace in 156 *see also* European Convention on Human Rights (ECHR)

IaaS (infrastructure as a service) 9–10, 11
identity cards 187
identity theft 37, 54
illegal immigration 126
ILO (International Labour Organization) Code of Conduct on protection of workers' data 156
impact assessments 135, 140, 161, 169
income levels 88, 98, 107–8, 111–13 *see also* privacy impact assessments (PIAs)
infomediaries 27
information privacy *see* generational and age-cohort views of information privacy
innocence, presumption of 38, 51
institutional contexts 58–60, 61
intelligentPIA tool for RFID applications 164, 166–7, 168
intimacy and intimate data 75, 103, 120
invasion of privacy 104, 109, 112–13, 121
Ireland 162

Jasanoff, S 67
Jefferis, C 15
judicial review 38
Julian, AL 154

Kaiser-Guttman rule 108
Keller, R 61
Kinect gaming console 74

KISS principle 169
Klein, HK 67
Kleinman, DL 67
knowledge 57, 61–2, 68, 74, 167, 169

Lancaster, LC 84
Lash, S 122
lawfulness, principle of 136–7
let alone, right to be 2, 103, 120
lex mercatoria digitalis 184
London bombings 2005 124, 125
Luckmann, T 61
luggage 36–7, 48–9, 52
Lwin, MO 105
Lyon, D 57–8

machine readable policies 24–6
Madrid bombings 123–4, 125
Madrid Resolution on International Standards 8, 16
Mannheim, Karl 83–4
margin of appreciation 45
marketing 103, 114
Marx, Gary 146
Matures 84
Mayer-Schönbeger, V 60
McCahill, M 106
Meadow, RG 87–8
middle-aged persons 82, 84, 88–98
Millennials (born after 1980) 82–3, 84, 89, 93, 95, 97
'mind-reading' 77
minimization of data 42, 49–50, 54, 135, 185–6
MIT Interactive Social-Emotional Toolkit 74
Mival, O 76
mobile communication 1–2, 14, 21–2, 124
monitoring 148 *see also* Spain, use of covert CCTV in workplace in; workplace monitoring
moving target, privacy as a 2–3
multifacted concept, privacy as a 2
multi-tenancy 10

nationality discrimination 45
necessity 40, 44, 186
neurodevices 71–2
neuro-physiological computing 73, 78
New Zealand: Google Street View PIA 173–4, 175–6; privacy impact assessments (PIAs) 161–3, 173–4, 175–6
newspaper articles 62–3, 65
Noble, DF 66
non-governmental organizations (NGOs) 60
Norris, C 59
'nothing to hide' argument 105, 114
Nouwt, S 146

INDEX

OASIS LegalXML 26
OASIS XACML 25
Oblinger, DG 84
Oblinger, JL 84
OECD (Organization of Economic Cooperation and Development) 14, 23, 188
offshoring 10–12, 23
older generation, attitudes of 84, 88–97
opinion polls and surveys 84–90, 98, 101, 105–8, 113–14
organized crime 36, 40, 126
outsourcing 10–13, 20, 23

PaaS (platform as a service) 9
Pantic, M 73
Paris Project 16–17
parliamentary debates and documents 62–3
Passenger Name Records (PNRs) 126
pattern recognition technologies 59
Pearson, Siani 164, 167
PEGS see PIA Evaluation and Grading System (PEGS), proposal for
personal data see data protection; sensitive personal data
personal responsibility, privacy as issue of 3–4
personally identifiable information (PII) 8–9, 11–15, 18–19, 21, 25, 28
personhood 103, 120
PETs see privacy enhancing technologies (PETs)
Pew Research Report 82–4
physiological computing 73, 78
PIA Evaluation and Grading System (PEGS), proposal for 163, 169–77; Australian EVI PIA 174–6; case studies 173–5; checklist, as 169–74, 177; criteria 169–77; data protection 175, 177; effectiveness 169, 177; KISS principle 169; New Zealand Google Street View PIA 173–4, 175–6; PIAF project 169; reports, evaluation and grading 163, 169–77
PIA Tool for Cloud Computing 164, 167–8
PIAF project (EU) 162–3
PIAs see privacy impact assessments (PIAs)
Picard, Rosalind 73
piloting aircraft 75
Pocs, Matthias 51–4
police 36–54, 133–6, 139, 141, 153
policy 3, 14, 21, 24–7, 30, 77–8, 83, 105, 125–6
political parties 88, 98
polls 84–90, 98, 101, 105–8, 113–14
Ponder 25
pragmatic majority 105, 121
precautionary principle 182–3
Preparatory Action for Security Research (European Commission) 126

Prins, C 146
PRISMS project 119, 127–9
Privacy and American Business surveys 85–6
privacy-by-design 14, 39, 47–8, 77–8, 135, 140–1, 182–3, 186, 188
privacy, definition of 103–4
privacy enhancing technologies (PETs) for data protection 181–91: accountability 186, 188–9; anonymity 182, 184, 186–7; audits 183, 185–6, 190; certification 187; criminal offences 182; data controllers 188–90; Data Protection Directive 182, 186, 189–91; Data Protection Regulation, proposal for 5, 181–2, 186–91; data protection through technology 182–3, 185–7, 189–90; design 5, 182–3, 185–8, 191; enforcement 182–3, 189; Germany 181, 185–8; inspect and report duty 188; mandatory requirements 187–8, 190–1; mixed approach 187; privacy-by-design 182–3, 186, 188; regulation 182, 186, 189–91; producers as target group 183–5, 188; pseudonymity 182, 184, 186–7; regulation 185–8; seals 187, 190; self-regulation 188; socio-technological system, PET as 184; target groups of concept 183–6; transparency 182, 184, 188; users as target group 183, 185, 188
privacy fundamentalists 105, 221
privacy impact assessments (PIAs) 161–77: accessibility 165, 168; accountability 23, 27–30, 167; AIPCA/CICA privacy risk assessment tool 163, 164, 166, 168; audits 28, 29–30; biometrics 38, 47–8; cloud computing 23, 27–30, 164, 167–8; contextual usability 165, 168; criteria 162–8; data protection 5, 47–8, 121, 161–2, 166; definition 161; effectiveness criteria 162–8, 177; enhancement 163–8; European Union 47–8; evergreening process 28; GS1 RFID Privacy Impact Assessment (PIA) tool 164, 165–6, 168; intelligentPIA tool for RFID applications 164, 166–7, 168; operational usability 165, 168; personally identifiable information (PII) 14; PIA Tool for Cloud Computing 164, 167–8; PIAF project (EU) 162–3; public sector 161; related work 163–4; RFID applications 161, 164, 165–7, 175; risk and trust assessment 27–8; security 163–5, 166–7; Security and Privacy Impact Assessment (SPIA) Tool of University of Pennsylvania 163–5, 166, 168; social impact assessments 161; thoroughness 165, 168; Vienna University intelligentPIA tool for RFID applications 164, 166–7; yardsticks 164, 167 see also PIA Evaluation and Grading System (PEGS), proposal for

203

INDEX

Privacy Incorporated Software Agency (PISA) project 26
Privacy Pathfinder projects 15
private and family life, right to respect for 42–6
productivity 145–7, 158
property rights 38
proportionality 39, 40, 44–5, 134, 140, 147, 150, 153–4, 156–9
pseudonymity 182, 184, 186–7
public attitudes to privacy 5, 100–14, 119, 161 *see also* demographics; opinion polls and survey; smart CCTV, public discourse on
public interest groups 14
public law 9, 14
public spaces, surveillance of 60, 77

quality of data 136–7, 183

Raab, C 104
Radio Frequency Identification (RFID) applications 47, 161, 164, 165–7, 175
Raines, C 84
rational choice theory 147
REALM project 26
rectification 135
Registered Travellers Programme 126
regulation: accountability 14–22, 28, 30–1; biocybernetic adaptation 4, 74, 77–8; biometrics 38–9; cloud computing 4, 7–9, 11–22, 28, 30–1; command and control regulation 7–8, 13; European Union 189–90; impact assessments 169; margin 189–90; privacy enhancing technologies (PETs) 182, 185–90; self-regulation 8, 9, 14, 30, 18–19, 188
responsibility, allocation of 21–2
RFID (Radio Frequency Identification) applications 47, 161, 164, 165–7, 175
right to privacy 2, 5–6, 45, 120–4, 152, 188
risk assessment 11–14, 27–8
Rogers, Y 77
Roper Surveys 85

SaaS (software as a service) 9–10, 138, 167
Safe Harbor Agreement between EU and US 18, 20
science and technology by legal technology design, governing 38–9, 47
Science and Technology Options Assessment panel (STOA) (European Parliament) 71–2
seals and marks 187, 190
searches 153
secrecy 103, 120
security: accountability 25; biometrics 42, 50, 54; cloud computing 4, 11, 21; data

protection 105, 185–6; freedom, security and justice, area of 127, 136; privacy impact assessments (PIAs) 163–5, 166–8; public attitudes 101, 105–6 *see also* security and privacy trade-off paradigm
Security and Privacy Impact Assessment (SPIA) Tool of University of Pennsylvania 163–5, 166, 168
security and privacy trade-off paradigm 2, 3, 5, 119–29: balancing exercise 123–6; biometrics 125; data protection 123–4, 126–7, 129; European Union 119–22, 125–9; human rights 120, 125; PRISMS project 119, 127–9; public attitudes 119; right to privacy 120–4; right to security 122–4; surveillance 5, 122–3, 126–7; terrorism 119–20, 123–7
self-determination 38–9
self, limited access to 103, 120
self-regulation 8, 9, 14, 30, 18–19, 188
semantic video surveillance 59
semi-public spaces 60
sensitive personal data: accountability 25; biocybernetic adaptation 72–3, 74–6, 78; biometrics 37–8, 44, 46, 54; cloud computing 25; Data Protection Regulation, proposal for 78; ethnic origins 44, 46; health 44, 46; hiding data 25; highly sensitive data 75–6; public exposure and availability 76; social networking 76
sensory processing disorders, children with 74
Sentry Insurance 86
September 11, 2001, terrorist attacks on United States 123–4, 125, 136
server farms 10
service level agreements (SLAs) 11, 23–4, 27, 30
Silent Generation (born from 1928–1945), attitudes of 84, 89, 90–7
site inspections 10–11
situational crime prevention 147
SKAD (sociology of knowledge approach to discourse) 61–2
Slobogin, C 113
smart CCTV, public discourse on 4, 57–68: appropriate and working solution, smart CCTV as 64–5; blogs and online magazines 62–3, 65; crime 64–6; culture 58, 61–2, 67–8; data protection 60, 65–7; definition of smart CCTV 58–9; Germany 4, 58, 60, 62, 65–8; human failure 64–6; inappropriate technology, smart CCTV as 65, 68; institutional context 58–60; newspaper articles 62–3, 65; parliamentary debates and documents 62–3; police 60, 65, 67; semi-public spaces 60; simple CCTV, comparison with 64–5; social groups,

INDEX

classification of and discrimination against 66–7; terrorism 60, 64, 66–7; theoretical framework 61–2
smart grids 4
Snider, Laureen 155
social construction of privacy 4, 58–9
social control 38, 58, 105
social groups, classification of and discrimination against 66–7
social impact assessments 161
social inequality 57
social networks 1, 3–4, 76, 82–3, 135
social unrest 84, 89
social value of privacy 104, 120, 123–4
socio-economic status 88, 106, 114
sociology of knowledge 61–2, 68
soft law 78, 185
Solove, DJ 103–5, 120
Spain, Madrid bombings in 123–4, 125
Spain, use of covert CCTV in workplace in 145–59: absenteeism 151; accountability 159; consultation and information procedures 156; crime prevention/detection 5, 149, 150–5, 157, 159; culture 153–4; data protection 156, 159; dishonesty 149, 150–5; due process 153; employee representatives 156; ethical perspective 5, 147, 157–8; European Convention on Human Rights 150, 153; European Union 159; exceptional monitoring 147; good faith 155–6, 159; justification 150, 158; necessity test 150; notification 156–7; ordinary monitoring 147; productivity 146–7, 158; proportionality 147, 150, 153–4, 156–9; Spanish Constitutional Court ENSIDESA decision 148–52, 159; suitability test 150; transparency 147, 150, 152–7; trust, morale and motivation 147, 153–5, 157; utilitarianism 157–8; victimization 150
SPARCLE project 26
Stach, B 51–3
Stalder, F 57
standards 8, 11–12, 16, 21, 27–9, 47, 72, 106, 187
Stanton, JM 154
Steeves, VM 57
stigmatization 40, 42, 51
Stillman, D 84
Stockholm program 125
Strauss, AL 61
Strauss, W 84
subsidiarity 190
supremacy of EU law 43, 46
surveillance: algorithmic surveillance 59; biometrics 38–9, 41–2, 44–6, 52; culture 58; data protection 100; definition 105; discrimination 57; government 101; privacy

57–8; public attitudes 5, 100–14; public spaces 77; security and privacy trade-off paradigm 5, 122–3, 126–7; semantic video surveillance 59; wiretapping 89, 90–3, 96–8, 113 see also smart CCTV, public discourse on; Spain, use of covert CCTV in workplace in
surveys 84–90, 98, 101, 105–8, 113–14
synthetic biology, pursuit of standardization in 72

Tampere program 125
Tancock, David 164, 167
technology, data protection through 182–3, 185–7, 189–90
telecommunications 185
telephone tapping 89, 90–3, 96–8, 113, 124
terrorism: biometrics 36, 40; Data Protection Regulation, proposal for 136; European Union 126, 136; London bombings 2005 124, 125; Madrid bombings 123–4, 125; public attitudes 111, 113; security and privacy trade-off paradigm 119–20, 123–7; September 11, 2001, terrorist attacks on United States 123–4, 125, 136; smart CCTV 60, 64, 66–7; social groups, classification of and discrimination against 66–7
thought, conscience and religion, freedom of 2
tracking devices on cars 153
trade-off see security and privacy trade-off paradigm
Traditionalists 84
transparency: accountability 15–21, 25, 28; biometrics 41–2, 44, 46, 48–9, 51–2, 54; cloud computing 13, 15–21, 25, 28; data protection 2, 41–2, 134, 138–9, 142, 156; PIA Evaluation and Grading System (PEGS), proposal for 175; privacy enhancing technologies (PETs) 182, 184, 188; private sector 18; public attitudes 102; right to privacy 121; Spain, use of covert CCTV in workplace in 147, 150, 152–7
travel, right to 38, 51
trust: accountability 21, 24–8; cloud computing 21, 24–8; Croatia 105, 109, 111–12, 114; market forces 187; privacy impact assessments 27; public attitudes 105, 109, 111–12, 114; Spain, use of covert CCTV in workplace in 147, 153–5, 157; Trust Authorities 24–7; trusted virtual machines 25
Truste 18–19, 26
truth-claims 61–2

unconcerned group 105–6, 121

INDEX

uniform personal identifiers (UPIs) 42, 50, 54
United Kingdom: cloud computing 15, 20;
Information Commissioner PIA Handbook
162; London bombings 2005 124, 125;
privacy impact assessments (PIAs) 162–3
United States: cloud computing 8, 15, 18–20,
22; Federal Trade Commission 19–20;
health 76; opinion polls and surveys 105–6;
Passenger Name Records 126; privacy
impact assessments (PIAs) 161–4;
pragmatic majority 105, 121; privacy
fundamentalists 105, 121; public attitudes
82–9, 101; reasonable expectations 45; Safe
Harbor Agreement with EU 18, 20;
searches 153; September 11, 2001, terrorist
attacks 123–4, 125, 136; surveillance 124,
153, unconcerned group 105–6, 121
utilitarianism 157–8

validation 77, 126, 128, 169
van der Ploeg, I 57
Veterans 84
victimization 146, 150
Vienna University intelligentPIA tool for
RFID applications 164, 166–7
Vietnam War 84
virtual machines (VMs) 9–10, 12, 25
visualization 9–12, 73
von Hirsch, A 157

W3C P3P 25
Wang, C 25
wanted lists 37–40, 49
Warren, Earl 103, 121
watched, feelings of being 41
Weckert, J 154
Weitzner, Daniel 16, 20, 26
Westin, Alan 88, 103, 120
whole genome sequencing 71
Wii gaming console 74
wifi information, collection of 173–4
Williams, JD 105
wiretapping 89, 90–3, 96–8, 113, 124
Wirtz, J 105
workplace monitoring 88, 145, 148 *see also*
Spain, use of covert CCTV in workplace in
Wright, David 161, 163, 172

younger people, attitudes of 82–3, 84, 88–9,
93–7

Zedner, Lucia 124
Zemke, R 84
Zureik, E 58, 120